GW01312932

T. Lobsang Rampa
and Other Characters
of Questionable Faith

Also by R.B. Russell

Short Story Collections
Putting the Pieces in Place, 2009
Literary Remains, 2010
Leave Your Sleep, 2012
Death Makes Strangers of Us All, 2018

Novellas
Bloody Baudelaire, 2009
The Dark Return of Time, 2014
The Stones are Singing, 2016

Novels
She Sleeps, 2017
Waiting for the End of the World, 2020
Heaven's Hill, 2022
The Woman Who Fell to Earth, 2024

Collected Edition
Ghosts, 2012

Non-fiction
Occult Territory: An Arthur Machen Gazetteer, 2019
Past Lives of Old Books and Other Essays, 2020
Sylvia Townsend Warner: A Bibliography, 2020
(with J. Lawrence Mitchell)
Robert Aickman: A Biography, 2022
Fifty Forgotten Books, 2022
Fifty Forgotten Records, 2025

Translation
Le Grand Meaulnes by Alain-Fournier, 1999
(with *Miracles*, translated by Adrian Eckersley)

T. Lobsang Rampa
*and Other Characters
of Questionable Faith*

R.B. Russell

Tartarus Press

T. Lobsang Rampa,
and Other Characters of Questionable Faith
by R.B. Russell

First published 2025 by Tartarus Press at
Coverley House, Carlton-in-Coverdale, Leyburn,
North Yorkshire, DL8 4AY, UK

© R.B. Russell, 2025

Painting © Les Edwards, first published on the cover of
As It Was! by T. Lobsang Rampa, Corgi, 1976.

ISBN 978-1-912586-67-7

This edition limited to 300 copies

Acknowledgements:
Ossian Brown, Kady Drorbaugh (UCLA Library Special
Collections), Dr Robert A. Gilbert, Danny Goring,
Liz Hodgkinson, Thomas Hoebel, Stephen Holman,
Donald S. Lopez, Jr, Bob Mann, David Michie,
Mutahara Mobashar (Manuscript Division, Library of
Congress), Mark O'Kane, Rosalie Parker, Jim Rockhill,
Alicia and David Spangler, Tore Sørensen,
Matthew Levi Stephens, David Tibet
and Mark Valentine.

Contents

Introduction . . . v

T. Lobsang Rampa: The Unbelievable Lama

A Note on Writing a Biography of Lobsang Rampa . . . xiii
1. *The Third Eye* . . . 1
2. Ireland . . . 19
3. The Burgess Investigation . . . 25
4. The Exposé . . . 41
5. The Explanation . . . 60
6. Inspiration for *The Third Eye* . . . 68
7. The Aftermath . . . 80
8. The Legacy . . . 109
9. Conclusion . . . 124

T. Lobsang Rampa and the New Age . . . 131

Bibliography of Books by T. Lobsang Rampa . . . 140
Other Works Consulted . . . 142

Appendices
1. Burgess Report . . . 145
2. *Daily Mail,* 1st February 1958 . . . 147
3. *Daily Mail*, 3rd February 1958 . . . 153
4. *Daily Express*, 3rd February 1958 . . . 157
5. *Daily Express*, 4th February 1958 . . . 159

The Brotherhood of the Cross and Star

The Brotherhood of the Cross and Star ... 163
Olumba Olumba Obu ... 171
The Succession ... 188
Russell vs The Gorings ... 193
Addendum:
Is the Brotherhood of the Cross and Star a cult? ... 198
Works Cited and Consulted ... 201

Scientology

A Question of Personality ... 205
References ... 224

Thee Temple ov Psychick Youth

Thee Temple ov Psychick Youth ... 227
A Note on the Satanic Panic ... 251
Books and online resources consulted ... 255

Conclusion

Conclusion ... 259
General Reading ... 263

Index ... 264

Introduction

My interest in 'alternative beliefs', the New Age and 'new religious movements' goes back to 1980 and my third year at secondary school when one of our teachers, Mrs Wilson, took over Religious Education lessons and taught *all* the world religions, not just Christianity, as had previously been the case. After only a very short time, it appeared obvious to me that historically, despite the wildly different ideas of God (or Gods) and the many stories that were told in their support, each of the traditional religions had been simply trying to make sense of the world around them, as well as the world beyond our lived experience.

It also seemed clear that despite all the elaborations, cross-fertilisation, and even the possible co-opting of real characters from history, none of the religions could be seen as anything other than collections of allegories or fables, many of which were often fascinating and sometimes quite beautiful. It was impressed upon us that these different beliefs all deserved respect, despite the fact that they were all in disagreement with each other over not just minor details, but on fundamental, age-old questions such as 'Where do we come from?' and 'Why are we here?'

Mrs Wilson's basic but panoramic survey of world religions suggested to me, logically, that they could not all be right, meaning that several billions of people around the world, over thousands of years, had all been duped. At the time, it was a revelation to me that *no* faith was likely to be found correct in its explanation of either the natural or supernatural worlds.

I was intrigued that so many people held such apparently irrational beliefs, although I assumed that for the vast majority this was the result of the cultures in which they had been brought up. Religion has invariably informed the shape of society and especially systems of education, just as it had mine. All through primary school I had sung Christian hymns and listened to Bible stories, and people from other cultures pre-

Characters of Questionable Faith

sumably had their own experiences which might also be described, pejoratively, as indoctrination. Religion has always been difficult, if not sometimes dangerous, to question, especially when it has been the basis of prevailing ideas of morality, and systems of governance and justice. I found all this fascinating, although I may have been the only one in our class who did.

At this time I happened to be regularly visiting secondhand bookshops looking for cheap paperbacks of ghost stories and other strange and outré fiction. Very often, shelves of genre short stories would merge into a supposed non-fiction section which was often classed as 'Mind, Body and Spirit' or 'New Age'. Moving on from the sensational short stories of Arthur Machen and H.P. Lovecraft, I would find 1960s paperbacks about 'real' ghosts, UFOs, Ley Lines and Atlantis; books by Colin Wilson, Aleister Crowley, Wilhelm Reich and Erich von Däniken. One of the earliest books I bought from these disreputable shelves was T. Lobsang Rampa's *Wisdom of the Ancients* (1965), because it seemed to offer an informal encyclopaedia of all kinds of mystical and supernatural phenomena. I have to admit that I didn't know quite what to make of it, and I soon replaced it with Colin Wilson and John Grant's *Directory of Possibilities* (1981), which was far more wide-ranging and rather better-written. I also thought that Wilson and Grant were not quite so likely to believe in *everything*, as Rampa appeared to do.

I was intrigued to discover, as the result of my rather random and uninformed researches, that many people worldwide seemed to embrace these alternative and unlikely beliefs with sincerity at least equal to those who considered themselves conventionally religious. However, if these alternative beliefs were ever discussed, it was usual for people to laugh and scoff at the credulity of those who embraced them. It struck me that the only real difference between these alternative ideas and those of traditional religions was that the latter had history on their side, and a greater number of followers.

My thought processes might have been somewhat naïve, but I was essentially distrusting of any system of faith that required a belief in that which could not be empirically tested. I hope,

Introduction

however, that I have always been able to treat any such beliefs, new or old, conventional or alternative, with respect. But respect does not mean that anyone who dogmatically espouses their faith should not expect to be closely questioned, especially if they claim their beliefs to be superior to those of others.

I continued to come across Lobsang Rampa's Corgi paperbacks over the years, although they have slowly become rare on the bookshelves reserved for alternative thinking (now stocked in favour of such modern concepts as 'Mindfulness'). After *Wisdom of the Ancients*, I tended to ignore Rampa, assuming that his other books were, more or less, just a personal elaboration of Buddhist beliefs with added spaceships. It wasn't until I bought a copy of Christopher Evans' *Cults of Unreason* (1973), to read about Scientology, that I learned just how far Rampa deviated from orthodoxy, and that his life story was quite different from the one he claimed for himself. That the truth was outwardly mundane didn't make it any the less fascinating: Rampa's obviously real interest in Tibet caused him to create a fictional role for himself—a role he would continue to play for the rest of his life. I noticed that even before the internet began to proliferate so many half-truths about Rampa, his story was often mangled in reference books for the purposes of a quick laugh at his expense. In deciding to write an essay on Rampa, I ended up discovering far more about him than I expected, and the biographical study included here is by far the largest part of this book.

The second study in this collection of essays goes back to the 1990s when an old school friend announced he had joined a Christian church of which I had not previously heard. I suppose my surprise makes it clear we had not been quite as close as I had thought. What I had not seen coming was his certainty that Christ was here on earth again, come this time to save us from physical Armageddon at the advent of the new millennium. In the run-up to the year 2000 I had already become interested in the proliferation of millennial churches and cults, and the *Sunday* programme on BBC Radio Four each week always seemed to feature yet another millenarian group. With my

Characters of Questionable Faith

friend now a fully paid-up member of such an organisation, I took an interest in his beliefs, although this was not as easy as I had hoped. It is always frustrating trying to engage with a committed believer because, even if they are willing to tell you about their ideas and explain their point of view, they are rarely willing to actually *debate* their faith. I told myself that come the year 2000 one of us would have to concede they had been mistaken, but it didn't quite turn out like that.

I have also included here an essay about Scientology, the first really alternative 'faith' that I brushed up against in real life when, as a teenager, I was invited to take a free 'personality test' by a group of very presentable young people in the Brighton Lanes. I think it has always rankled with me that they concealed their identity and did not explain their agenda. Others have written in greater detail about the often terrible practices of The Church of Scientology, and in my essay I consider only one small aspect of their activities; their apparently quite harmless first attempt to make converts. Their initial approach is built upon just a few small untruths and it is in many ways an innocuous deception, but it strikes me that it is indicative of Scientology's complete disregard for honesty. Maybe I am something of a romantic idealist, but when a 'church' lies about its intentions, activities and even their documented history, it suggests that something is rotten at the heart of their philosophy.

At the same time I came across Scientology and Rampa, I also heard the music of Psychic TV. I enjoyed the band's first two albums, but was not persuaded to join what appeared to be their fan club, Thee Temple ov Psychick Youth (TOPY). Their 'Message from the Temple' sounded rather too preachy and New-Agey and was an uncomfortable fit with an equally off-putting pseudo-militaristic fashion sense. Through school, university and beyond, I always seemed to know people who were members of TOPY, and there seemed to be something a little suspect about many of them, although being put-off by their practice of 'sex magic' probably says more about me being a prude. What I didn't realise until the 1990s was that the driving force behind TOPY, Genesis P-Orridge, had deliberately based the 'fan club'

Introduction

on his fascination for the activities of Charles Manson, The People's Temple at Jonestown, and the Process Church of the Final Judgment. P-Orridge's claims that his own organisation was founded ironically didn't make it less potentially dangerous. My motivation for writing about them now is, to a certain extent, my memories of personal comments made by friends who were close to P-Orridge—comments which came back to me when I read the often hagiographic obituaries of P-Orridge following his recent death. Many pundits have tried to portray him as a transgressive saint, which seems to ignore the damage that was done to some members of TOPY. Yes, P-Orridge pushed at a large number of boundaries, but he was very far from sanctity. With the formation of TOPY, P-Orridge showed just how easy it can be to create a cult, and how willingly some people will join it.

My conclusion to this book is in no way meant to be an apology for foolish thinking or irrational beliefs, or an attempt to downplay the very real damage that religions/cults can do. However, in researching this book I have come to look at alternative beliefs and especially cults with a slightly different perspective.

Lobsang Rampa:
The Unbelievable Lama

A signed photograph of T. Lobsang Rampa, c. 1958.

A Note on Writing a Biography of Lobsang Rampa

In researching the life of Tuesday Lobsang Rampa, a man also known as Cyril Hoskin, Kuan-suo and Dr Carl Kuan, I had first to disassociate him from others with the same name(s). For example, a contemporaneous Cyril Hoskin seems to have taken part in amateur dramatics in Rampa's native Devon in the 1930s, and it was most likely this other Hoskin who was reported in the *Western Morning News* in January 1938 as having been fined £2 for driving without due care and attention (he hit a pram). With Rampa's predisposition to get into scrapes with the police, I did have to look into this, but I found the addresses didn't match with the Cyril Hoskin I have been researching.

Rampa later reported in *Candlelight* that while he was living in Windsor, Ontario, a man claiming to be him,

> . . . was trying to collect 'disciples' and he was encouraging them to take mescalin and peyote [sic], saying it was good for their psychic development, etc., etc., . . . Inevitably the Los Angeles fraud was reported in the Press, and there was a great commotion about it.[1]

Rampa reported that eventually it was proved that he had never been in California, and 'the uproar died down'. But even after his death, there were stories in an American newspaper of a man stealing a car and, rather than admit his real identity, declaring his name was Lobsang Rampa.[2] There would also be

---

[1] Rampa, *Candlelight*, 65.
[2] Spartanburg *Herald-Journal*, 3rd December 1993.

recordings and even a correspondence course that bore his name, which he denied were his.

But, really, there was only ever one Tuesday Lobsang Rampa. The main problem for his biographer is that Rampa has frequently been included in books of fraudsters and perpetrators of literary hoaxes, and the same few details have been repeated time and time again, allowing small errors and fanciful details to creep in. It should be stated that Rampa's name was not originally Albert Price[1] (it was Cyril Henry Hoskin, without an 's' at the end of his surname[2]), he was never a plumber[3] (that was his father), he was not Irish,[4] nor did he come from Surrey[5] (he was born and raised in Devon), and his 'transmigration' did not occur as the result of a car accident[6] (he apparently fell out of a tree, at least once). Furthermore, I can find no evidence that he held séances[7] in London, and he did not set up an ashram[8] in Canada.

As for whether he was ever a Tibetan lama who travelled to Venus, please read on . . .

[1] Liz Hodgkinson: *Reincarnation: The Evidence*, Piatkus, 1989, 105.
[2] This error was initiated by the *Daily Mail*, 1st February 1953.
[3] Various sources, including Bharati, 'Fictitious Tibet', 1974.
[4] Bharati, 'Fictitious Tibet', 1974.
[5] James Randi, *An Encyclopedia of Claims, Frauds, and Hoaxes of the Occult and Supernatural*, St Martin's Press, 1995, 198.
[6] Harrer, *Beyond Seven Years in Tibet*, 245.
[7] *ibid*, 245. Burgess is credited with attending a 'séance' at which Rampa 'wore a mighty beard, and was lying in bed stroking two Siamese cats. Among the students were several members of the English aristocracy.' I have been unable to locate a copy of Burgess's original report, but all this is possibly fanciful.
[8] Bharati, 'Fictitious Tibet', 1974.

Promotional photograph of T. Lobsang Rampa, c. 1958 from the back of the dustjacket of reprints of *The Third Eye*.

1.
The Third Eye

On 7th July 1956 *The Bookseller* magazine included an advertisement from the respectable British publisher Secker & Warburg for a forthcoming book, *The Third Eye* by T. Lobsang Rampa, described simply as 'The autobiography of a Tibetan Lama'. When it was published in November the book purported to describe the life of a young nobleman who, aged only seven years old, had been sent to a medical lamasery at Chakpori where he was taught not just medicine, but was given religious instruction, trained in the martial arts, and learned the secrets of Tibetan science. He discusses the practice of levitation and invisibility, the latter being something he was apparently unable to master. The most startling part of Rampa's story was a description of how his psychic powers were awakened through the physical operation to open his 'third eye', thus stimulating the psychic centre of his brain:

Characters of Questionable Faith

. . . the instrument penetrated the bone. . . . a very hard, very clean sliver of wood which had been treated by fire and herbs to make it as hard as steel . . . slid down so that it just entered the hole in my head. . . . I felt a stinging, tickling sensation apparently in the bridge of my nose. It subsided, and I became aware of subtle scents which I could not identify. That, too, passed away and was replaced by a feeling as if I was pushing, or being pushed, against a resilient veil. Suddenly there was a blinding flash, and at that instant the Lama Mingyar Dondup said 'Stop!' For a moment the pain was intense, like a searing white flame. It diminished, died and was replaced by spirals of colour, and globules of incandescent smoke. . . . The sliver of wood remained, it would stay in place for two or three weeks . . . the Lama Mingyar Dondup turned to me and said: 'You are now one of us, Lobsang. For the rest of your life you will see people as they are and not as they pretend to be.'[1]

Rampa declared that his patron was the Thirteenth Dalai Lama, and he explained in *The Third Eye* how he had witnessed such marvels as men flying in kites (maximum load, two men and one boy), huge feline temple guardians, yetis, the mummified body of an earlier incarnation of himself, and the gilded mummies of giant gods who had once walked the earth. *The Third Eye* is a well-written and lively book full of convincing everyday details which lead persuasively towards the author's more astounding revelations.

Given the sensational nature of the claims made by Rampa, it is not surprising that *The Third Eye* was a popular success. Even Winston Churchill read a copy. In an undated letter to his wife in 1956/7, the celebrated British wartime leader wrote that the book 'promises well',[2] although we do not know if he finished it and what his considered opinion might have been.

---

[1] Rampa, *The Third Eye*, 100-101.
[2] Gilbert, *Never Despair*, 1251.

The Third Eye

First Secker & Warburg edition of *The Third Eye*, 1956.

The Third Eye sold so well that it required reprints in quick succession, and it was translated into French, German, Italian, Spanish, Swedish and Finnish. Large parts of the book were reprinted in the French magazine *Jours de France* along with (uncredited) photographs from Tibet which added authenticity to the text.[1]

The publisher stated that by the end of 1957 they had sold over 45,000 copies.[2] By 1958 it was already in its ninth Secker & Warburg hardback edition. It was a best-seller in translation in Germany,[3] and was published in America by the reputable Doubleday and Company.

However, while *The Third Eye* was a great commercial achievement, it was not a complete critical success. Reviews were mixed; some commentators took the book at face value:

---

[1] *Jours de France*, No. 147, 7th September 1957, 18-22.
[2] Warburg, *All Authors Are Equal*, 237.
[3] *Der Spiegel*, 12th February 1958, quoted in Brauen, *Dreamworld Tibet*, 258.

Characters of Questionable Faith

. . . the prevailing effect is credible and unassuming.[1]

Very few books have been written by 'insiders,' born and educated there, hence every such publication is of great interest. Recommended for specialized libraries, though the taste of the public for books of this nature seems to be increasing.[2]

Secker & Warburg quoted for publicity purposes the *Times Literary Supplement*'s assertion that *The Third Eye*:

. . . comes near to being a work of art.

But the *TLS* quote was taken out of context. What the reviewer had actually written was:

There is no doubt that this book was worth publishing, since, though it would be a matter of extraordinary difficulty to say whether it is a work of truth, it comes near to being a work of art.[3]

The *TLS* reviewer obviously had some doubts about the authenticity of the book, and there was scepticism among other reviewers, but a few reactions were openly hostile. Hugh Richardson's response, published in the *Daily Telegraph* suggested that:

A book which plays up to public eagerness to hear about 'Mysterious Tibet' has the advantage that few people have the experience to refute it. But anyone who has lived in Tibet will feel after reading a few pages of *The Third Eye* that its author, 'T. Lobsang Rampa' is certainly not a Tibetan.

---

[1] *Kirkus*, 25, no. 62, 15th January, 1957. Quoted in Lopez, *Prisoners of Shangri-La*, 98.

[2] *Library Journal*, 82, no. 670, 1st March 1957. Quoted in Lopez, *Prisoners of Shangri-La*, 98.

[3] Review of *The Third Eye*, *Times Literary Supplement*, 30th November 1956.

The Third Eye

Local colour has apparently been borrowed from standard works, but is applied as inappropriately as the decoration of a magpie's nest. There are innumerable wild inaccuracies about Tibetan life and manners which give the impression of Western suburbia playing charades.

The samples of the Tibetan language betray ignorance of both colloquial and literary forms; there is a series of wholly un-Tibetan obsessions with cruelty, fuss and bustle and, strangely, with cats. Moreover, the turn of phrase in the slick colloquial English is quite unconvincing when attributed to a Tibetan writer.

Given that this is the work of a non-Asian mind—and if I am mistaken, I should be happy to make amends to the author in person and in Tibetan—one can regard only as indifferent juvenile fiction the catchpenny accoutrements of magic and mystery: the surgical opening of 'the third eye'; the man-lifting kites; the Abominable Snowman; the Shangri-la valley and eerie goings-on in caverns below the Potala.[1]

Hugh Richardson was a commentator with some authority on the subject of Tibet, having served in the British mission in Lhasa in the 1930s and 40s.

When *The Third Eye* was translated into German and discussed in *Der Spiegel*, they wrote:

The reception the book received from English critics when it was published 15 months ago was also positive—much friendlier, at least, than in Germany. . . .

For a large number of German critics it was perfectly clear that this book must be a forgery. In particular, the head of the Indological Seminary in Munich, Professor Helmut Hoffmann, pointed out in the West Berlin *Tagesspiegel* that numerous statements in Rampa's text contradicted all Buddhist teachings.[2]

[1] *Daily Telegraph*, 30th November 1956.
[2] *Der Spiegel*, 11th February 1958.

Characters of Questionable Faith

Given the doubts cast by many reputable critics as to the genuineness of *The Third Eye*, it is reasonable to ask why Secker & Warburg published the book; their imprint giving it a stamp of authenticity. They obviously felt they had covered themselves by providing a Foreword in the first edition which begins:

> The autobiography of a Tibetan Lama is a unique record of experience and, as such, inevitably hard to corroborate. In an attempt to obtain confirmation of the Author's statements the Publishers submitted the MS to nearly twenty readers, all persons of intelligence and experience, some with special knowledge of the subject. Their opinions were so contradictory that no positive result emerged. Some questioned the accuracy of one section, some another; what was doubted by one expert was accepted unquestioningly by another.[1]

Secker & Warburg also declared:

> Lobsang Rampa has provided documentary evidence that he holds medical degrees of the University of Chungking and in those documents he is described as Lama of the Potala Monastery of Lhasa.

Having thus absolved themselves of any responsibility for the dependability of the author's account, the Foreword still concluded:

> . . . the publishers believe that *The Third Eye* is in its essence an authentic document.[2]

This suggests that Secker & Warburg had an essential belief in *The Third Eye* and in its author, T. Lobsang Rampa. However, Frederic Warburg, who personally accepted the manuscript for publication, did have very serious doubts about the book,

---

[1] Rampa, *The Third Eye*, 5-6, *et seq.*
[2] The Publisher's Foreword is removed from later Secker and Warburg editions of *The Third Eye*.

The Third Eye

despite his enthusiasm for it. The story of the publication of *The Third Eye,* related in his autobiography *All Authors Are Equal*, is a fascinating one.

> The affair began about 11 a.m. on April 15 [1955], when the telephone operator rang to ask whether I would speak with Cyrus Brooks.[1]

The equally prestigious literary agency, A.M. Heath, was offering Warburg the autobiography of a Tibetan lama and required an ambitious advance on royalties of £1,000. Warburg claims to have asked at the very beginning, 'How do you know it's genuine?' but says that Brooks reassured him. The agent explained that the author's name was Dr Kuan (shortened from Dr Kuan-suo), a Chinese name he had found convenient to adopt, but that he intended to sign his book with the Tibetan pseudonym, T. Lobsang Rampa; 'T' standing for 'Tuesday', it apparently being a Tibetan custom to name children after the day of the week on which they are born.[2] Dr Kuan had ostensibly only agreed to write his autobiography 'after severe pressure on a number of occasions' from Brooks.

At this time, Brooks had only about 30,000 words of typescript 'on about 100 flimsy canary-yellow sheets of paper'. Warburg wrote that:

> If the author succeeded in completing it with the same degree of skill as he had shown in the sections before me, and if the material could be authenticated, then there could be no question that I had in my hands one of the biggest sellers of all time. If, on the other hand, the material was not authentic, we had a fascinating work with a strong if limited appeal, which my firm might or might not publish.

---

[1] Warburg, *All Authors Are Equal*, 220.
[2] Rampa, *The Third Eye*, 34. He never explains why, in Tibet, they might use the English name for this particular day of the week.

Characters of Questionable Faith

From the beginning there emanated from Dr Kuan's master-piece a magical aroma of enchantment.[1]

Warburg was later quoted by the *Daily Express* as saying that when he first received the manuscript of *The Third Eye*,

My excitement was intense; I read it greedily. It had every-thing it takes to become the world best-seller it is today . . . But other doubts were there . . .[2]

Warburg states that terms were agreed with Brooks in just ten days, and with pride he wrote that the large advance was negoti-ated down to £800.[3] Brooks admitted to Warburg that before offering *The Third Eye* to him, it had been sent to Gollancz who had accepted it, but were unable to agree to the advance the agent required. Robert Hale had then also accepted the book, but insurmountable personal differences had arisen between the author and their editor. William Collins was the next publisher to see the manuscript, but they had been too sceptical to proceed with it. Warburg points out in his autobiography that for a manuscript to receive several rejections and setbacks before finally being accepted and published was quite normal, and he was encouraged to learn that the American firm of E.P. Dutton were also going ahead with the book for U.S. publication and had also agreed an advance. Warburg knew the president of Dutton, Elliott Macrae, and was aware that the firm had recently published several well-received books about Tibet.

'Everyone seemed delighted, author, agent and publisher,' wrote Warburg, and a meeting was arranged for 3 p.m. on April 26th. The publisher was impressed by Dr Kuan:

Slightly below the medium height, well-shaped head with a domed forehead, hair rather scanty, cut tonsure-like round the

---

[1] Warburg, *All Authors Are Equal*, 222.
[2] *Daily Express*, 3rd February 1958.
[3] Which equates to approximately £18,000 in 2025.

The Third Eye

crown of his skull, a long nose and full mouth, a swarthy face with prominent ears. Nothing remarkable, nothing which I could wholly associate with what I knew of Tibetan physiognomy. But the eyes were strange, large, luminous, penetrating, under heavy lids and heavy bushy eyebrows. Between the eyes, slightly to the left of centre, a small purplish-red mark could be seen, almost the size of a collar button, the scar no doubt of that remarkable incision. Dr K. looked like a monk. He seemed a man not to be trifled with. He appeared composed, relaxed, indifferent, with a tendency to jest.[1]

Publication of Dr Kuan's manuscript was discussed, and rather than *Passionate Priest* or *Autobiography of a Tibetan Lama* (as Kuan proposed) it was decided to call the book *The Third Eye* (suggested by the publisher's wife, Pamela). Frederick Warburg asks:

> What was my state of mind at this point? It seemed to me, I must admit, almost (but not absolutely) certain that what we had in our possession was an authentic account of the early life of a lama from Tibet, touched up maybe a bit here and there, as is not uncommon with autobiographies.[2]

In his own book, Warburg defensively makes a point of writing that others around him were also convinced by Dr Kuan, writing as T. Lobsang Rampa: Mark Bonham-Carter of Collins, Cyrus Brooks of A.M. Heath, Charles Gibbs-Smith at the Victoria and Albert Museum, Elliott Macrae of Dutton, and several others. Above all, Warburg liked Dr Kuan, and thought his book was wonderful, and with the potential to sell well.

All was proceeding without complication, with chunks of the advance being released to the author as he completed the remaining chapters of his autobiography. Warburg recalled approvingly:

---

[1] Warburg, *All Authors Are Equal*, 224-6.
[2] *ibid*, 226.

Characters of Questionable Faith

A map of Lhasa was prepared by the author 'accurate, although done entirely from memory. There is NO map of Lhasa in the British Museum, to their astonishment and mine.' So wrote Dr. K. on May 12th.[1]

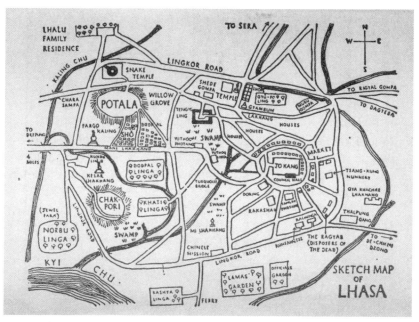

Above, Rampa's Sketch Map of Lhasa from *The Third Eye*, apparently drawn from memory.

Rampa's assertion, though, was simply not true. In 1955 a library card would have given any researcher access to books on Lhasa by Das, Candler, Waddell and Landon, to mention only a few published between the years 1902 and 1905. All of these included maps that Rampa would have been able to work from.

---

[1] Warburg, *All Authors Are Equal*, 227-228.

The Third Eye

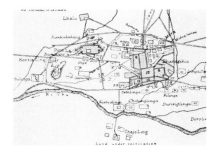 

Maps of Lhasa from (left) *Journey to Lhasa and Central Tibet* by Sarat Chandra Das (1902), and (right) *Lhasa and its Mysteries* by Laurence Austine Waddell (1905).

On 31st May 1955 Elliott Macrae wrote to Warburg:

> Our editors have raised a number of questions which we sent to Dr Kuan . . . the good doctor was rather sarcastic in answering them, and dismissed most of them with a wave of his hand . . . I think we may have a very good book here, but it is important that we establish beyond a shadow of doubt Dr Kuan's background, the year he graduated, the names of several important people that he knew or worked with, etc.[1]

Warburg responded:

> We have no doubts about the author's authenticity, and even if the book were a fake, which it is not, it would be one of the greatest fakes of our time. . . .

If Macrae had doubts, Frederic Warburg admitted that his wife, Pamela, was entirely sceptical. She suggested to her husband that he demand to see Dr Kuan's passport, which he refused to do, presumably because it would be something of an insult, and this caused problems between husband and wife. ('We quarrelled over it, often, bitterly.'[2]) At a later meeting with the author, Warburg found Kuan aggressive and boastful, but

---

[1] Warburg, *All Authors Are Equal*, 228, *et seq.*
[2] *Daily Express*, 3rd February 1958.

still impressive, not least because Kuan is meant to have read Frederic's palm with uncanny accuracy:

> He told me I had been involved recently in a big legal case.[1]

as though a 'big' legal case might not have been reported in the newspapers.

Frederic Warburg (left) and Elliott Macrae (right).

Kuan completed and delivered the manuscript in early August, and the balance of the advance was paid to him. But September 'proved to be a month of crisis', for Warburg as his doubts increased. He received a letter from Macrae, dated 15th September 1955:

> 'I have now had three outside reports, and all three readers agree that there are many inaccuracies in the manuscript . . . serious questions have been raised as to the author's accurate knowledge of Lhasa—both in the geographical sense and from the standpoint of customs, traditions and monasteries, as well as

---
[1] The *Daily Express*, 3rd February 1958.

The Third Eye

his knowledge of Buddhist and Tibetan religious belief and the Tibetan language. . . . One of these readers believes that the author may have been in Lhasa, but that he came there from one of the outlying provinces, possibly in China, and may have read up books about Tibet and presented some of the material from them as personal experiences and observations.'[1]

Macrae forwarded a report from another reader that stated:

Having read it, I can say that the English construction, grammar, idiom and vocabulary are most unlikely to have been achieved by any Tibetan.[2]

Warburg wrote in his autobiography:

Macrae in his letter added, most reasonably, 'I think that both we and Secker & Warburg would be in a very embarrassing position if we cannot authenticate the material we publish.' The same thought was present in the minds of my colleagues and myself. The situation demanded instant action. We sent Macrae's material to Dr K for his comments, and arranged that he should meet my directors with his agent three days later.

At the meeting, Dr Kuan accepted some of the readers' criticisms and admitted to mistakes. He alleged in a written statement that:

Pema Choki (Macrae's Reader One) is particularly virulent. Rather a pity, because she used to be quite a nice girl. Perhaps she wants to get her book published first.

Having attacked one of his main detractors, whom he claimed to know personally, Kuan continued to insist on his authenticity. Warburg recorded:

---

[1] Warburg, *All Authors Are Equal*, 230.
[2] *ditto*, 231, *et seq.*

Characters of Questionable Faith

So I pinned my faith or what was left of it on Dr K's identification of Reader One as Pema Choki. Three days later a cable came from Macrae, 'Pema Choki is not one of our readers, completely unknown to us.'

Warburg cancelled the contract with Kuan, although he agreed to Brooks' suggestion that the publisher meet the author once more. At this later meeting, Warburg accused Kuan of having no knowledge of the Tibetan language and of having copied Tibetan script from other freely available sources. On showing him an example,

A look of horror passed over Dr K's swarthy face and he covered his eyes with his right hand as if suffering from a violent spasm of migraine.[1]

Warburg's account in his autobiography is taken almost verbatim from a statement he gave to the *Daily Express* in 1958. The story has often been re-told, but in an embellished form, and it has passed into folklore that, to test Kuan, Warburg asked phonetically in Tibetan, 'Did you have a nice journey, Mr Rampa?' In some versions, Kuan does not immediately react because he does not recognise his own language. Whether he realises he has been addressed in Tibetan, or has to be told, he is then meant to have fallen to the floor in apparent agony. (The story is also re-presented in a version where Rampa's aversion to Tibetan is meant to have been revealed during a radio interview, in which he is unable to speak, although no names, dates, etc have ever been given to corroborate this.[2])

However violently affected by whatever manifestation of what was meant to be his native language, when Kuan was sufficiently recovered, he explained that during World War II the Japanese had endeavoured to gain his secret knowledge of

---

[1] Warburg, *All Authors Are Equal*, 232.
[2] See, among others, David Bramwell, 'On the Art of Deception', *The Idler*, Idler Books, 2014, 188.

The Third Eye

Tibet and that he had been forced to use self-hypnosis to block his understanding of Tibetan so as to foil them. He claimed that the memory of it brought back the pain of the harrowing ordeal, and now he only knew a few simple, residual words.

Kuan was also asked about his peculiar voice, which was noted by several commentators as having an strong West Country accent, and he blamed this on Japanese wartime torture.

Warburg was obviously still not convinced, but he liked the book and offered to publish *The Third Eye* as a work of fiction. Dr Kuan, however, was adamant his book was true, despite acknowledged mistakes. He then claimed to be suffering from an incurable disease.

Warburg was moved by Kuan's plight, but did not relent in his refusal to publish. A few days later, Dr David Snellgrove, Lecturer in Tibetan at the School of Oriental Studies at London University, sent in a report on *The Third Eye:*

> The book is a complete fantasy culled from the writing of others. Nowhere does he demonstrate personal acquaintance with his subject. . . . The fellow is a complete impostor.[1]

Snellgrove would begin his published review of *The Third Eye* in 1957, 'This is a shameless book'.[2] Another expert consulted was Marco Pallis, writer and Himalayan explorer,

> Pallis declared the book to be a wild fabrication and a libel on both Tibet and its religion.[3]

These reports were followed by a letter from Macrae who had another reader with different concerns about Kuan's book. They believed the author had some knowledge of Lhasa, although they doubted his claims about his parentage. Later, Warburg was to use these 'discrepancies' (as he chose to inter-

[1] Quoted in Warburg, *All Authors Are Equal*, 234.
[2] Summer 1957 issue of the magazine *Oriental Art*.
[3] Lopez, *Prisoners of Shangri-La*, 97.

Characters of Questionable Faith

pret reports which simply highlighted different areas of concern) to suggest that even the experts could not agree whether Kuan was authentic.

At the time, however, Warburg wrote to Macrae:

> In my opinion, we and you have been the victims of one of the most remarkable and interesting fakes in modern times.[1]

Rampa doubters: Marco Pallis (left) and Heinrich Harrer (right).

Another of the experts who saw galley proofs and commented was Heinrich Harrer, to whom Warburg had actually suggested that Kuan was probably a fraud. Harrer was an Austrian Tibetologist who had genuinely been tutor to the Dalai Lama before writing the best-selling *Seven Years in Tibet* (1953).

> After half an hour I delivered my verdict . . . The author was a fraudster, the book a literary deception and the contents a complete fabrication. Since Lobsang Rampa claimed to have lived in Lhasa at the same time as me, I asked Hart-Davis to telephone his friend Frederic Warburg and request a meeting with Lobsang Rampa to enable me to chat to him in Tibetan about our mutual acquaintances . . . That afternoon we received

---

[1] Warburg, *All Authors Are Equal*, 234.

The Third Eye

word that the lama was meditating at present and could not be disturbed under any circumstances. A few days later another message arrived saying that, regrettably, Lobsang Rampa was now on a ship bound for Canada.[1]

Another commentator who was sent the manuscript was Agehananda Bharati, who later wrote:

> I was suspicious before I opened the wrapper: the 'third eye' smacked of Blavatskyan and post-Blavatskyan hogwash. The first two pages convinced me the writer was not a Tibetan, the next ten that he had never been either in Tibet or India, and that he knew absolutely nothing about Buddhism of any form, Tibetan or other.[2]

Warburg, unhappy about the whole affair, noted that Dr Kuan did not return his advance on royalties, as requested. In the New Year, the author wrote that he was leaving England, 'a very sick man indeed'.[3] But Warburg was strangely loath to give up a book that seems to have captivated him, and he commissioned yet another report, this time from the Orientalist John Morris, who wrote:

> My own opinion is that the author is some sort of psychopath living in a private neurotic world of his own. It is even likely that he has persuaded himself that all this occult nonsense is true.[4]

[1] Harrer, *Beyond Seven Years in Tibet*, 244. Heinrich Harrer's review of *The Third Eye* when published in Germany was so scathing, he was threatened with a libel suit by Kuan's German publisher. Heinrich Harrer, himself, was to become a controversial figure when, in 1997, the newspaper *Die Stern* exposed him as a former member of the Nazi Party and the SS, which he denied until documentary evidence was produced. Harrer later publicly expressed regret for his Nazi affiliations.
[2] Agehananda Bharati, 'Fictitious Tibet', 1974.
[3] Quoted in Warburg, *All Authors Are Equal*, 235.
[4] *ibid*, 235.

Characters of Questionable Faith

At this time, Warburg was told by Kuan that he was in Canada, although Warburg doubted this. Kuan was certainly in England when Warburg went against so much advice to the contrary and made the decision to publish *The Third Eye* after all.

In his autobiography, Warburg goes into such detail about the events leading up to the publication of Kuan's book that there is little reason to doubt any of it, not least because the publisher does not come out of the story well, admitting that he was fooled by Dr Kuan. His argument that, 'I thought [that by publishing], the truth will somehow emerge'[1] is not a convincing excuse for marketing the book as factual, even though the idea turned out to be correct. One can only believe that Warburg knew he had a controversial bestseller on his hands and presumably did not care that it was essentially fiction. It is difficult to assume he was motivated by anything other than 'the bottom line', i.e. making money.

Elliott Macrae at Dutton chose not to publish *The Third Eye*.

---

[1] Warburg, *All Authors Are Equal*, 236.

First Corgi/Transworld paperback edition of
The Third Eye, 1963.

2.
Ireland

In January 1957, Scotland Yard is said to have requested that Kuan present himself with either a Tibetan passport or a residence permit.[1] It just so happened that at this time Kuan, said that he was suffering from an attack of coronary thrombosis[2] and was advised to leave London. A specialist is meant to have said:

'Your life is in danger here. Get away to a different climate.'[3]

Quite how superior the climate of Dublin in Ireland was to that of London can be debated, but with his wife Sarah and a

---

[1] From Lopez, *Prisoners of Shangri-La*, 98. No source cited. The story is repeated elsewhere, including by Shravasti Dhammika in *The Strange Case of the Three-eyed Lama*, 2020.
[2] In *Time* magazine he is reported to have claimed both heart disease and cancer. 17th February 1958, 52.
[3] Rampa, *The Rampa Story*, 204.

Characters of Questionable Faith

young woman named Sheelagh Rouse (who was described by Kuan as his adopted daughter, and by the press as his secretary), he found accommodation in Nassau Street, above a florist, opposite Trinity College. Kuan complains in several of his books that the demands of the taxman were excessive wherever he lived, and Sheelagh Rouse makes it clear in her memoir, *Twenty-Five Years with T. Lobsang Rampa*, that he decided to move:

> Somewhere where perhaps the taxes would not be so exorbitant for writers as they were in England'.[1]

Ben Edair on Balscadden Road, from *Der Stern*.

Whatever the combination of factors that caused him to leave London, Kuan and his entourage later rented a house in Howth (ten miles from Dublin city centre) called Ben Edair[2] towards the end of the Balscadden Road, overlooking the sea. By this time

---
[1] Sheelagh Rouse, *Twenty-Five Years with T. Lobsang Rampa*, 105.
[2] Sheelagh Rouse, *Grace: The World of Rampa*, 31.

Ireland

he would have been receiving substantial royalties from *The Third Eye*,[1] and Sheelagh Rouse wrote that their time in Ireland was initially quite idyllic, although they were all busy with correspondence from readers from all over the world wanting to make contact with 'Chen' as she called the author. ('Chen', in turn, called Sheelagh 'Buttercup', Buttercup called Mrs Kuan, 'Ra'ab', and Ra'ab called Kuan 'the Guv'.) They were often plagued by visitors who wished to meet the Lama in person. According to the *Daily Express*:

> At first they only had half the house, and in his desire for solitude, Dr Kuan persuaded the other occupants to leave. Then he realised he would be seen in his garden by passers-by and when clambering up and down the cliffs beneath his house. He had an 8ft-high concrete wall built.[2]

This is the one period in the life of Kuan in which he appears to have had any other friends. When *The Rampa Story* was published in 1960 it was dedicated to several individuals in Howth: Mr and Mrs O'Grady (who lived just up the road), Mr Loftus (the local policeman) and his family, as well as Dr Chapman, and Brud Campbell (a builder).

Kuan's health problems presumably improved; the climate obviously did agree with him. And the incurable disease he told Warburg about seems to have no longer been an issue. Rouse wrote:

> When we lived in Howth, Chen did an astonishing amount of things, he was never idle. He often rowed himself over to Ireland's Eye [an island in Balscadden bay] . . . He kept a small rowing boat pulled up on the shingle directly below our house. Occasionally he would hire a larger motor boat.[3]

[1] Various figures are given for book sales and royalties by different sources. *Time* magazine (17th February 1958, 52) suggested he had earned £50,000, which would be equivalent to £1 million today.

[2] *Daily Mail*, 3rd February 1958.

[3] Rouse, *Twenty-Five Years with T. Lobsang Rampa*, 125-6.

Characters of Questionable Faith

Rouse's memoir is necessarily a partial one, and she makes it clear that she did not always get on with Ra'ab (and in her memoirs Ra'ab doesn't mention Rouse at all). In Rouse's mind they were helping the great man fulfil his main ambition, which was to produce equipment that would photograph the 'aura' they believed mystics like Kuan could see surrounding the human body. It is something Kuan would discuss in *Doctor from Lhasa* (1959), and he later wrote in *The Rampa Story* (1960):

> My task in life, I had known from the start, was in connection with the human aura, that radiation which entirely surrounds the human body, and by its fluctuating colour, shows the Adept if a person is honourable or otherwise. The sick person could have his or her illness seen by the colours of the aura. Everyone must have noticed the haze around a street light on a misty night. Some may even have noticed the well-known 'corona discharge' from high tension cables at certain times. The human aura is somewhat similar. It shows the life force within. Artists of old painted a halo or nimbus round the head of saints.[1]

Rouse appears to be sincere in accepting this to be a worthwhile undertaking, and doesn't seem to realise that mentioning the trouble they had finding models to pose for Dr Kuan's photographic research might look suspicious. He explained to her that women had the brightest auras and were therefore the best as models, and that they had to be willing to be photographed naked.

Rouse wrote:

> . . . photography was ongoing. We continued to have models come out on the bus from Dublin . . . We still were constantly changing or upgrading equipment, and we bought a small three-wheeled car . . . As well as photography, which was essentially work, Chen became passionate about constructing a model rail-

---

[1] Rampa, *The Rampa Story*, 21.

Ireland

road, an ambitious and fascinating hobby with tracks all round his room and beyond, sophisticated and realistic, and the Dublin trips were a necessity for a time to choose and purchase the almost daily additions of track, engines, freight cars, passenger carriages [etc.][1]

Money was obviously not an issue, and Rouse remembers Kuan being generous with gifts to local people. Even the *Daily Mail*, which would later take satisfaction in exposing Kuan as 'bogus', reported that:

> The few people who have met him say he is quiet and kindly.[2]

and said that he had given gifts of bicycles to local lads. He even offered to pay for the education of some children at an academy in Texas.

As well as his photographic 'work', Kuan was writing his sequel to *The Third Eye*. It began with the working title *A Medical Lama*, but was eventually published as *Doctor from Lhasa*. He would also have two articles published in the British magazine *Flying Saucer Review*, 'Saucers over Tibet'[3] and 'Flying into Space',[4] extraordinary accounts of visiting Venus by flying saucer (taking off from Tibet). These articles would be reprinted in various flying saucer magazines including the *Saucerian Bulletin*, published by an interesting character called Gray Barker. Barker claimed 'Saucers over Tibet' to be an excised chapter from *The Third Eye*.[5] It had not been described thus in any of the earlier printings of the article, and this may have been an

---

[1] Rouse, *Twenty-Five Years with T. Lobsang Rampa*, 126.
[2] *Daily Mail*, 3rd February 1958.
[3] *Flying Saucer Review*, March-April, 1957.
[4] *Flying Saucer Review*, May-June, 1957.
[5] A note was added by Barker to the *Saucerian Bulletin* # 16, Vol 3 No1, 1st April 1958 (note the date) stating that he has just heard that *The Third Eye* might be a carefully written hoax and that he was checking.

assumption on the part of Barker, or just clever marketing. It is possible that because The Saucerian Press would publish the American edition of *Doctor from Lhasa* in 1959[1] that Barker had inside information. If 'Saucers over Tibet' and/or 'Flying into Space' had been included in the original manuscript of *The Third Eye*, surely they would have been too much even for Warburg. If they had been a part of the published book they would certainly have strained the credulity of his most sympathetic reviewers.

Flying Saucer Review, April-March 1957, containing 'Saucers over Tibet', reprinted in *Flying Saucers*, 1957.

Saucerian Bulletin # 16, April 195, and #19, October 1958.

[1] The Saucerian Press edition of *Doctor from Lhasa* (1959) must have had a small print run, because it rarely appears on the secondhand book market. However, this may also be because books from this publisher have a cult following and are very collectable.

Promotional photograph of T. Lobsang Rampa, c. 1958.

3.
The Burgess Investigation

In theory, all the relevant information about the life of Dr Kuan, writing as T. Lobsang Rampa, should have been available in his autobiography, but for some readers the book raised more questions than it answered. Until his death in 1981, Rampa (he changed his name, legally, to Tuesday Lobsang Rampa in 1963) felt he had been unfairly treated. Those who defend him and his writings today believe there was an embittered cabal working to undermine him.

A 1964 edition of *The Third Eye* contained a Foreword by the author which ended with the statement:

> My specific reason for insisting that all this is true is that in the near future other people like me will appear, and I do not desire that they should have the suffering that I have had through spite and hatred.

Characters of Questionable Faith

'Spite and hatred' are strong words for an author to use, no matter how harsh the condemnation of his book had been from some critics, but by this time the author was not simply reacting to negative reviews. Rampa later reported:

> An Agency in Switzerland had put a wholly misleading advertisement in *The Times* reading, 'If Lobsang Rampa will communicate with — he will hear something to his advantage.'[1]

This 'fishing' advertisement was replied to by Cyrus Brooks at A.M. Heath & Company, who, Rampa reported, was told that it had been placed by 'an author in Germany to find out all'. Rampa said that he was followed and spied on, but this observation was most likely made with the benefit of hindsight. Heinrich Harrer wrote:

> . . . the British diplomat and writer, Hugh Richardson had also been racking his brains wondering who the mysterious author of the book might be. In an attempt to determine the validity of Lobsang Rampa's tale, a committed Buddhist by the name of Marco Pallis hired a detective, Clifford Burgess.[2]

It has been suggested that Pallis, Harrer and other experts on Tibet were not just aggrieved by Kuan's misrepresentation of Tibetan culture and religion, but motivated by a belief that he had taken much of his detail from their own books. Whatever their reasons, they engaged Clifford Burgess, an ex-Scotland Yard detective, now a private investigator from Liverpool. After a month of enquiries, he came back with a report stating that the author of *The Third Eye* was not a lama from Tibet, called either 'Tuesday Lobsang Rampa', 'Dr Carl Kuan' or 'Kuan-suo'; he was, in fact, Cyril Henry Hoskin.[3] On 1st February 1958, the *Daily Mail* was the first to publish the details.[4]

[1] Rampa, *Candlelight*, 63.
[2] Harrer, *Beyond Seven Years in Tibet*, 245.
[3] Burgess's report is included in full as an appendix to this book.
[4] See page 147.

The Burgess Investigation

Before going on to the press coverage, it is worth unpicking the report delivered to Pallis by Burgess, as Lobsang Rampa was later to do himself in Chapter Eight of his book *As It Was!* (1976). Burgess made a few mistakes, but none that undermined the central message of the press stories that proclaimed Rampa to be an Englishman, rather than a Tibetan, and that his 'autobiography' was a work of fiction.

Cyril Henry Hoskin's birth certificate.

Burgess reported correctly that Tuesday Lobsang Rampa was born Cyril Henry Hoskin on 8th April 1910, at Plympton St Maurice in Devon, England. The details given of his parents and his sister were also accurate. Hoskin's father, Joseph, initially kept a plumber's shop in the Ridgeway at Plympton although, later, he was also a dealer in bicycles and electrical equipment.

In *As It Was!*, Rampa would confirm that his grandfather, William Henry Hoskin (1853-1931) had several children and was an important man locally, living in the Mayoral House.[1]

---

[1] Rampa's wife, writing in *Tigerlily* as 'Mama San Ra'ab Rampa', also retells Cyril's early life, confusing the generations in his family by appearing to suggest that William was Cyril's father, rather than grandfather.

Characters of Questionable Faith

William was the chief of the local waterworks and was also in charge of the small town's historic fire engine. Rampa believed that being reported to be the 'son of a plumber' by the media showed their snobbery, which was true to a certain extent. What Rampa failed to acknowledge, however, was that they were contrasting his family's trade and his rather conventional upbringing in Devon with that of his professed claim to have come from Tibetan nobility and to have been educated in a lamasery at Chakpori.[1]

Cyril did leave school at fifteen, as Burgess reported, although this was not unusual in 1925.[2] In *As It Was!* Rampa gives a nostalgic account of his upbringing and early life which accords with various surviving records and sounds highly probable. He seems to have been close to his father, but disliked his mother, Eva. He says upon leaving school he was apprenticed to a motor engineering business which supplied and serviced cars and motorcycles. The business, R. Humm and Co, was at 80-81 Old Town Street in nearby Plymouth. It was not a job Cyril Hoskin enjoyed, although it gave him a working knowledge of vehicles and engines that was later useful. It was apparently while out collecting a motor bike on behalf of his employer that he had his first run-in with the police, who suspected him of stealing the bike. Minor problems with the constabulary seem to have been a recurring theme in his life under his various names and aliases, although he insisted he was never at fault.

Rampa also recalled that his father had a crystal radio set and later expanded his business to make radios for clients, and undertook other electrical work. Cyril seems to have been

---

[1] Rampa wrote in *As It Was!*, 151: 'Surely it doesn't matter what a person's father was, why is it such a disgrace to have a parent who was a tradesman? . . . I am always amused because Jesus, it is said, was the son of a carpenter. How was that a disgrace?'

[2] It is slightly misleading when commentators such as Donald S. Lopez Jr (in 'The Mystery of the Three-Eyed Lama') write Hoskin off as a 'high school dropout'.

The Burgess Investigation

employed by his father for a while, and he retained an interest in electrical equipment and gadgets throughout his life.

Burgess reported that Cyril was 'odd', 'a crank' and 'lazy', but admits that he had been a delicate child. Cyril's various attempts to find employment outside his father's business appear to have been hampered by ill-health. He says he contracted tuberculosis as a young adult, and also had serious problems with his eyesight. He began taking correspondence courses in an attempt to increase his employment prospects, and says he also trained as a radio operator at a school outside Southampton. There is no particular reason to dispute his claim that he passed his examinations to receive a license as a first-class wireless operator, and he may well have worked as such,[1] but we only have his word for it that he learned how to fly aircraft at the same time and gained a licence. Rampa's story of learning to fly a plane in *Doctor from Lhasa* is so naïve that it seems unlikely Hoskin ever did so.

He wrote:

> I could not pass the medical examination for a commercial license and so I was grounded before my career started.[2]

Rather more believable is his assertion that he later attended classes at the Royal Sanitary Institute in London and passed their examination, receiving a certificate as a smoke inspector. (Air pollution in British cities was horrific before the Clean Air Acts of 1956 and 1968.)

Burgess reported that when Cyril's father died in 1937, Cyril's mother moved to live with her daughter, although in the 1939 Register (essentially, an emergency Census) she was living at 1A Teignmouth Parade, Ealing, Middlesex with her son. By this time, Cyril had found a job with a surgical appliance manufacturer in Perivale, Middlesex, and though he again makes an

---

[1] Hoskin is noted as a wireless operator in the 1936 UK *Postal Service Appointment Book*.
[2] Rampa, *As It Was!*, 146.

Characters of Questionable Faith

ambitious claim that he was immediately appointed as works manager, that is how he is described on the Register.

Rampa said that when the owner of the surgical appliance business discovered he could write good advertising copy, Cyril was also made advertising manager. He took courses in surgical fitting, becoming a surgical fitting consultant, and was promoted from working in Perivale to become 'chief fitter' in central London.

Burgess's date for Cyril's marriage to Sarah Anne Pattinson, a nurse at a Richmond hospital, appears to be incorrect. The wedding was reported in the 1940 *Penrith Observer* on 23rd April 1940, which stated that the ceremony had taken place the previous weekend. In this marriage notice, Cyril Henry Hoskin is reported to have obtained certificates as both a Master of Arts and a Bachelor of Science, and is described as having travelled extensively, and being 'prominent in aviation and engineering circles'. This appears to be the earliest printed record of his having gained dubious, likely unearned distinctions.

In 1941, Mrs and Mrs Hoskin were living at 22 Ovington Court SW3, London. Early in the Second World War, Cyril was, for a time, on fire watch—a distinctly dangerous undertaking, especially during the blitz. Twenty-nine when war broke out, he would not have been immediately 'called-up' for active service. He and Sarah lost their accommodation due to bombing, and the surgical outfitters premises were also destroyed by enemy action. While trying to get to his place of work after it had taken a direct hit, Cyril reported that 'a most officious policeman came up and accused me of looting', and Hoskin's employer had to smooth things over.

Again, Burgess would appear to be slightly inaccurate in his report, because when the surgical goods manufacturers relocated, the Hoskins could not afford to follow, and Cyril found work at the offices of the correspondence school with whom he had previously taken courses. To become a 'correspondence clerk' he had to move to Weybridge in Surrey, and initially the Hoskins took a flat provided by the firm, over a garage.

The Burgess Investigation

Rampa reported that, 'Life at Weybridge was not happy'.[1] He resented not just having to undertake onerous duties for his new employer, but having to maintain the boss's cars. He became an air raid warden and says he aroused jealousy in another warden (he does not specify why) and was reported by this rival when a faulty switch in his flat caused him to be showing a light during an air raid:

> So there was a Court appearance and a fine. And that is a thing I have resented ever since because it was so utterly unnecessary, and 'the enemy' warden was the one who had reported it. After that I resigned from the A.R.P.

At this time, Cyril Hoskin received his call-up papers. He presented himself, as required, to the Board of Medical Examiners, who sent him to hospital, doubting that he had ever really suffered from T.B. (It is a recurring irony throughout his life that nobody ever believes anything he says.) Hoskin would end up being classed as 'Grade Four'; unfit for military service.

Immediately after World War Two, in the 1945 and 1946 telephone directories, the Mr and Mrs Hoskin are listed as living at Stoneleigh flat, St George Avenue, Weybridge, with the telephone number Weybridge 3012. This is all quite normal, but this is the point in Rampa's story when it becomes really rather strange and difficult to understand. Burgess stated that Hoskin became 'more peculiar in his manner', began taking his cat out for walks on a lead, called himself Kuan-Suo, and shaved off all the hair from his head.

A researcher, John Pitt, a journalist from the *Psychic Times*, later took an interest in Hoskin and talked to previous neighbours who still remembered Cyril and Sarah Hoskin. Mrs Ablett, from Weybridge, recalled him as,

> . . . full of strange stories about China where he had been taken as a child. He had been very interested in occult matters, would

---

[1] Rampa, *As It Was!*, 152, *et seq.*

cast horoscopes for all and sundry and was generally a good conversationalist, if a bit inclined to tell contradictory stories about his past.[1]

Christopher Evans, in *Cults of Unreason*, mentions a Mr Boxall who was reported by John Pitt as saying,

> He told me in 1943 or 1944 that he had been a flying instructor in the Chinese air force. . . . He said he had been badly smashed up in a plane crash when the parachute failed to open.
>
> A rather similar picture came from a Mr Lorraine Sutton of East Moseley, who met Hoskin in 1948, shortly after he had changed his name to Carl Kuan Sou. By that time the former Hoskin was describing himself as Dr Kuan and saying that he was born in Tibet—a fact which rather surprised Mr Sutton somewhat since 'The Doctor' both talked and looked remarkably like an Englishman.'[2]

Frederic Warburg himself went to see Mrs Ablett and Mrs Boxall in 1960:

> They had not, they said, liked Dr K. overmuch, but they knew him reasonably well. It was in 1942 that he told them he proposed to revert to his 'real' name of Kuan Suo in place of Cyril Henry Hoskins [sic]. He had cards printed in this style and insisted he be called by his 'proper' name. His mother, he said, was Chinese and, though he detested English children because they were so badly brought up, he loved Chinese ones. He demanded to be treated with the greatest respect, and could not endure to be told off by anyone, even in a superior position to himself. He loved cats, and had a collar and lead for his own which he took driving in his car at night hanging round the back of his neck. He took many snaps of her, for he loved photography—and trick mirrors. He was also interested in numerology

---

[1] Mutton, 'T. Lobsang Rampa: New Age Trailblazer', Part 1, 50.
[2] Evans, *Cults of Unreason*, 246.

The Burgess Investigation

and palmistry. He showed little interest in women, but was married to an ex-nurse or hospital sister. He was not much interested in men either, for he was solitary and secretive. He was, however, these two women informed me, a marvellous teller of tales.[1]

Hoskin had changed his name, officially, to 'KuonSuo' on the official Register on 16th February 1948. Burgess reported that following his decision to make his first change of name, Hoskin had written to his supervisor at the correspondence school:

> 'You may wonder why I go on so
> But will you please remember I am Kuan Suo.'[2]

The period is described by Kuan's wife in her book *Tigerlily* in terms that make it sound quite reasonable that a cat should be taken out for walks with a harness and on a lead. Both he and Sarah were obviously 'cat mad' and had a number of beliefs that even the most ardent admirers of the species might find difficult to share. Their cat, Sarah said, did not like being taken for rides in their car simply because their vehicle was haunted. She admitted that taking it out on a rowing boat may have been a step too far. From their own later accounts, it is reasonable to suggest husband and wife were both equally eccentric.

As for shaving off all his hair being a part of Hoskin's peculiar behaviour, to judge by the one surviving photo from this time, from a relatively young age he only had a small amount of hair on either side of his head to remove. He would, though, begin to affect stereotyped 'Eastern' dress.

Rampa reports that he had problems with his teeth, necessitating a period of recovery in a nursing home, and says that his employers were not sympathetic.

---

[1] Warburg, *All Authors Are Equal*, 244-245.
[2] *Daily Mail,* 1st February 1958.

Characters of Questionable Faith

Cyril Hoskin.

> There were quite a number of unpleasant little incidents, needlings and all that sort of thing, and unjust accusations. There is no point in going into all the details, raking up muck, because, after all, I am not a pressman. But there were false accusations, so my wife and I talked it over and we decided that we couldn't stick it any longer, so I handed in my notice.[1]

Rampa says that he and Sarah moved to Thames Ditton, at which time he could not find work, in part because he had voluntarily left his previous employment, and, as he wrote, preference was given to returning servicemen. The couple would seem to have lived in a lodging house at first, and then moved to Rose Croft, on Western Green Road, opposite the cottage hospital. They had the upstairs flat, with a balcony at the rear and access to the large back garden.

Rampa describes this period as one of poverty and unhappiness. On the 24th March 1950 there was another official change of name and 'KuanSuo' became, 'Carl Kuan', on the Register.

---

[1] Rampa, *As It Was!*, 156.

The Burgess Investigation

His frequent addition of the title 'Dr' does not appear in any official record.

Cyril Hoskin's conditions may well have caused him to consider that a radical change might improve his circumstances. However, what neither he nor his wife admitted in their subsequent memoirs, and Burgess does not appear to have discovered, was that in 1953 Sarah Hoskin, calling herself Sanya Ku'an, was running a fashionable boutique called Rene Clair in Kensington Church Street. Quite how they were able to afford to buy a business in Kensington and maintain a furnished flat off Ladbrooke Grove, is not accounted for in their own records. In a *Daily Express* story it was claimed that they had told neighbours they had a wealthy backer in Manchester.[1]

The local newspaper, the *Kensington News*, happily gave Sanya's business good publicity. In November 1953, under the headline 'A Nurse Takes to Fashion', Anne Campden wrote:

> This week I met Madame Sanya Ku'an who has taken over the business of Rene Clair, the attractive boutique at the northern end of Kensington Church Street. Madame Ku'an is a State Registered Nurse as well as having a passionate interest in clothes and fashion. . . . Madame Ku'an first started to make corsets when she realised the misery and embarrassment many women suffer when they have to wear a heavy, ungainly and unsightly corset under fashionable clothes. . . . Sanya Ku'an in addition to being a nurse, a corsetiere and a fashion enthusiast, finds time to devote to her fascinating hobby of graphology or the art of handwriting . . . and to care for her two adorable Siamese kittens, who in the kingly way of such creatures allow her and her husband to share their Kensington flat.

In January 1954 there was a follow-up article, presumably also by Campden:

---

[1] *Daily Express*, Tuesday 4th February 1958.

Characters of Questionable Faith

Star attraction of the week is the 'TV' show which is screened several times a day at a Kensington Church Street dress shop. Dr C. Ku'an, husband of Sanya Ku'an who runs Rene Clair's 'boutique' made the film himself—in colour—and the star roles are divided equally between models showing Rene Clair fashions and Dr and Mrs Ku'an's two delightful Siamese kittens, Ku'ei and Su-wei.

The film is projected from behind on a 'TV Set' screen which has been made by Dr Ku'an from a tea-chest and walnut veneer paper, but is indistinguishable from the real thing.

Obviously, Cyril Hoskin's interest in electrical appliances was being usefully combined with his interest in photography and film. In February 1954 there was another article in which the readers were reminded that Sanya is a nurse:

And has practiced psychological work with her doctor husband.

although what kind of psychological work she and the 'doctor' were undertaking is unclear. Rampa later wrote:

I did certain psychological work among people who could get no assistance from orthodox medicine and I did quite well, I really did. I cured a number of people but then one day there was a man who tried to blackmail me.[1]

Rampa does not give details of the attempted blackmail. (He mentions another, different blackmail attempt in *Candlelight*.[2])

When scandal later broke, Campden wrote an article stating:

I met Dr C. Kuan and his wife Sanya in the winter of 1953-54, when they bought a women's dress and lingerie shop in Kensington Church Street. They lived in a furnished flat off the

---

[1] Rampa, *As It Was!*, 176-177.
[2] Rampa, *Candlelight*, 91.

The Burgess Investigation

Ladbrooke Grove, with their two Siamese kittens, to which they were devoted. . . .

Dr Kuan lavished presents on her, expensive compacts, jewellery—mostly European and mystic in appearance, and round her neck she wore a wooden medallion. In her turn she would lavish presents on those who would accept them. She said she was Scotch and a State Registered Nurse, and in addition to the boutique she and her husband sold medical corsetry.[1]

Then Dr Kuan introduced himself as a Tibetan lama. Tall, pale, with a wispy beard, he wore well-cut lounge suits and had a great sense of humour despite the fact that he could talk with great seriousness of auras, transmigration, levitation and other Eastern mysticisms.

He showed heavily sealed documents which he said were degrees from Eastern Universities where he had obtained degrees of Dr of Medicine, M.A., Dr of Science and B.Sc in Civil Engineering.

Rampa is rather vague about the period before the writing and publication of *The Third Eye*, but because of his animus towards petty authority, he tells two related stories to show his superiority over the average British policeman. In the first he says he was travelling for work with anatomical models in his car and was stopped by the police because somebody had seen the naked legs of women showing through the back window. In the second, he was in his place of work, presumably an office block, when the police came and accused him of making mysterious signals out of the window, which he easily explained as waving goodbye to his wife. The policemen had been observing him from a building opposite and also wanted him to account for what he was up to on the floor below with 'naked females', which turned out to be manikins in a showroom.[2]

Rampa also tells a story about another job at this time, developing photographic film for undisclosed undesirable types. It

---

[1] Important but unromantic work, 'medical corsetry' is a euphemism for trusses—support used by men suffering from hernias.
[2] Rampa, *As It Was!*, 173-176.

may have been based on experience, for Burgess reported that during this period Hoskin was a 'Criminal and Accident Photographer'. The subject matter of the work he was doing may well have inspired the embellishments about run-ins with gangsters whom he was able to get the better of through his knowledge of martial arts.[1] Suffice to say, the first three books by Rampa display a quality of breathless physical adventure and repeated hardships that are surprisingly robust experiences for a religious mystic.

Burgess was back on Hoskin's track in 1954 when he was living in Bayswater. Harrer, in *Beyond Seven Years in Tibet*, claimed that Burgess '. . . slipped into one of the lama's séances in the guise of a student. He reported that Lobsang Rampa wore a mighty beard, and was lying in bed stroking two Siamese cats,'[2] but I can find no corroboration that Kuan ever undertook séances.

Along with Cyrus Brooks and Frederic Warburg, the journalist Campden was obviously also shown impressive certificates by Dr Kuan to prove his credentials. In his book *Prisoners of Shangri-La*, Donald S. Lopez claims that the 'diploma' shown to Warburg:

> . . . was in English rather than Chinese, badly typed and festooned with what appeared to be bottle caps.[3]

It is unlikely that Brooks, Warburg or Campden would have been able to understand what they were shown if the certificates

---

[1] Rampa, *The Rampa Story*, 189.

[2] Harrer, *Beyond Seven Years in Tibet*, 245.

[3] Lopez, *Prisoners of Shangri-La*, 98. No source is cited, but the earliest reference to the certificate being 'badly typed' with 'bottle tops' seems to be 'T. Lobsang Rampa—Lama, Mystic and Plumber', a BBC Radio 4 documentary first broadcast 4th Nov 1995, which is very entertaining, but contains a number of fictional embellishments.

The Burgess Investigation

had not been in English, although it is likely that they would have been able to recognise bottle caps, had they been attached.

It was after this period of comparative affluence that the Kuans first met Sheelagh Rouse, who was to have an indirectly major influence on their lives. Rouse was married to John Rouse with whom she had two children, and she admits in her memoir that her marriage was unfulfilling at the time she met Kuan. She seems to have given up her husband and children without any qualms, along with all her former friends, to move in with the man she believed to be a Tibetan lama. She even gave birth to her third child in the Kuan's flat, which caused a complaint to be made, necessitating another visit from the police who suspected the couple of running an unregistered nursing home. Kuan told Rouse that the complaint had been made by her parents.[1] She gave the baby to her husband and his family to raise, and Rouse was to live with the Kuans for the next twenty-five years.

Rouse had been immediately struck by Kuan when she was first introduced to him through her housekeeper, Mrs Wood. Sheelagh was told he was a Tibetan doctor and that he was looking for work. She remembered him and his wife being very poor at this time. Obviously, their circumstances had altered; Sanya was no longer being lavished with expensive gifts by her husband, and she was unable to give equally expensive presents to friends.

In an attempt to help Kuan, Sheelagh persuaded her husband to write a letter of introduction for the 'doctor' to their friend, Charles Gibbs-Smith at the Victoria and Albert Museum. Rouse is very uncomplimentary about Gibbs-Smith, who was an expert in the history of aviation, and who would have been fascinated by Kuan's tales of man-bearing kites in Tibet. Gibbs-Smith helpfully sent Kuan on to Cyrus Brooks at the literary agents, A.M. Heath.

---

[1] Rouse, *Twenty-Five Years with T. Lobsang Rampa*, 104-5.

Characters of Questionable Faith

In one recollection, Rampa claimed he was hoping to find work as a ghostwriter.[1] *Time* magazine reported that:

> When he was sacked some time later, he took to 'spivving' it and writing occasional magazines and articles.[2]

but I have been unable to locate any literary work published by Rampa/Hoskin/Kuan-suo before *The Third Eye*. In another recollection, Rampa wrote that when he visited Brooks:

> I thought I was going to get a job with him reading and commenting on authors' typescripts, but no, he knew a bit of my story and very, very much against my will I allowed myself to be persuaded into writing a book. One cannot be too particular when starvation is just around the corner.[3]

Warburg reported:

> K. wanted Brooks to find him work writing advertising material for medical supplies. Why *medical* supplies, Brooks had inquired? At this point K. had taken from his briefcase a certificate of considerable elaboration . . .[4]

As it was, Brooks believed that Kuan had more to offer with his recollections of having once been a Tibetan lama.

[1] Rampa, *The Third Eye* (New York: Ballantine, 1964), 8.
[2] *Time* magazine, 'Private v. Third Eye', 17th February 1958, 52.
[3] Rampa, *As It Was!*, 177.
[4] Warburg, *All Authors Are Equal*, 221.

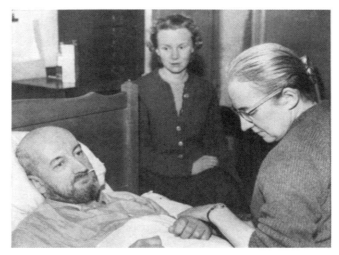

Kuan in bed at Ben Edair, tended by his wife, with Sheelagh Rouse.[1]

4.
The Exposé

The first newspaper to act upon the Burgess report was *The Daily Mail*. Before publishing their story, Hugh Medlicott appears to have conducted a number of interviews, not just with the Rampa household in Howth, but also with their friends and relatives. The Rampas later declared that their reported statements were fabricated, but it is very possible that Medlicott, interviewing them, might not have told them everything that Clifford Burgess had discovered. The *Daily Mail* certainly used subterfuge when they asked Irish freelance photographer Pat Maxwell to visit the household on the Balscadden Road. Maxwell recalled:

> They warned me not to declare that I was from the *Mail*, as he was reluctant to have any pictures taken.[2]

---

[1] Photographed by Pat Maxwell, *Time* magazine, 17th February 1958.
[2] Maxwell, *Stories Behind My News Pictures*, 1, *et seq.*

Characters of Questionable Faith

When Maxwell knocked on their door, he was greeted with suspicion by Mrs Kuan, and he told her he wanted to photograph the author reading his book, suggesting that the publicity would increase sales of *The Third Eye* among Irish readers. All three residents seem to have been happy for him to do so.

Mrs Kuan and Sheelagh Rouse examining different editions of *The Third Eye*, in a photo taken by Pat Maxwell.

Maxwell was shown into Kuan's bedroom:

> The room was rather cold despite the fact that a fire glowed in the corner. A large double bed was situated alongside big picture windows which, in daylight, must have given a wonderful panoramic view of the sea. Sitting up resting against a nest of pillows was Mr Hoskins.

Maxwell made a mental note that there was no sign of anything that might suggest a third eye. He took his photos and returned to his office, by which time it was 6 pm. However, there was a message waiting for him from *Time* magazine, who had also called to ask him to take photos of Kuan.

The Exposé

. . . as I had only taken enough pictures to service the *Daily Mail*, I had no option but to travel back and get some different pictures.

On his second visit that evening, Maxwell explained to the family that his first set of photos had been ruined during processing, and they allowed him to take more. Maxwell explained that Rampa was falling asleep after taking a sedative, when he was photographed reading his own book.

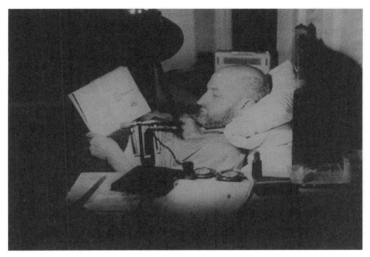

Rampa reading *The Third Eye*, in bed at Howth.

Maxwell says the story was published in the *Daily Mail* the day after the photos were taken, on 1st February 1953. The story was a long one at 1,500 words, and told the public all about the 'Mayfair wife' and the 'bogus Lama'. Although the story only made it to the front page of the Scottish edition of the *Daily Mail*, there was a more lavish spread, with extra photographs, inside the London edition. Described as 'a brilliant hoaxer', the author of the best-selling *The Third Eye* was revealed to be 'plain Mr Cyril Henry Hoskins' [sic]. Rouse was described as 'once a gay member of West End Society' who 'has been presented to the Queen at a Buckingham Palace tea party'. There is

43

no overt suggestion of sexual impropriety (readers could, no doubt, draw their own conclusions), but it was a gift to the newspaper that alongside a fraudulent lama, they could bring into the story a pretty young society woman (Sheelagh Rouse's photograph is by far the most prominent on the page), accuse her of un-maternal feelings, *and* mention the Queen.

Inside the *Daily Mail*, London edition, 1st February 1958.

The Exposé

Medlicott reported that when he had talked to Madame Kuan, she had said of *The Third Eye*:

> 'The book is fiction. He had tried to get a number of jobs without success. We had to have money to live. So he was persuaded to write the book. We depend upon its sale for money.'[1]

Medlicott wrote that 'Dr Kuan was too ill to see me when I called at the white-and-green villa . . .' but,

> His wife invited me into the house . . . [where] she and Mrs Rouse at first denied that Dr Kuan was Cyril Henry Hoskins [sic]. . . . Then they told me he adopted the name of Kuan to hide the identity of the real Dr Kuan, who wrote the book and lives in fear of Communism.
>
> Madame Kuan said: 'He will not tell anyone who the real Dr Kuan is. He will sacrifice everything to protect him.'
>
> Mrs Rouse added: 'We were prepared for snoopers to come and pry out the facts. I have seen the real Dr Kuan but I will not tell you where he is.'

Madame Kuan, from the *Daily Mail*, 1st February 1958.

[1] *Daily Mail*, 1st February 1953, *et seq.*

Characters of Questionable Faith

Then,

> Madame Kuan telephoned me and said: 'I've got to tell you. This will hurt him very much.' . . . 'He is not a Tibetan. That is his photograph on the cover of the book. He has written another one on the same lines.'

But later,

> From his sick bed Mr Hoskins [sic] sent me a message maintaining the authenticity of the book.
> It said: 'This story is true but for very special reasons the identity of the Tibetan author cannot be revealed.'

Neither of the above stories accords with the explanation that Kuan was later to offer, and to assert for the rest of his life, albeit that his later story also contained various alterations.

John Rouse, *Daily Mail*, 1st February 1958.

The household on Balscadden Road might not have even realised they had been interviewed by somebody from the press, and that they had allowed photographs to be taken to accompany an exposé. From their quiet seclusion in Ireland they

The Exposé

were probably unaware that Medlicott had also talked to Sheelagh Rouse's husband, John, 'an ex-Regular Army officer' who,

> . . . said at his City office last night:
> 'I know the stories that are circulating about Lobsang Rampa, but I believe none of them and I do not want to discuss them. I have known him for two and a half years and I am convinced he is thoroughly genuine. He has been a guest in my home, a good friend of my wife and myself, and I am quite sure he is no phoney.'

Medlicott had also talked to Rouse's mother, Mrs Margery Isherwood, who said that her daughter 'believes implicitly that he belongs to a high-ranking Tibetan family', and Hoskin's sister, Mrs Winifred Illingworth-Butler, who said: 'I know nothing about it.' Cyrus Brooks had also been interviewed and said: 'I am surprised', a response echoed by Frederic Warburg who also added, 'I thought he was Chinese'. With reference to *The Third Eye*, the *Daily Mail* quoted members of the 'cabal' including Snellgrove: 'I am of the opinion it's not authentic'; Richardson: 'It's quite obvious it's not written by a Tibetan'; and Pallis: 'To anyone who has been there, the book proves itself to be false.'

It is probable that Medlicott and Maxwell were the first visitors from the press to Ben Edair on Balscadden Road in Howth, but many more of their profession were soon knocking on the Kuans' door. There are two other separate accounts of this time; by Sheelagh Rouse in her memoir, and by the travel writer Eric Newby in *A Traveller's Life*.

Rouse remembers that, presumably on 1st February, she left the house early and noticed that there were an unusual number of people at The Cliff Hotel, in the near distance, and she only later realised they were reporters. When she went down to the village shop she guessed from the attitude of the locals that something untoward had happened, but it was only when she picked up the newspaper that she realised what it was. Her main memory was of being:

> ... met by a half page photograph of myself, taken years ago by Pearl Freeman, a society photographer, on my engagement to John for inclusion in *The Tatler*. It was still, so many years later recognizable. The caption, however, was the disturbing part: 'Society Hostess Flees with Bogus Lama,' it read in large, black print.[1]

Sheelagh Rouse, *Daily Mail*, 1st February 1958.

She wrote of the newspaper article:

> This allusion to myself was merely in the trumped up story to make Chen out to be the worst kind of lecher possible, and to pander to scandal mongers. The story inside the newspaper was lengthy, and I was unable to bring myself to read it in full. I got the gist, though—it was insulting, hurtful, and untrue.

When she returned to the house she found:

> Men crowded around the steps leading to the front door, and Ra'ab standing on the top step outside the door, looking

[1] Rouse, *Twenty-Five Years with T. Lobsang Rampa*, 138-9, *et seq.*

The Exposé

fearful and agitated. Then it dawned on me. The press! My God, it was the press, all those people at the Cliff Hotel, that was what it was, the press waiting to pounce. But why so many?

Rouse's immediate reaction was to fly to London to consult a friend of her estranged husband. A QC, Brian Carruthers told Rouse there was nothing she could do about the newspaper stories because Rampa was obviously the fake they claimed him to be, and she admitted to living with him and his wife, having deserted her family. All he could suggest was that she should leave the company of the Kuans, which she refused to do. At her club she was informed that her parents would like to see her at Brown's Hotel. When she dutifully met them they were, as might be expected, unhappy about the stories in the newspaper, but:

> What happened next was almost surreal. As if summoned by the devil, a little man suddenly appeared in our midst. Had he come from a hole in the floor, or had he dropped from the sky? Neither, he had emerged from behind the screen, like a character in a comedy.
>
> 'Mrs Rouse, allow me to introduce myself—Jeremiah Smythe, private detective.'
>
> Ignoring his attempt to shake hands with me, I remained standing, watching him. Jeremiah Smythe! No one was called Jeremiah Smythe outside Dickens . . .[1]
>
> 'Ah, I see you haven't heard of me. Well, let me tell you, my dear young lady, I have spent months tracking down your friend, and he isn't what he says he is, he's been fooling you. . . . He's a plumber![2] A common plumber!! An English plumber who has never been outside this country.'[3]

---

[1] It would appear that Clifford Burgess is called Jeremiah Smythe only so Rouse could make the joke that it was an unlikely Dickensian name—a joke that falls flat as it was her own invention.

[2] Neither Burgess, nor the newspapers at the time, accused Cyril Hoskin of being a plumber himself.

[3] Rouse, *Twenty-Five Years with T. Lobsang Rampa*, 147-149.

Characters of Questionable Faith

It is surprising that by the time she wrote her memoir, nearly fifty years later, Rouse hadn't realised that Smythe (Burgess) was hired by Pallis and his associates, although it is very reasonable, given her prominence in the story, that she should feel that it was as much of an attack on her own character as it was on that of Dr Kuan. She was reported by the *Daily Express* as saying that her marriage was over without hope of reconciliation and that:

> 'Someone employed a private detective to discredit the Lama and win me back.'[1]

She is also meant to have said:

> 'I never want to see my parents again.'[2]

However, the *Daily Express* did report that her parents had contacted the police themselves because they were concerned for her, and this might be a cause of her confusion. Their own investigation seems to have been separate to the one carried out by Burgess.

The personal aspect of the story hurt, but as for attacks on Kuan, Rouse obviously blamed Harrer, who,

> . . . may have been jealous or he may have been moved by a mistaken but genuine desire to keep the lamastic life sacred. . . . Whoever it was did a grave disservice, and it would not be going too far to say a grave disservice to mankind. The fact is . . . Lobsang Rampa's true identity is not important. WHO Lobsang Rampa was is not the consequential issue, the message he imparted is. But to say he was an English plumber—plumbers then being regarded as illiterates—or an Englishman of any kind who had never been out of his country is so ridiculous as to be ludicrous.[3]

[1] *Daily Express*, 3rd February 1958.
[2] *ditto*.
[3] Rouse, *Twenty-Five Years with T. Lobsang Rampa*, 139.

The Exposé

Rouse was able to fly back to Dublin and return to Howth the same evening.

> There had been people around the house all day, they went through the dustbins, they crept along the cliff path under his window with mirrors on long poles, they waylaid anyone who approached the house.[1]

The activities of the press in Howth were corroborated by Eric Newby, author of the successful *A Short Walk in the Hindu Kush*, published by Secker & Warburg. Newby was asked by Frederic Warburg to go to Kuan as an official emissary, to ask for a statement. (Although Warburg might have required information, he should not have been completely surprised by the turn of events.)

> By this time the *Daily Express* had been on the line to Warburg. They were furious at having been scooped by the *Daily Mail* and were anxious, if at all possible, to prove that the Lama was a Lama and not the son of a plumber in Plympton. They wanted one of their reporters to accompany me to Ireland for this purpose and Warburg thought this would be no bad thing.[2]

Newby points out that at such a moment it must have seemed to Warburg that any allies were better than none. Newby and the reporter arrived in Dublin too late to call on Rampa, and set out the next morning to Howth:

> I had never seen the gentlemen of the press in action before —and frustrated gentlemen at that—and now doing so I found it difficult to believe my eyes. Some of them had constructed primitive periscopes, using bamboo poles with mirrors attached to them, with which they were trying to look in through the windows . . . others were apparently happily engaged in going through the dustbins.

[1] Rouse, *Twenty-Five Years with T. Lobsang Rampa*, 154.
[2] Newby, *A Traveller's Life*, 176, *et seq.*

Characters of Questionable Faith

Newby was not admitted to the house at first, but after a brief discussion with Madam K through the letterbox, was told to come back later. At that time he was,

> . . . allowed in to the hall of the house, which was furnished with a wooden Buddha and a brass tray made in Birmingham on a rickety black ebony stand. It was a depressing room, rather like the set for an oriental interior in a play to be performed in a village hall.

He met Madam K, and:

> A fresh-faced, very English-looking girl who told me that she had left her husband (who was a member of Lloyds), and her three children in order to live as a disciple in the Lama's house. She was 'upset' at being, like the Lama, subjected to a lot of undesirable publicity.
>
> The Lama, Madam K said, was dying . . . and it was unlikely that he would live for more than a couple of days.

When Newby returned the next day he was given cassette tapes made by Kuan for Frederic Warburg. Unless there were others, these were presumably the ones quoted from by the newspapers and later passed on to a television company which broadcast them. Essentially, Dr Kuan gave details of the take-over of Cyril Hoskin by Tuesday Lobsang Rampa through the process of transmigration. It would become his long-term explanation of events, as given in detail first in *The Rampa Story* (1960) from the point of view of the lama, and then later, with some details altered, in *As It Was!* (1976) from the position of Cyril Hoskin.

The Rampas issued an official statement which was widely reported in the press:

> In his statement, Mr Ku'an makes a 'solemn declaration that his book *The Third Eye* is absolutely true.' He says that his wife knew at the time 'that another entity had taken over his body.'
> . . .

The Exposé

In the statement, Mr Ku'an speaks of his 'memories of life as an Englishman fading' and later losing all memory of life before and having instead the 'full memory of a Tibetan from baby-hood onwards.

'A strong entity is able to take possession of another body—replacing the original soul—this is called transmigration.' . . .

Mrs Ku'an says that after an accident in 1949 her husband 'was no longer the same man. Since that summer of 1949 his whole makeup and manner has been that of an Easterner. His general appearance and colouring have also shown a marked change.[1]

Eric Newby did finally manage to talk his way into Rampa's bedroom. As he left, Mrs Rampa had also been persuaded to let the *Daily Express* reporter see Rampa as well, having explained that they intended to show the author in a more favourable light. They also admitted another photographer who would later phone Newby and the reporter to say:

> 'You know those pictures I took of the Lama? Well, I've printed them oop and do you know what? There's a ruddy great 'alo round 'is 'ead.'[2]

Pat Maxwell even returned to the house for a third time to take pictures for the *Daily Mirror*. The intention was for a reporter to knock on the door, and to throw a copy of *The Third Eye* at whoever answered, while shouting '*Rubbish!*' This was to be photographed by Maxwell. The planned photo opportunity does not seem to have been successful.[3]

---

[1] *The Birmingham Post*, 8th February 1958.
[2] Newby, *A Traveller's Life*, 181.
[3] *In Stories Behind My Pictures*, Maxwell claims that the interruption of the Irish Garda meant an alternative photo was taken and was published on the front page of the *Daily Mirror*. However, no edition of the *Daily Mirror* from this period archived by the British Library has such a photo.

Characters of Questionable Faith

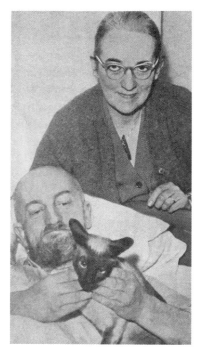

Mr and Mrs Kuan from *Der Stern*.

On 3rd February 1958 the *Daily Mail* continued the story of 'the Third Eye Hoaxer', but only in the London edition. They quoted from the cassettes as 'The Bogus Lama speaks from his sick-bed'. In response to the accusation two days before that he had been 'reading the stars' and giving 'advice on spiritual and health problems for a fee',

> He denied that he had ever taken any money for giving advice to people about their health and spiritual problems.[1]

Medlicott reported that Madam Kuan,

> ... asked me not to call on her husband again as my aura was penetrating the house and making him ill.

[1] *Daily Mail*, 3rd February 1958, *et seq.*

The Exposé

The *Daily Mail*, 3rd February 1958.

The *Daily Mail* also reported that the television producer, John Irwin, had met Rampa soon after the publication of *The Third Eye*. He told them:

'No normally intelligent person could meet him and believe he was Tibetan or Chinese. He was thoroughly Western.
 'He is over 6ft tall, bald, and clean-shaven.
 'He seemed to be a gentleman, but harmless and lonely and completely lost in the fantastic role he had set himself.

Characters of Questionable Faith

'He was a sad man and, while I am sure he has no magic powers or strange knowledge, if he did write this book he has remarkable powers of imagination.'[1]

The *Daily Express* was finally able to print a story on the same day. In an attempt to undermine the *Daily Mail*, they reported Sheelagh Rouse ('former Mayfair hostess') as saying,

'I regard myself as the Lama's daughter and I am here of my own free will.'[2]

Their headline ran:

The FULL truth about the bogus Lama

The *Daily Express*, 3rd February 1958.

They reported:

The Lama—he claims that he has been possessed by a Tibetan monk—said from his sick bed, 'I saw this girl's marriage breaking up. I wanted to help.'

---

[1] *Daily Mail*, 3rd February 1958.
[2] *Daily Express*, 3rd February 1958.

The Exposé

They then gave the details of the literary controversy, although their attempt at being even-handed didn't do Kuan's case a great deal of good. They nevertheless pointed out, with regard to the *Daily Mail* accusing him of charging the public for dubious clairvoyant skills:

> 'I have taken no money from the hundreds of people who write to me. Why should I? My book is a best seller.'

The *Daily Express* also printed Frederick Warburg's account of the publication of *The Third Eye*. In his autobiography he proudly wrote that the newspaper bought his 1,000 word article at the 'stiff price' of £250.[1]

The *Express*, obviously mindful that a sensational story was probably more important than undermining their competitor reported, on the 4th February:

The Three-Eyed Lama Once Sold Corsets

Daily Express, 4th February 1958.

---

[1] Warburg, *All Authors Are Equal*, 244.

Characters of Questionable Faith

The *Express* had managed to find details of the shop that the Kuans had previously run in Kensington Church Street, calling Cyril 'a character in a street of London "characters".'[1]

> The lama . . . and his wife sold books, antiques, corsets, and women's clothes.

and mentioned the shadowy 'wealthy backer in Manchester'. They reported,

> Dr Kuan enthralled his neighbours with tales of his past.

According to the *Express*, when they left Kensington the Kuans said they might be going to America.

Sheelagh Rouse in *Der Stern*.

A comment made by Rampa in the Ballantine paperback edition of *The Third Eye*, suggests that when the Burgess report was made public, the press in Germany were also hounding the Kuans.[2] *Der Spiegel*, however, gave no more details than the British *Daily Mail*, and although *Der Stern* devoted several pages to the story (with many pictures[3]), *Die Zeit* was quite matter of

---

[1] *Daily Express*, 4th February 1958, *et seq*.
[2] Rampa, *The Third Eye* (Ballantine, 1964), 5.
[3] Although a photograph of Marco Pallis is mistakenly captioned 'Ex-Scotland Yard Detective Clifford Burgess'.

The Exposé

fact in its report of the exposé, and sounded quite weary of the affair:

> The whole thing is by no means a scandal, but a fairly everyday occurrence. . . . It is no different with many other events on the slippery slope of philosophy, art and religion, and it will always be the same.[1]

In America, when the story was reported in the journal *Tomorrow*, the authority on Buddhist philosophy Professor Chen-Chi Chang wrote a review of *The Third Eye* that pointed out that Rampa's knowledge of Buddhism and Tibetan occultism was 'inaccurate and superficial', and he characterised the book simply as 'interesting and highly imaginative fiction—but certainly not a source of authentic information on Buddhist teachings of training.'[2]

The story of the Bogus Lama was reported in newspapers in all the countries where *The Third* eye had been published, but not every British national newspaper bothered with reporting the exposé. Anne Campden, however, took the opportunity to remind her readers in the *Kensington News* that when she had reviewed *The Third Eye* for them in December 1956 she had written:

> Even if I was not acquainted with T. Lobsang Rampa, *The Third Eye* would be an incredible story. As I have met him, and know him to be a tall, pale-faced 'un-Eastern looking' man, with Western speech, manners and business knowledge, I found the book almost impossible to believe.[3]

---

[1] Martin Beheim-Schwarzbach, 'The Pseudo-Tibetan', *Die Zeit*, 6th February 1958.

[2] 'Tibetan Phantasies', *Tomorrow* vol 6, no 2, Spring 1958, 13-16.

[3] The original article was published in *The Kensington News* 28th December 1956, and was quoted by Campden after the scandal broke on 7th February 1958.

5.
The Explanation

When the press first requested a clarification of the identity of the author of *The Third Eye*, Mrs Kuan appears to have initially insisted that her husband was *not* Cyril Hoskin. That might not necessarily invalidate later explanations because he had already assumed another name, but she appears to have also admitted the book was fiction. This was quickly changed to a story (agreed by both Kuans) that it had been ghost-written for a suspiciously 'unavailable' Dr Kuan of Tibet, although they later claimed this story to have been an invention of the press. Perhaps it was? Who is to say that the spirit of invention did not affect many of those who found themselves in the small village outside Dublin in that first week of February in 1958?

In *The Rampa Story*, Kuan wrote that Cyril Hoskin's 'first actual "contact" ' with Tibetan lamas took place at Rose Croft, Thames Ditton. After describing, unnecessarily, the trouble he had cutting the lawn one day, he wrote:

The Explanation

I was interested also in photography, and for some time I had been trying to take a photograph of an owl which lived in an old fir tree nearby, a fir tree well encased in climbing ivy.[1]

Suddenly seeing the owl in the tree, 'blinded by the bright sunlight' he went and got his camera, climbed the tree, and then, unfortunately, fell out of it.

I lay a crumpled inert mass beneath the branches of the old fir tree, but quite suddenly I became aware that I was disengaging myself from the physical body . . . Gingerly I got to my feet, and looked about me. To my horrified amazement I found that my body was lying prone upon the ground. . . . Approaching me across the grass was the figure of a Tibetan lama dressed in the saffron robe of the High Order. His feet were several inches from the ground

Communicating telepathically, the lama explained:

'I have come because I want your body for one who has to continue life in the Western world, for he has a task to do which brooks no interference.'

I looked at him aghast. The man was mad saying that he wanted my body! So did I, it was my body. I wasn't having anyone take off [with] my property like that. I had been shaken out of the physical vehicle against my wish, and I was going back.

The Tibetan then pointed out to Cyril:

'What have you to look forward to? Unemployment, illness, unhappiness, a mediocre life in mediocre surroundings, and then in the not too distant future death and the start all over again. Have you achieved anything in life? Have you done anything to be proud of? Think it over.'

---

[1] Rampa, *The Rampa Story*, 172 *et seq.*

Characters of Questionable Faith

The Tibetan said to him, 'But your body cannot be taken unless you are willing', at which Hoskin considered, not unreasonably:

> I really did not like the idea at all. I had had my body some forty years, and I was quite attached to it.

The Tibetan countered by asking: 'Have you no thought for humanity?' and eventually persuaded him, saying that he would return in a month, by which time Cyril would be expected to have grown a beard.

On the next visit, Rampa wrote that the lama was accompanied by three other astral-travelling lamas. Cyril Hoskin was waiting. ' "I am *determined* to go through with it," ' he said.

With a wonderful sense of the absurd, Cyril was asked to climb the fir tree again and throw himself out of it, 'falling to the earth with a satisfying "*thud*",' which effected the transmigration: Rampa took over Cyril's old body, while Cyril was released into Paradise.

From *Rampa's* point of view, it would take some time to come to terms with controlling the recently vacated body of *Hoskin*, mastering the language, and explaining everything to his newly acquired wife:

> From the house came a woman running, saying, 'Oh, what have you done now? You should come in and lie down.'

In the second version of events, published in *As It Was!*, sixteen years later, Rampa claims the 'first contact' occurred while living in Weybridge, not Thames Ditton, where he had access to a large garden with a wooded copse, where he:

> . . . tripped over an exposed root and went down with a horrible thonk. Literally it jerked me out of myself! I stood upright, but then—God bless my soul! I found that 'I' wasn't 'me' because I was standing upright and my body was lying flat on its face. I looked about in utter amazement, and I saw some strange

The Explanation

looking people around me. Monks, I thought, what the devil are monks doing here?[1]

In this version of events, the monks had arrived because they had divined that Hoskin was so unhappy he was considering suicide, something that he had denied in *The Rampa Story*. He apparently found the situation difficult to believe (!) but, in preparation for the transmigration, he went along with their suggestion that he change his name, and also grow a beard (which comes as an afterthought this time). Cyril next hears from the monks when in the garden at Rose Croft, Thames Ditton, who tell him that they will come for him the next day, giving him the exact moment to throw himself out of the tree. In this version, the rigmarole of falling twice from the same tree is discarded, as is the pivotal role of the sun-blinded owl:

> . . . a minute or two before the appointed time I went out into the garden and walked over to the tree. I pulled on a branch of ivy, or whatever it is that ivy has, and reached up to the branch as directed. And then I felt as if I had been struck by lightning. I had no need to pretend to fall, I did fall—whack down![2]

At which point the transmigration took place with 'a sucking sort of noise and a plop'.[3]

It is strange that there are differences in such an important and pivotal moment in Rampa's life. Over the course of sixteen years we are all likely to remember details of our past differently, but it must be noted that the subject of his own story had previously written it down and published it in a book that would have been easily to hand.

A third, streamlined version of events was published in the Introduction to the American Ballantine paperback edition of

---

[1] Rampa, *As It Was!*, 155 *et seq.*
[2] *ditto*, 158.
[3] *ditto*, 158.

Characters of Questionable Faith

The Third Eye in 1964 which also takes the story back to late 1947 when Hoskin:

> . . . had strange impressions and absolute compulsions to adopt Eastern ways of living.[1]

And then:

> On the thirteenth June 1949, he had a slight accident in the garden [and] . . . lost all memory of the life before and instead had the full memory of a Tibetan from babyhood onwards.

This third version has the benefit of lacking so much detail that might otherwise have been queried by sceptical readers. In all the versions of events, Mrs Kuan appears to react to the takeover of her husband's physical body by a Tibetan lama with admirable equanimity. She offers unquestioning support (apart from the one wobble with the press in February 1958), and in her statement printed in the Ballantine edition of *The Third Eye*, she doesn't once express any regret that her original husband had effectively abandoned her. Rampa is at pains to point out that although they apparently live alongside each other, ostensibly as man and wife, there are no sexual relations between the couple. A blind lama guide had apparently explained to him:

> 'You and the lady may live together in a state of companionship, for do not our own monks and nuns live at times under the same roof?'[2]

In later years he was asked about his domestic arrangements by Alain Stanké, and answered:

---

[1] Rampa, *The Third Eye* (Ballantine, 1964), 7, *et seq.*

[2] Rampa, *The Rampa Story*, 162. In fact, the *Snow Lion Newsletter*, Autumn, 1991, reports, 'For the most part monasteries for men and those for women were distinctly separate. In exceptional cases, communities of monks and nuns would be located nearby one another.'

The Explanation

My sex life has sparked a surprising amount of interest. I can easily satisfy everyone's curiosity. It's very simple: I don't have a sex life. I live like a hermit. You could say, and it has been said that I am like a boarder in my own home.[1]

Quite what Mrs Kuan thought of that, does not seem to be on record.

The story told by Lobsang Rampa is an incredible one, and it may be unnecessarily pedantic to analyse minor discrepancies in his accounts when the general thrust of his claim, that Cyril Henry Hoskin's body was taken over by an astral-travelling lama from an 'alternative reality' version of Tibet, would appear to be such an obvious hoax. For those who are minded to believe Rampa (and his supporters have always existed), the differences between the two main accounts can probably be explained using Frederic Warburg's suggestion that autobiographies are inevitably 'touched up maybe a bit here and there'.[2]

The trouble with the original version of events told in *The Rampa Story* is that Hoskin changed his name to KuonSuo in February 1948 while he was still in Weybridge working for the correspondence school, from which he resigned in September, 1948. However, the 'first contact' was described as occurring in Thames Ditton, implying that he had changed his name *before* first encountering any astral-travelling lamas. This was tidied up sixteen years later in *As It Was!*

The actual transmigration is meant to have happened on 13th June 1949.[3] Having officially changed his name to Kuansuo in 1948 (at the behest of the lamas), the man who now declared himself to be Rampa waited until 1950 to change his name to Karl Kuan, not Tuesday Lobsang Rampa. He did, however, claim the Tibetan doctor's right to call himself a Doctor of Medicine. Quite how Rampa was able to acquire Hoskin's

---

[1] Stanké, *Rampa: Imposteur ou initié?*, 149. (My translation.)
[2] Warburg, *All Authors Are Equal*, 226.
[3] Newby, *A Traveller's Life*, 178.

Characters of Questionable Faith

questionable M.A. in Science and B.Sc in Civil Engineering, referred to at the time of his marriage notice in the *Penrith Observer* is unclear. At some point, critics must have asked how Rampa came by the impressive certificates which presumably didn't travel with him when he transmigrated, but he answered this in 1964 by saying that he sent to Tibet for them.[1] (If the astral-travelling lamas had been more thoughtful, they would have posted them to him in Thames Ditton as soon as they had returned to Tibet, without having to be asked.)

The business with the beard is also a curious one. Because biologists calculate that the cells in our body regenerate at least once every seven years, Rampa explained that by then the Englishman called Hoskin would have completely assumed the appearance of the Tibetan now inhabiting his body. The beard, therefore, would hide the physical damage apparently inflicted on Rampa's jaw by the Japanese during the war. Sceptics might argue that, equally, a beard could hide a lack of such evidence.

In 1958 Mrs Hoskin told the newspapers that her husband's 'general appearance and colouring have also shown a marked change'[2] in the previous nine years—explained by the changes at a cell level due to the take-over. However long it took for the physical transformation to happen, Anne Campden recollected that when she met him some four or five years *after* the trans-migration she saw 'a tall, pale-faced "un-Eastern looking" man, with Western speech, manners and business knowledge.'[3] Irwin similarly reported, 'No normally intelligent person could meet him and believe he was Tibetan or Chinese. He was thoroughly Western.'[4]

In fairness, Warburg described Rampa as having a 'swarthy' face, although 'Nothing remarkable, nothing which I could wholly associate with what I knew of Tibetan physiognomy.'[5]

---

[1] Rampa, *The Third Eye* (Ballantine, 1964), 8.
[2] *The Birmingham Post*, 8th February 1958.
[3] *The Kensington News* 28th December 1956.
[4] Daily Mail, 3rd February 1958.
[5] Warburg, *All Authors Are Equal*, 224-6.

The Explanation

When Newby met Rampa in Howth, he described Rampa as making a 'powerful impression' and that in his 'high, domed forehead' was 'a slight dent which could have been the result of the "third eye" operation'. However, Newby noted that his accent was Devonian:

> It certainly wasn't oriental in any way, neither were the expressions which came from his lips those of an oriental person.[1]

[1] Newby, *A Traveller's Life*, 179-180.

6.
Inspiration for *The Third Eye*

Even before *The Third Eye* was published, commentators pointed out errors and fabrications in Rampa's book, all of which suggest that the author had no personal experience of Tibet, let alone life inside a Tibetan monastery. These ranged from mistakes about simple matters of diet, dress, custom and tradition, through to his declarations that there were gold and jewel-filled caverns under the Potala, and his descriptions of yetis and the gilded mummies of extra-terrestrials.

The errors relating to the more mundane matters of Tibetan life are surprising because there were a number of very detailed accounts of Tibet, the city of Lhasa, and even the Potala available to anyone with a library card in the 1940s and 1950s. (One can only imagine how many more such errors were in the early drafts of *The Third Eye*, before Rampa accepted certain corrections.) It is perhaps the least interesting of the faults in the book that do the most to undermine its authenticity, rather than the obvious fabrications, because Rampa would point out that doubters, especially 'so-called experts', had not been initiated into the mysteries that he had experienced. It is impossible to argue with somebody who relates their activities on the astral plane, for example, but when an author makes egregious mistakes about commonplace, verifiable facts, it has to cast doubt on their other assertions.

This is what *Der Stern* did in Germany. Among other details they explained, with the help of Heinrich Harrer:[1]

> 'We learned to write on slates', reports Lobsang Rampa in his book. Harrer saw many schools in Tibet and did not find a single one where slate tablets were known. The children use whitewashed wooden boards into which they scratch the characters.

[1] All quotes, *Der Stern*, 1st March 1958, 13-14.

Inspiration for *The Third Eye*

Hoskins [sic] complains that he was pulled by his pigtail tail as an inattentive student.

'As the alleged son of a prince, he cannot wear a braid,' explains Harrer, 'because the sons of nobles have their heads shaved like lamas. This will make them immune to all evil forces.'

'It wasn't until I was twelve that the Dalai Lama appointed me a lama!' Hoskins [sic] is crucially wrong here. 'A Tibetan is a lama the moment his incarnation is established,' say Harrer and Pallis.

Lingkhor road encompasses the Tibetan capital Lhasa. 'This is where my house of fun stood,' claims the imaginative author Lobsang Rampa. 'My father's house had four floors.' Heinrich Harrer and Marco Pallis, who both know Lhasa like the back of their hands, explain: 'There is not a single four-story house on the Lingkhor. Hoskins talks about three rings of roads in his book; but Lhasa only has two such streets! He was never there!'

One of many questions that arise from *The Third Eye*, is why Rampa attached so much importance to the position of cats in Tibet. What Kuan did not seem to realise is that Tibetans actually have very little interest in cats and much prefer to keep dogs. The simple reason for this is that cats tend to take the lives of other animals, and to Buddhists this is anathema. (Perhaps he was confusing the ancient Egyptian veneration of cats?) A photo of the author and his wife in *Der Stern* has a caption that reads:

Today he lives with his wife near Dublin (Ireland), where he is known as Dr Kuan-suo. However, as a lama priest he is not allowed to be married, and as a Tibetan he cannot possibly have a thick beard (Tibetans hardly have any body hair). The 'real Tibetan cat' in his arm comes from Siam, because there are no cats in Tibet.

So, where did Hoskin's information on Tibet come from, apart from his imagination?

Characters of Questionable Faith

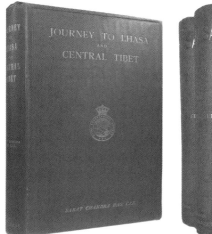

Journey to Lhasa and Central Tibet by Das,
and *Lhasa* by Perceval Landon.

Non-Fiction

Although Marco Pallis, Heinrich Harrer[1] and other experts on the subject of Tibet may have believed that Dr Kuan used their work to help him write *The Third Eye*, there were many other books that could have caught the attention of Dr Kuan in the decade before the publication of *The Third Eye* in 1956, during which time he had obviously become fascinated by China and Tibet.

---

[1] Harrer even mentions Yetis in *Seven Years in Tibet*, although he is dismissive: 'On the tree line I once found deep footprints in the newly fallen snow, which I could not account for. They might have been made by a man. People with more imagination than I possess might have attributed them to the Abominable Snowman.' See 66. In his article 'My Seven Years in Tibet' published in *The Geographical Journal*, Vol. 120, No. 2, June 1954, 148, Harrer writes: 'Personally I believe the tracks to be of bears in winter and of the huge lanur monkey during summer.'

Inspiration for *The Third Eye*

Beguiling accounts of 'mysterious and inaccessible' Tibet became popular not long after the foundation of Theosophy in 1875, and more believable reports of The Younghusband Mission to Tibet[1] (1903-04) were also important for stimulating interest in the country. From the start of the twentieth century there were authoritative volumes published detailing the geography, people, customs and beliefs of Tibet, including *Journey to Lhasa and Central Tibet* by Sarat Chandra Das (John Murray, 1902), *The Unveiling of Lhasa* by Edmund Candler, (Edward Arnold, 1905), *Lhasa and its Mysteries* by Laurence Austine Waddell (John Murray, 1905), and *Lhasa* by Perceval Landon (Hurst and Blackett, 1905). All of the above contained maps and photos that could have aided Kuan in putting together his own story.

Other more popular accounts included *My Journey to Lhasa* by Alexandra David-Néel (Heinemann, 1927), and books by Edmund Candler, F. Spencer Chapman and Theos Bernard, among others, all before the point where Marco Pallis, Heinrich Harrer and other experts were beginning to publish their books.

Donald S. Lopez, Jr. also suggests as a possible source Edwin John Dingle's *My Life in Tibet* (1952),[2] a book in which the author claimed to be a reincarnated Tibetan lama, although it does not appear to have had a wide circulation in Britain.

Precedents in Fiction

There is also the possibility that Kuan had been inspired by fictional accounts of Tibet. John Geddie's *Beyond the Himalayas* (1882) portrayed Tibet with accuracy, even if Laurence

---

[1] An expedition that was, in effect, a temporary invasion by British Indian Armed Forces, intended to counter the Russian Empire's perceived ambitions in the East.

[2] Lopez, *Prisoners of Shangri-La*, 103.

Characters of Questionable Faith

Oliphant's short story 'The Sisters of Thibet',[1] published in 1887, did not. Oliphant allows his narrator with psychic abilities to travel to Tibet in his astral body (which is rather the reverse of Rampa's story). Among other sensational and popular early fiction was Guy Boothby's *Dr Nikola* (1896) in which the unscrupulous central character attempts to steal the secrets of a Chinese esoteric society in Tibet.

Other less fantastic early novels included *War on the World's Roof* (1906) by Gordon Stables and *A Wife from the Forbidden Land* (1907) by A.P. Crouch. Other authors could not resist the temptation to make passing references to 'mysterious' Tibet, as in Arthur Conan Doyle's first chapter of *The Return of Sherlock Holmes* (1905), in which the famous detective tells Watson where he had been since his showdown with Moriarty:

> I travelled for two years in Tibet, therefore, and amused myself by visiting Lhassa and spending some days with the head lama.[2]

Alexander Macdonald's *Through the Heart of Tibet* (1910) is full of adventures, but Claverdon Wood's *The Stolen Grand Lama* (1917) has been identified by Dr R.A. Gilbert as potential inspiration for Dr Kuan:

> . . . it is this novel that introduces a Potala riddled with secret tunnels, vast caverns and hidden exits. Not only are these an essential feature of the plot, but they are also the most likely source of Lobsang Rampa's subterranean Potala.[3]

A great deal of other Tibet-inspired fiction was published in the first half of the twentieth century, including *The Lama's*

---

[1] *Fashionable Philosophy and other Sketches* by Laurence Oliphant, William Blackwood, Edinburgh & London, 1887.
[2] Sir Arthur Conan Doyle, *The Return of Sherlock Holmes*, George Newnes, 1905.
[3] Gilbert, 'Beyond the Lost Horizon', 8.

Inspiration for *The Third Eye*

Secret in 1922 by William Murray Graydon in which Sexton Blake rescues an abducted child from a Tibetan monastery. In *Nine Lives* by Mark Channing (1937) a lama moves between Tibet and Egypt by thought, and Tibet was the background to several novels by Talbot Mundy, including *Om: The Secret of Ahbor Valley* (1924), *The Devil's Guard* (1926), *The Thunder Dragon Gate* (1937) (which introduces the character 'Lobsang-Pun'), and *Old Ugly Face* (1939).

In *Darkness and Light* by Olaf Stapledon (1942) Tibet plays an important role in a tale of future history, and in *The Great Mirror* by J. Arthur Burks (1952), Tibetans have access to Mars via matter transmitters. In most cases, Tibet is the backdrop because it allows authors to project all their fantasies on a country which is still sufficiently unknown that anything can be considered to happen there.

But also qualifying as fiction are those books that were downright impostures. Pre-dating *The Third Eye,* Theodore Illion (1898–1984) was a German author who said he had lived and travelled in Tibet in the mid-1930s, and his book, *In Secret Tibet* (1937) described lamas performing miracle cures, and also feats of endurance. (Rampa, too, described vicissitudes, albeit once he had left Tibet.) In his follow-up, *Darkness Over Tibet* (1938), Illion described an underground city run by a spiritual elite. Both books are preposterous, but there was yet another attempt to pass off fiction as a factual account in Murdo MacDonald Bayne's *Beyond the Himalayas*. This was published in 1954, just two years before *The Third Eye,* and Dr Gilbert has written:

> [Bayne] claimed to have entered Tibet through the Chumbi Valley, presumably in the 1930s, and may actually have done so. But the narrative that follows is pure fiction . . . Once in Tibet MacDonald Bayne meets, talks with and is taught secret doctrines and practices by various lamas and Masters.[1]

---

[1] Gilbert, 'Beyond the Lost Horizon', 3, *et seq.*

Characters of Questionable Faith

Dr Gilbert points out that Bayne was, like Illion, a 'liar rather than a fantasist':

> The significance of this outrageous fraud is the false image of Tibet that his book conveys, and which is believed by his New Age followers.

It can be argued that Rampa was guilty of exactly the same crime. Given his interest in Tibet, Kuan may have read both Illion and Bayne, although, ironically, he may not have realised that they were fraudulent accounts.

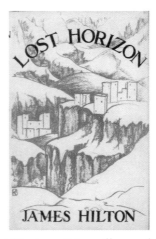

First edition of *Lost Horizon*, Macmillan and Co, London, 1933.

There another book that it is difficult to believe Hoskin had not encountered. James Hilton's best-selling novel *Lost Horizon* had been published in 1933, and was successfully filmed in 1937. The book describes characters surviving an aeroplane crash close to the lamasery of Shangri-La, and portrays Tibet as mysterious and spiritual. In Tibetan Buddhist tradition, Shambhala (also spelled Shambala or Shamballa) is a spiritual kingdom that becomes Shangri-La in the Western imagination. *Lost Horizon* will have had a far wider effect on the prevailing view of Tibet at the time than any other (real or fictional) accounts, until, perhaps, the publication of *The Third Eye*.

Inspiration for *The Third Eye*

Mysticism

In theory, given his alleged educational experiences, all of Rampa's thinking should have been underpinned by Tibetan Buddhism, which evolved from the later stages of mainstream Buddhism, preserving many Indian practices, while allowing for various developments.

From the beginning, commentators found fault with Rampa's claim to be any kind of Buddhist at all. Apart from the ease with which he weaves into his beliefs so many other esoteric concepts unknown to Buddhism, his writings deviate importantly from Buddhist thought.

Agehananda Bharati was patently annoyed that Rampa could write in *The Third Eye*, 'for we know there is a God':[1]

> A Buddhist makes many statements of a puzzling order at times, and he may utter many contradictions; but this statement he will not make . . . the statement 'there is a God' is and remains impossible for any Buddhist. . . . But this was only one of the inane impossibilities of *The Third Eye*. Every page bespeaks the utter ignorance of the author of anything that has to do with Buddhism as practiced and Buddhism as a belief system in Tibet or elsewhere.[2]

As David Mitchie has written on his blog, *The Dalai Lama's Cat*:

> Rampa gets a number of essential concepts completely, you might say, hilariously wrong. Here he is on inner development: 'According to Buddhist belief, all animals, all creatures in fact, have souls, and are reborn to earth in successively higher stages.' (*The Third Eye*, Chapter One). There is no concept of a 'soul' in Buddhism—but we'll let that slide as a translation issue. The idea of successively higher stages, however, is just not Buddhist.

[1] Rampa, *The Third Eye*, 135.
[2] 'Bharati, 'Fictitious Tibet'. This objection was raised in the original review in *Der Spiegel*.

Characters of Questionable Faith

It would suggest that, irrespective of your behaviour in this lifetime, things for you in the future are going to get better and better.[1]

Michie also points out that Rampa's conception of Hell and Karma simply make no sense in Buddhist teaching.

> As for earth being hellish, it may be for many beings. But Buddha described a precious human birth, of the kind most of us have, as being of the most incredible rarity, something to be greatly treasured. Not a sentiment that comes across in Lobsang Rampa's books.

In another blog post, Michie explained:

> As important was what he missed out, with no reference to some of the main teachings of the Dharma, such as the cultivation of bodhichitta. Who wants to read boring stuff about the importance of generosity, ethics and patience when you can go astral travelling instead?![2]

Tibetan Mahakala Mask, Late Qing Dynasty, from Lhasa displaying a third eye on the forehead.

---

[1] Michie: 'The enduring fascination with Lobsang Rampa', *et seq.*
[2] Michie, 'A Few Words on Lobsang Rampa'.

Inspiration for *The Third Eye*

In fairness to Rampa, the concept of the third eye *is* known to Buddhism, but it is a spiritual, not a physical concept. As has been previously noted, transmigration is also an accepted part of Buddhist teaching, but Rampa has taken such concepts further than any genuine Buddhist might expect.

Helena Blavatsky in 1877.

Rampa synthesises various religious ideas and traditions, but appears to have drawn most heavily on Theosophy, rather than Buddhism. Theosophy was founded in New York in 1875 by Russian mystic and spiritualist Helena Blavatsky and is based on her own writings which draw on various traditions including Gnosticism, Neoplatonism, Hinduism and Buddhism. Blavatsky taught that there is an ancient and secretive brotherhood of spiritual adepts based in Tibet called the Masters. Theosophists believe these Masters are attempting to revive knowledge of an ancient religion. Unfortunately, Blavatsky's correspondence from the Masters turned out to have been written by herself.

As Bharati writes of Rampa:

> . . . his whole work reeks of Blavatskyisms; and of course, he doesn't quote sources—fakes never do.[1]

---

[1] 'Bharati, 'Fictitious Tibet'.

Characters of Questionable Faith

A more obvious source than Buddhism for Rampa's conception of the third eye is Blavatsky's description of it in *The Secret Doctrine*. Blavatsky claimed that early human beings were three-eyed and that the additional eye permitted a spiritual inner vision. However,

> When we learn that the Third Eye was once a physiological organ, and that later on, owing to the gradual disappearance of spirituality and increase of materiality, the spiritual nature being extinguished by the physical, it became an atrophied organ, as little understood now by Physiologists as is the spleen.[1]

Blavatsky claimed that the third eye had since become the pineal gland, but that in states of trance and vision it could be revitalised.

A further borrowing from Blavatsky by Rampa was the idea of the 'silver cord'. In *The Third Eye*, Rampa writes:

> The spirit is kept in contact with the physical body by a 'silver cord' which is there until the moment of death.[2]

Blavatsky writes of a 'magnetic or odic chord',[3] or a string connecting the head of the astral and that of the physical body, which she equated with the silver cord in the Old Testament (*Ecclesiastes* 12:6). This is also recognised in the Rosicrucian tradition as a thin, shining, silvery cord. In *The Third Eye*, the silver cord was the only link between Rampa's astral body and his lifeless body during the three-days when he became an 'initiate' with the ability to see the past and to know the future. The silver cord has absolutely no part in Buddhism, Tibetan or otherwise.

Another direct use of Theosophy in Rampa is his insistence that he was able to access the Akashic Record which:

[1] Blavatsky, *The Secret Doctrine*, Vol II, 309.
[2] Rampa, *The Third Eye*, 97.
[3] Blavatsky, *The Secret Doctrine*, Vol I, 606.

Inspiration for *The Third Eye*

. . . tells all of the past and of the immediate present everywhere and all the probabilities for the future.[1]

The 'Akashic Record' is not to be found anywhere in Buddhism, either, simply because it was another invention of Blavatsky. Not that this would have mattered to Rampa, for Buddhism has equally little to say about astral travel, UFOs or life on Venus.

Even Rampa's 'life's work', to photograph the human aura, was a concept first popularised by the Theosophical Society's Charles Webster Leadbeater.

A rather bewildering array of additional concepts are also brought into Rampa's books, although many can be credited to the author's own imagination. For example, I can find no other source than Rampa for the concept of the Gardeners of the Earth, a group of extra-terrestrial, trans-dimensional beings that regularly arrive here in UFOs to watch over us humans. It is telling that the Guardians first make an appearance in Rampa's book *Beyond the Tenth* in 1969, and they are only brought retrospectively into the Rampa story in *The Hermit* in 1971. In this book a young monk is tutored by a mystic who had been blinded by the Chinese but was rescued in an alien spaceship belonging to the Gardeners of the Earth in order to teach him about the fate of Atlantis. It is strange that such a significant concept was never revealed to Rampa at the time of his initiation, as related in *The Third Eye*.

As a postscript, one might also mention that Alexandra David-Néel's *My Journey to Lhasa* (1927) was followed by *Magic and Mystery in Tibet* (1936), and it would also have been available to Rampa through his local library. David-Néel played an interesting and important part in letting the West know about Tibet, but she was also a Theosophist, having joined the Society in 1892.

[1] Rampa, *The Rampa Story*, 11.

Doctor from Lhasa, Souvenir Press (London), 1959.

7.
The Aftermath

Secker & Warburg had an option on Kuan's second book, *Medical Lama* (which would be re-titled for publication, *Doctor from Lhasa*), which was written in Ireland, but they declined to take it up. Rampa became frustrated that Doubleday, in America, were taking their time in making a decision. Rampa wrote 2nd June 1958 to Ken McCormick at Doubleday:

> I would like to dedicate *Medical Lama* . . . 'To Mr Henry Miller Esq. of Big Sur, California, a Gentleman of America.'[1]

Henry Miller had reviewed[2] *The Third Eye* in America, and was '. . . struck by the book and sang its praises'.[3] Rampa sent the

---

[1] Letter from Rampa letter to Ken McCormick, 2nd June 1958. (Library of Congress.)
[2] *New York Review*, Spring 1958, 7-9.
[3] See *Henry Miller: A Personal Archive*, a sale catalogue compiled by Jackson and Ashley, 1994, 147.

The Aftermath

proposed dedication to Miller, who passed it on to McCormick and at the same time queried:

> [Rampa] says he is still waiting to hear if you are publishing 'Medical lama'—for the whole of the English speaking world.[1]

On 16th June 1958 McCormick replied to Miller that they were hoping to publish the book in 1959, but on the same day he wrote to Cyrus Brooks.

> We've been doing a lot of hard, deep thinking about *Medical Lama*. We're very much indebted to T. Lobsang Rampa for his willingness to let us publish this book . . . We have finally decided that we will have to forego this pleasure. *Medical Lama*, as you know, is nowhere as good or believable a book as *The Third Eye*. It is filled with incredible incidents, has not the aura of believableness that *The Third Eye* so hauntingly had.[2]

McCormick went on to explain that *The Third Eye* had been published by Doubleday in all good faith and would continue to sell to an appreciative audience, but that because the sequel was 'inferior and also smacks of the bogus', publication would damage the reputation of its predecessor. He also requested that the advance paid to Rampa for *Medical Lama* be credited against future royalties for *The Third Eye*.

Brooks replied that he had written to Rampa to explain the situation,

> But he and I are not on particularly good terms at the moment. I am in fact tying up any loose ends on Medical Lama and shall not be representing him for future books, if any.[3]

---

[1] Letter from Henry Miller to Ken McCormick, 9th June 1958. (Library of Congress.)
[2] Letter from Ken McCormick to Cyrus Brooks, 16th June 1958, *et seq.* (Library of Congress.)
[3] Letter from Cyrus Brooks to Ken McCormick, 20th June 1958. (Library of Congress.)

Characters of Questionable Faith

McCormick wrote to Miller admitting that they had sat on the fence too long, but that,

> . . . revelations that have taken place, puts a little different responsibility on our shoulders. I don't know whether you've read this book, but it is not nearly so good as *The Third Eye*. It doesn't have the same conviction and it simply doesn't ring true. . . . The temptation to toss scruples to the wind and make a fast dollar is one we have overcome. . . . *Medical Lama* has a real counterfeit air about it.[1]

A.M. Heath found the Souvenir Press to publish the British edition of *Doctor from Lhasa*, although this was not without some difficulty. A letter from Brooks to McCormick in November makes it clear that the book was not accepted without revisions being made. It was published by the Souvenir Press on 15th June 1959, and they followed with *The Rampa Story* in 1960. The Saucerian Press would publish the American edition of *Doctor from Lhasa* in 1959, and though Rampa hoped that Doubleday would distribute it, they declined.[2] From then on, Rampa would be published by the mass market paperback publishers Corgi/Transworld in the UK, and by various different publishers, randomly, in the US.

Doctor from Lhasa was almost as dramatic as *The Third Eye*, but contained fewer 'revelations'. As the blurb on the Corgi reprint asks:

> Can a mortal man discipline his mind and body to survive starvation, fear and torture? Captured during World War II, soon after travelling from a remote Tibetan monastery . . . Rampa

---

[1] Letter from Ken McCormick to Henry Miller, 2nd July 1958. (Library of Congress.)

[2] Letter from Rampa to Henry Miller, 15th January 1960. (UCLA Library Special Collections.) Ken McCormick seems to have made the decision personally, and Rampa wrote to Miller, 'a pox on him!'

The Aftermath

suffered what must have been the most terrible atrocities ever committed by the Japanese. Yet he survived to tell his story... With hypnotic readability he reveals the fantastic powers of the Tibetan lamas, their rites, their beliefs. Whether it be true, as some believe, or myth as others claim, *Doctor from Lhasa* is as exotic and controversial a book as its widely discussed predecessor.[1]

T. Lobsang Rampa from the frontispiece of
Doctor from Lhasa, Souvenir Press, 1959.

The book is written in a similar style to *The Third Eye*, but the imparting of esoteric knowledge comes through repeating stories from the previous book, and the addition of several lectures on auras, special breathing, the use of crystals, etc. The action is often unbelievable, such as teaching himself to fly by stealing an aeroplane (his previous kite-flying experiences were apparently helpful), or downright masochistic (such as the tortures apparently inflicted on him by the Japanese). Reviews were not encouraging. *The Illustrated London News* wrote:

[1] Back cover of Corgi, 1963 paperback edition of *Doctor from Lhasa*.

Characters of Questionable Faith

Turning from [*No Room in the Ark* by Alan Moorehead] to *Doctor from Lhasa*, by T. Lobsang Rampa, was like being transported from the finest zoo in the world, that of Nature itself, to a sideshow in a third-rate circus. If an Englishman chooses to believe that he is possessed by the spirit of a Tibetan lama, I cannot help it. But I do not want him to go on and on about it— at least, not in my hearing. (Nor do I believe that any real lama would be quite so boringly self-conscious about his high rank and religious distinction.)[1]

Michael Dillon and T. Lobsang Rampa.
(Private Collection of Liz Hodgkinson.)

Following the press exposé of the prosaic early life of Cyril Hoskin, a man called Michael Dillon played a small part in the Rampa story. Dillon was a British Merchant Navy doctor remembered today for his pioneering transition from female to male (between 1939 and 1949), before he took the name Lobzang Jivaka and became a Buddhist monastic novice. He, too, would be subject to an intrusive and painful exposé when

---

[1] *The Illustrated London News*, 5th September 1959.

The Aftermath

he was 'outed' in the newspapers in 1958 as having undergone a sex-change.

Sheelagh Rouse called Dillon 'Naughton'[1] in her memoir. She says she knew he was a qualified medical doctor, but reports that he was working on a diagnostic device that had not been accepted by the medical establishment, and that he hoped Kuan would be able to help him with it. Rouse says she was pleased when Dillon left London, but he later turned up in Howth where she claims he made threats against her life.

Dillon's autobiography does not entirely accord with Rouse's memoir. He never mentions a diagnostic device, but states that he wanted to learn about Buddhism, and at the time he took the *Third Eye* story at face value, and liked the author.

Moreover he had quite definitely psychic powers.[2]

Later,

Rampa had written to suggest my coming over for a week or two's holiday, since he had a flat in Howth overlooking Dublin Bay and Ireland's Eye. . . . Whether he was really a Tibetan Lama or not did not trouble me . . . For the next two weeks we were much together. We went out in a hired dinghy with outboard engine and explored the cliffs and islands; we ran round the countryside in a car and all the time we talked. Much of what he told me purporting to be of his life I now know to be false, because life in Tibetan monasteries is not like that, but what he said of the Universe and man's place in it made good sense and merely continued my own line of thinking.[3]

---

[1] Names seem to have been changed arbitrarily by Rouse. There was no need to hide the identity of Clifford Burgess or Cyrus Brooks, but she left unchanged the name of Charles Gibbs-Smith although her comments might be almost described as libellous. Changing the name of Dillon would have made sense considering what she says about him, if he had not already died by the time she published.

[2] Dillon, *Out of the Ordinary*, 199.

[3] *ditto*, 199.

Characters of Questionable Faith

Rouse asserts that *after* Rampa's unwelcome press coverage, Dillon apparently reappeared, saying that he had bought from their landlord the house the Rampas were renting. This is not discussed by Dillon, although a sea-going doctor was mentioned as the Kuans' landlord by the press at the time of the exposé.[1]

Rouse was afraid that Dillon was attempting to inveigle his way into their lives once more. She suggests that the purchase of their house by Dillon persuaded Kuan that they should move away, although Dillon doesn't acknowledge this, and Rampa says, instead, that he was forced to move by the Irish taxman.[2]

Dillon would later call Kuan dishonest, but said that he would not have considered entering a monastery if it had not been for Rampa suggesting it, and for that he was forever grateful.

In leaving Ireland, Rouse wrote that North America was their goal, but that realistically Canada was more likely to accept Kuan than the USA, due to his ill-health. It is not known quite what passport he would have shown at customs, but Newby attests to the fact that he had not required one when flying from England to Ireland, and Canada was, at that time, still a member of the British Commonwealth.

Rampa's life thereafter became a peripatetic one, albeit mainly within Canada. He would continue to write his books, which became increasingly fantastic and rambling. When he was living in Calgary, *The Bookseller* ran the following story which suggests that despite poor reviews, sales of *Doctor from Lhasa* were strong:

> According to the [*Daily*] *Mail* Rampa now drives a large American car and carries with him copies of *The Third Eye* which he autographs for admirers. Mr Ernest Hecht, managing director of Souvenir Press, told the *Mail* that he had decided to publish the book after giving the matter very careful considera-

[1] *Daily Mail*, 3rd February 1953.
[2] Rampa: *The Rampa Story*, 211-212.

The Aftermath

tion and that he was not completely satisfied that Lobsang Rampa was a hoaxer. . . . Souvenir Press have ordered a first printing of 10,000 for the book which is now almost sold out.[1]

Whatever the literary merits of the book, *The Bookseller* obviously still relished reporting the Rampa story:

> There has been a lively exchange in the columns of the *Times Literary Supplement* between Mr Frederick Warburg, publisher of *The Third Eye*, by T. Lobsang Rampa, and Mr Ernest Hecht, whose firm, Souvenir Press, recently published *Doctor from Lhasa* by the same author. . . . An unfavourable comparison by the *Lit. Supp.* reviewer of the later book [*Doctor from Lhasa*] with *The Third Eye* prompted Mr Warburg to suggest that the Devonian spirit of Cyril Henry Hoskins [sic] had become jealous of the success of T. Lobsang Rampa and started to expel the invader from his body in order to write his own books in the future. 'The mind boggles at the idea of two authors in one body struggling with each other to write his own book and to choose his own publisher. Yet what other hypothesis will fit the facts?'
>
> Mr Warburg added that he proposed to fast and then to concentrate his thought processes for three nights to ensure the supremacy of the Tibetan over the British author.[2]

The back cover of the Corgi paperback of the third book, *The Rampa Story*, states that it offers:

> The full background to the earlier books—further revelations of the strange mystic powers with which the author is endowed —and his answer to those critics who accuse him of being a crank, a charlatan, or worse . . . [publisher's ellipsis]

Interestingly, Secker & Warburg had stated in print that *The Third Eye* was copyright without saying in whose name, while

---

[1] *The Bookseller*, 9th May 1959.
[2] *The Bookseller*, 15th August 1959.

87

Characters of Questionable Faith

Doctor from Lhasa was credited as copyright 'C. Kuan Suo', which was the author's legal name at the time. Oddly, in *The Rampa Story* the copyright has regressed to the persona of 'Kuansuo', but by the time of his fourth book, *Cave of the Ancients* (1963) the author is officially 'T. Lobsang Rampa'.

It is quite likely all of Rampa's books after *The Third Eye* were dictated to Sheelagh Rouse (the author often remarks that he forgot to mention something that should have come earlier in the text, but this is not corrected and the material is left to be printed out of sequence.) Corgi appear to have had less editorial input than Rampa's previous publishers, and his books suffer for this. For all their obvious faults, his first three books have a verve and headlong style that Rampa cannot reproduce later in his oeuvre. It was either inspiration or desperation when Corgi allowed him to publish *Living with the Lama*, which purported to be a book dictated to Rampa telepathically by his cat, Mrs Fifi Greywhiskers. It should be noted, though, that their feline companion wrote a far better book than any of those by Rampa's wife, Mama San Ra'ab Rampa, who later attempted to extend the Rampa franchise.

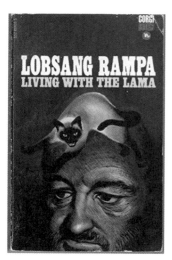 

Left: *Living with the Lama*, dictated to Rampa by his Siamese cat, Mrs Fifi Greywhiskers. Right: Mama San Ra-ab Rampa from the cover of a reprint of her book, *Autumn Lady*.

The Aftermath

Publishing books seems to have been the main source of income for the three-person household (and various cats, all of whom were considered equal members of the family.) Piracy of his products plagued Rampa.

In the June 1960 issue of the magazine *Flying Saucers* there was an advert for a free copy of Gray Barker's *Saucerian Bulletin* containing the 'censored chapters from *The Third Eye*'. This was the reprint of Rampa's 'Saucers over Tibet' from *Flying Saucer Review*, and publication may not have worried Rampa unduly. However, by the February 1961 issue of *Flying Saucers* there was an advert for *Doctor from Lhasa* by Rampa, legitimately published by Gray, stating that each copy ordered would be posted with a free 'souvenir book' of the excised chapter.[1] In later editions of *My Visit to Venus* Barker would include a letter addressed to him personally from Rampa stating:

> This book should not have been published really, but I am prepared to believe that you published in good faith . . . To regularise your position I suggest this; you make two alterations suggested by me, and I will give you permission to publish and sell the book. I will not take royalties on this book, 'My Visit to Venus,' but instead you can send ten percent of your profits to the Save a Cat League.[2]

In *Feeding the Flame* Rampa refused to recommend *My Visit to Venus*:

> '. . . let me state here and now that I definitely, definitely, definitely do not recommend that 'book'. It is just a few pages containing some articles which I wrote years ago, and it contains some—well, I consider them off-beat—illustrations not done by me. This book containing parts of my work and filled out with a

---

[1] The date of publication for the standalone publication of *My Visit to Venus* is usually given as c. 1966, but must have been c. 1961. It included not just 'Saucers over Tibet' but 'Flying into Space'.

[2] From the 1988 Inner Light Publications edition of *My Visit to Venus*, [72].

Characters of Questionable Faith

lot of blurb was published entirely without my permission and entirely against my wishes.[1]

Rampa never claimed he did not write the text, but in the earlier years of his literary career he may have had mixed feelings about it being widely available.

Interestingly, Gray Barker, who was best known for writing books about UFOs and other paranormal phenomena, is remembered today for his 1956 book *They Knew Too Much About Flying Saucers* which introduced to 'ufology' the idea of the 'Men in Black'[2] (mysterious figures who apparently intimidate individuals into keeping silent about UFOs—a concept that inspired the successful film franchise of the same name). It would not be until *Wisdom of the Ancients* in 1965 that Rampa would begin to discuss UFOs in his books,[3] and in *Beyond the Tenth* (1969) Rampa mentions the 'Men in Black',[4] although he seems to misunderstand the concept.

Rampa disowned the vinyl record and cassette *The Power of Prayer*, released by Saucerian Records in 1967. Also available at the same time was a recording called *My True Story* by Rampa, in which he 'tells of his leaving Tibet'.[5]

One colourful interlude in their relatively quiet but comfortable lives was time spent in 1968 in Montevideo, the capital of

---

[1] Rampa: *Feeding the Flame*, 140.
[2] Barker seems to have been sceptical of UFO claims, but realised there was money to be made from them, and is believed to have not just publicised but actively participated in hoaxes to deceive investigators.
[3] Rampa first mentions the '. . . so-called "flying saucer" ' in *Wisdom of the Ancients*, 1965, 34. By 1969, in *Beyond the Tenth,* he would write: 'U.F.O.s are real, there are other people in space, people so highly evolved, so highly intelligent, that intelligent humans now are by comparison to these space people as stupid as a dress shop dummy', 28.
[4] Rampa, *Beyond the Tenth*, 81.
[5] Both recordings offered in *UFO Review,* number 3, April 1979, 15.

The Aftermath

Uruguay in South America. Rampa was invited by the head of a large publishing company to move to Montevideo at the expense of that company, where he could continue his work.

Señor Salas who taught the Rampas Spanish
when they were in Montevideo.

The Rampa's Uruguayan experience is described (with very little charm) by Rampa in *As It Was!* He began by discussing the dock strikes that delayed their disembarkation. There, unfortunately,

> . . . we found that the man with an immense business did not have such an immense business after all. Instead—well, to put it at its kindest, he was a man with ideas which did not always work out.[1]

They discovered:

> It was very expensive living in Montevideo.

and it was:

---

[1] Rampa, *As It Was!*, 180, *et seq.*

Characters of Questionable Faith

. . . most unfortunate that we had to leave because Montevideo was a nice place indeed. . . . We returned to Canada by sea, and then there was the question of making money so I had to write another book.

Because he could not legally receive post in Uruguay in the name of Rampa (his passport was presumably still in the name of Kuansuo), he had his name changed legally to 'T. Lobsang Rampa while in Canada in 1963.'[1]

The best portrait of the Rampa household while in Canada comes from Alain Stanké in his book *Rampa: Imposteur ou initié?* Stanké was to become Rampa's French language agent, and for a time was his neighbour at the spectacular 'Habitat 67', a Utopian 1960s housing complex at Cité du Havre, on the Saint Lawrence River, Montreal.

Sheelagh Rouse outside Habitat 67
(photograph by Rampa).

[1] The official documents are reproduced in Stanké, *Rampa: Imposteur ou initié?*, 112.

The Aftermath

Everywhere in the apartment there is a strong smell of incense. I don't have time to discover whether it is the scent of rose or sandalwood until we have already reached the goal. A rather small room, very sparsely furnished: a hospital bed, two mismatched chairs, a bedside table and a small bookcase. In a corner, an electric wheelchair, on the wall, a vast map of the world and a series of clocks, pendulums and alarm clocks. This is the ancient kingdom of Lobsang Rampa . . .

'Come and sit here,' he said in English, his index finger pointing pointedly at the end of the bed. I take my place next to him, zealously trying to appear calm . . . Lobsang Rampa smiles indulgently as he extends his hand to me and holds mine for a long time. 'You were right to add a few handwritten words at the bottom of your letter,' he continues in a stiff voice that is both protective and condescending. 'They allowed me to know better who you were.'

Mrs Rampa introduces into the room their Siamese cats, Miss Tadalinka and Miss Cleopatra, and it is agreed that Stanké will handle the publication of Rampa's next book. By the next evening Stanké is able to return to the Rampa's apartment with his wife. He writes of Rampa:

Sometimes he assumes the placid attitude of a saint (which can be seen in his photographs) with long glances cast at the ceiling. He is by turns clever and ironic, proud and very simple, crazy about contradictions. Like a child, he enjoys being inquisitive, disillusioned, naïve, stiff, jovial or grimacing. This man, famous and inaccessible as he is, allows himself the freedom to clown around, for the enjoyment of his audience.

Stanké recalled that Rampa received a great deal of correspondence which he replied to diligently, as long as return postage was enclosed. He received gifts, including money, but was himself often generous. Apart from replying to people from all over the world, he continued with making miniature trains, cars and boats. He was also interested in shortwave radio, and had

Characters of Questionable Faith

an impressive radio set with which he listened to broadcasts from all over the world.

> But his greatest passion is, without a doubt, photography. He has the most complete equipment for all types of photos. There are Polaroid and three-dimensional cameras and lenses of all sizes. Rampa confided to me one day that this passion is part of research work in which he is interested. He wants to photograph what he himself perceives with the naked eye: the human aura.[1]

Rampa in later life, in Canada, with a camera.

In *Feeding the Flame*, Rampa said that he had to give up his research into photographing the human aura through lack of money.[2] Apparently there was another project he had wanted to develop:

> ... it is absolutely possible to make a device which will enable one to 'telephone' the astral world. It has actually been done, but the man who did it had such a barrage of doubts, suspicions,

---
[1] Stanké, *Rampa: Imposteur ou initié?*, 36-37. (My translation.)
[2] Rampa, *Feeding the Flame*, 23.

94

The Aftermath

and accusations from the press that he got tired of it, he lost heart, and driven by the insane press he smashed his apparatus and committed suicide.

It is quite possible to make a telephone with which to telephone, the astral world.[1]

Rampa was obviously still making good money from the royalties on his books. Apart from his cameras, Rampa is remembered as having the money to buy other gadgets, such as a paper shredder, with which he would destroy manuscript drafts and his correspondence, because he was convinced that reporters would go through the rubbish he threw out.

Rampa with his paper shredder.

It is difficult to believe that Rampa was much happier in Canada than when previously residing in England or Ireland. In *Living with the Lama* he wrote, through his cat, Mrs Fifi Greywhiskers:

> Canada, we are agreed, is a most uncultured country, and all of us live for the day when we can leave it. However, this book

---

[1] Rampa, *Feeding the Flame*, 24.

Characters of Questionable Faith

is not a treatise on the faults of Canada that would fill a complete library, anyway![1]

Stanké interviewed Rampa for television in a program called 'Citizens of the World' (Tele-Metropole C.F.T.M, Montreal) in the early 70s. He was filmed in bed in his bedroom at Habitat 67, with his crystal ball, Tibetan prayer-wheel, books and two cats. The 20-minute show is transcribed and translated into French in *Imposteur ou initié?*, revealing the author had become very reactionary and quite bitter. He railed against strikers, unions and students, and grumbled about the state of the world, including the iniquitous taxation systems in different countries. He kept his deepest antipathy, however, for the press, who seemed to have caused him unremitting trouble:

> . . . the press continues to want to 'execute' me, as it has continued to do during these last fifteen years.[2]

and he persisted in insisting he was authentic and that his books were all true, as well as rebutting stories that he was living in luxury in a bigamous relationship with his wife and Rouse. Some of the stories about Rampa in the press were almost as imaginative and wild as those he offered in his own books, although it is understandable he would want to deny some of them. Stanké said to Rampa:

> Some claim that you were hired by Hitler to go to Tibet for training and then return to Hitler and advise him.[3]

To which Rampa replied:

---

[1] Rampa: *Living with the Lama*, 160. Alain Stanké declined Rampa's offer to dedicate the book to him because he had been so rude about Canada.

[2] Stanké, *Rampa: Imposteur ou initié?*, 145. (My translation.)

[3] *ditto*, 165 *et seq.* (My translation.)

The Aftermath

Do you seriously believe that I will answer such a question? Well, yes, I will answer it! Although you seem to me to have scoured the insane asylums to find people capable of asking the craziest questions!

No, I was never hired by Hitler to go to Tibet.

Photograph by Alain Stanké.

Stanké reported that he had asked Louis Pauwels (author of *Morning of the Magicians*) what he knew about the identity of Rampa:

> According to this famous French author, it is not impossible that T. Lobsang Rampa was part of the group of politico-mystics who went to Tibet under the personal direction of Himmler and at the request of Hitler.

Wanting to obtain further clarifications, we asked Simon Wiesenthal (the Nazi hunter who has arrested more than 1,000 war criminals—including [Adolf] Eichman). His Vienna Documentation Centre does not have any specific files on Rampa who, not being a criminal, is therefore in no way wanted. However, this specialist does not rule out the possibility that Lobsang Rampa could have been part of a certain organization such as under the name of Thule which Pauwels reports at length in *Morning of the Magicians*.

Characters of Questionable Faith

Another detail which, in the eyes of some people, gives weight to Pauwels' suspicions and to the rumours circulating about Rampa is that Rampa lived for some time in Uruguay. It is well known that at the end of the war, many Nazis took refuge precisely in South America.

Again, seems reasonable to suggest that Rampa was not the only one with a vivid imagination. He doesn't seem to have considered that he might have been encouraging such flights of fancy by publishing books full of outlandish stories. From the beginning he offered a unique mix of derring-do, hardship, pseudo-orientalism and various New Age beliefs, although there was also a great deal of home-spun philosophy with additional reactionary grumbling.

Rampa with a Siamese cat.

Rampa also complained that:

One of the big troubles I have had since *The Third Eye* is the number of people who write 'Approved by Lobsang Rampa' . . . I do not 'approve' things. Many people, too, have impersonated me, in fact, on quite a number of occasions I have had to call in the police. There was, for example, a man in Miami . . . [who]

The Aftermath

had been for some time ordering goods in my name and not paying. . . . There have been others such as the man who retired to a mountain cave, sat cross-legged with darn little clothing on him, and pretended to be me. He advised teenagers to have sex and drugs, saying that it was good for them. But the press, of course, seized on such incidents and made quite a commotion, and even when it was proved that these impostors were impersonating me the press never got round to reporting the actuality of what happened.[1]

By 1969 Rampa had an open letter to readers appended to his paperbacks. In it he asked potential correspondents not to write to him via his publishers, and gave an address in Canada at which he could be contacted. Quite reasonably, he stated that he would only reply if adequate return postage was included. He obviously had a good relationship with his publishers, who, from 1971 onwards, allowed Rampa-Touch-Stones Ltd to advertise 'Rampa's tranquiliser Touch-Stones':

> You are interested in the Higher sciences or you would not be reading this book. Have you considered how your tranquillity can be nourished by a Rampa-Touch-Stone? On page 123 of *Wisdom of the Ancients* you can read about these Touch Stones.[2]

---

[1] Rampa, *As It Was!*, 182.
[2] Published at the end of Rampa's *Feeding the Flame*, 1971 paperback. Rampa's answer to anyone who doubted the efficacy of the Touch-Stones was, neatly, 'if you don't believe in them, they won't be of any use to you.' (Stanké, *Rampa: Imposteur ou initié?*, 160.)

Characters of Questionable Faith

Rampa continued to insist that he didn't 'approve' things, telling Alain Stanké that he gave up all rights to his Touch-Stones to 'another person out of kindness',[1] who was then operating a business in Loughborough, England, and was also selling his 12" vinyl meditation record. Rampa states that he likewise had no financial stake in the mystical paraphernalia sold under his name through the magazine *Fate*, where, in addition to Touch-Stones and meditation records, they offered a 'Complete Home Meditation Kit', including personally made meditation robes, as well as a 'meditating figure', incense, incense burners and original prayers.

Adverts for Rampa merchandise from *Beyond*, September 1969, Vol 2, Issue 13.

By the time of the posthumously published 1988 edition of *My Visit to Venus*, Rampa's meditation recording was available on the more up-to-date format of the compact cassette tape. Either Rampa was not being entirely honest, or he was a very bad businessman.

[1] Stanké, *Rampa: Imposteur ou initié?*, 160. (My translation.)

The Aftermath

Rampa in bed in Canada with a Siamese cat,
a crystal ball and Tibetan prayer wheel.

Unauthorised merchandise continued to be offered for sale. Buckley writes in *Eccentric Explorers* that it was not just recordings:

> In California . . . a man did more than copy Rampa's voice: this impersonator claimed to represent the great sage himself. In 1979, Rampa complained in letters about a man in England who was offering a kind of other-worldly Rampa correspondence course.[1]

In 1971, Canada granted asylum to 500 Tibetan refugees from India, some of whom made it to Calgary, where they heard about a renowned Tibetan lama called Rampa. Some tried to meet him, but as with the press, Rampa apparently did his best to keep out of their way.[2]

---

[1] Buckley, *Eccentric Explorers*, 323.
[2] *ditto*, 321.

Characters of Questionable Faith

Stanké asked Rampa why he was so antisocial, living like a hermit, to which he replied that he was seen as a kind of Agony Aunt:

> . . . to whom any weak-minded person can come to ask idle questions. No one has the right to come see me without being asked. [1]

and went on to say that in both correspondence and in person people were forever making unreasonable demands upon him. He also claimed that he had once 'received' people,

> . . . many of whom distanced themselves from me, and completely falsified what had happened. Some went straight to the newspapers to sell them untrue information at a high price.

although the only people who seem to have given stories to the newspapers would appear to have been former neighbours in England at the time of the original exposé.

Stanké's portrait of Rampa is an important one because, apart from his wife and Sheila Rouse, very few people seem to have been close to Rampa. Although Rampa suggested that Mrs O'Grady from Ireland paid them a visit, there is no other talk of friends, and Stanké suggested that Rampa was not necessarily a happy man:

> I feel the loneliness of this man who is looking for a friend like no other. A friend who espouses his cause, who believes in his supernatural possibilities, who does not doubt his past for a single moment, who obeys his whims, a friend ready to defend him in the public square where he fears to go himself, a shield, a defender, a friend ready to neglect his own needs to defend Rampa's, a friend of good reputation, of good company, a friend who does not ask embarrassing questions. Will he ever find someone who can meet so many demands? . . . Rampa doesn't like people to stand up to him. He knows, he says, much

[1] Stanké, *Rampa: Imposteur ou initié?*, 157 *et esq.* (My translation.)

The Aftermath

better than everyone what is good for everyone. 'You should know that I have ways of knowing things!' he likes to repeat in critical and decisive moments.[1]

Presumably life had been good in Ireland because he made the acquaintance of locals, he was generous and friendly, and nobody would have had reason to question the story he told about himself. When he moved to Canada, however, and met Canadians, he would have found his reputation preceded him. As Stanké wrote, he did not like people questioning or doubting his claims to be a Tibetan lama, so close friendships seem to have been impossible. Stanké's suggestion that he was a lonely man echoed comments by television producer John Irwin in 1958 when he wrote that he was 'harmless and lonely . . . a sad man'.[2]

Alain Stanké's friendship with Rampa ended after a year and a half, in 1972, when Rampa asked his friend to defend him after a newspaper had mocked his claims to be the incarnation of a Tibetan lama. Rampa asked Stanké to write to the paper to state that he believed Rampa, but Stanké felt unable to do so. The journalist left for Africa, and the Rampa family abruptly left Montreal.

Rampa and his cats, in photos sent to Gray Bergin.

---

[1] Stanké, *Rampa: Imposteur ou initié?*, 81. (My translation.)
[2] *Daily Mail*, 3rd February 1958.

Characters of Questionable Faith

Among Rampa's regular correspondents was a Californian called Gray Bergin. He was one of several people thanked by Rampa, in *Feeding the Flame,* for asking questions that he sought to answer in his book. Bergin would write supportively to Rampa, often enclosing generous and regular gifts of money. Rampa offered advice in return, as well as sending photographs and complimentary copies of his books

Rampa wrote to Bergin on 7th June 1973 after receiving a visit from the Fraud Squad of the Royal Canadian Mounted Police. They were investigating a complaint from a Mrs Betty Jesse, to whom Rampa had previously dedicated *The Thirteenth Candle.* Rampa reported that Mrs Jesse:

> . . . alleges that I have been forcing her by thought to be upset about sex and, according to the police, I am trying to make Miss Jesse send me money.[1]

Rampa explained that the complaint arose only because Jesse was a:

> '. . . maiden lady' who is now at the change of life stage, and I suppose she finds her glands are stirring up desires which she has all her life repressed.

He suggested to Bergin that because he was also named in *Feeding the Flame,* the Police might well be in contact with him. In reply, Bergin happily wrote a letter addressed 'To whom it may concern', explaining that Rampa had at no time attempted to influence him financially or sexually. Rampa's story of his run-in with the R.C.M.P. would later be told in Rampa's July 1973 newsletter.

Rampa came to be considered by many a harmless eccentric, although he continued to find followers. Commentators like James Randi would become annoyed by Rampa's claims,

[1] Letter from Rampa to Gray Bergin, 7th June, 1973, *et seq.*

The Aftermath

although others didn't think it was even worth the effort of debunking him. For example, Clint Porter in the Californian *Seaside Post* in 1972 was able to write about Rampa, assuming his readers knew exactly who he was:

> [Rampa] is still writing. You will see that he hasn't finished his work on earth yet. And he has worn out two bodies trying to do it. And his Master has revealed to him that he will stay here on earth until his work is done. And he is tired too. So very, very tired. But he just keeps on working and living in Montreal, doing his 'thing' for all mankind.[1]

Late photos of Rampa in Canada.

The author and his wife, San Ra'ab, had become Canadian citizens in 1973, as had Sheelagh Rouse. The three moved homes together within the country frequently. As James Martin put it in *Calgary: The Unknown City*, Rampa moved,

> . . . from Ontario to New Brunswick to Quebec to, at last, Calgary. Architectural aestheticism did not play a role in his

---

[1] Clint Porter, *Seaside Post*, 2nd March 1972, 4.

Characters of Questionable Faith

decision to trade Montreal's groovy Habitat for apartment #2808 in the bland O'Neil Towers (700-9th St. SW, the tall building with Baby Blues pizza parlour on the main floor), but the move did afford him precious anonymity. Until his death from heart failure in 1981, Rampa was known to Calgarians mostly as that weird guy in the motorized wheelchair who was constantly cruising up and down 8th Avenue. This is apparently exactly how he liked it; Rampa dedicated his . . . book (*As It Was!*, 1976) to 'the City of Calgary, where I have had peace and quiet and freedom from interference in my personal affairs. Thank you, City of Calgary.'[1]

Rampa's final book, *Tibetan Sage* was published as a Corgi paperback in 1980, and offers a hitherto unrecorded episode in the early life of the author while a student in Tibet. With his old teacher the Lama Mingyar Dondup they go to help a Hermit who is in trouble, and there is something of Enid Blyton's 'Famous Five' about the way young Lobsang inadvertently stumbles upon a secret passage to the 'Inner Temple', and then the way he blunders into secret rooms full of wonderful technology. Not that Enid Blyton's characters ever discovered an intact two million year old UFO. Blyton would never have strained the credulity of her readers by having Mingyar Dondup able to read the ancient alien instruction manual, but *Tibetan Sage* is so naïvely written as to suggest that the author didn't really expect to have any grown-up readers. His joy in describing alien vending machines that dispense sweets sounds like something only a child might think other people will be interested in.

After twenty-five years with the Rampas, Sheelagh left them just as Chen was dying. In her memoir, she says that Ra'ab had come to have the upper-hand in the household as Chen became weaker. He asked Rouse to stay with Ra'ab after he had died, which Sheelagh said she could not agree to. She had never got

[1] Martin, James, *Calgary: The Unknown City*, 124.

The Aftermath

on well with Ra'ab, having always found her 'a difficult person'.[1] Rampa promised Rouse a share of his money if she agreed, but she refused. We only have her word for it that,

> It was not a case of walking away from responsibilities—I was being sent away, forced away, one could say.[2]

T. LOBSANG RAMPA

T. Lobsang Rampa, author of the best seller *The Third Eye* and other works on Tibetan mysticism, died in Canada on January 25, at the age of 70.

The Third Eye, published in 1956, created great interest when it appeared. It described the author's life as a boy in a Tibetan lamasery and his receipt of mystic powers.

The publishers were at some pains to check the authenticity of the manuscript and consulted some 20 knowledgeable readers in the hope of getting a clearer answer to the question: was it a work of autobiography or fiction? A reviewer in *The Times Literary Supplement* had no doubt that whereas it was difficult to say whether it was a work of truth, it came near to being a work of art.

Some research into Rampa's background and upbringing was done by a private detective, and it was claimed subsequently that T. Lobsang Rampa was born Cyril Henry Hoskins, son of a Devonshire plumber. Rampa replied that the body of Hoskins had been taken over completely by the spirit of a Tibetan mystic.

He wrote in all nearly a score of books on mysticism. He and his wife became Canadian citizens in 1973.

Rampa's obituary in *The Times*, 31st January 1981.

Tuesday Lobsang Rampa (to give him the dignity of the name he used for many years) died in Calgary on 25th January 1981, at the physical age of seventy.

There has been one interesting posthumous publication, claimed to be by Rampa. According to the publisher, Timothy Green Beckley, back in the 1950s Jim Rigberg, who ran the Flying Saucer News Bookstore in New York had befriended Rampa. Beckley claimed that Rigberg actually paid him a royalty for publishing *My Visit to Venus*, and that Rampa would occa-

---

[1] Eaton, Barry, *Radio Out There*, March, 2021.
[2] Rouse, *Twenty-Five Years with T. Lobsang Rampa*, 226.

Characters of Questionable Faith

sionally send him his rejected writings. Among these was meant to be a story by Rampa detailing his journey into a Hollow Earth. This previously 'lost manuscript' has since been published as *My Visit to Agharta*.[1]

In the story, Rampa flies in a UFO (naturally), to the Himalayas where he is reunited (again) with his old master, Mingyar Dondup. Various adventures befall them after they enter a secret passage, and a hovercraft is involved in taking them deeper into the earth. Here they enter Agharta, where the capital city is Shambhala.

It should be noted that Timothy Green Beckley was not only a proponent of the hollow-earth theory himself, having written *Subterranean Worlds Inside Earth* (1992), but he also wrote *Silencers: Mystery of the Men in Black* (1991), and *My Visit to Agharta* does not just have Rampa visiting a hollow Earth, but the Men in Black are discussed. (This time with a proper understanding of the concept.) The book closes with adverts for 'Products Inspired by Rampa'.

Karen Mutton reported:

> . . . suspiciously, Rampa's secretary Sheelagh Rouse has no recollection of ever typing it or anything of that genre.[2]

---

[1] Inner Light Publications, 2003.
[2] Mutton, 'T. Lobsang Rampa: New Age Trailblazer', Part 2, 54.

 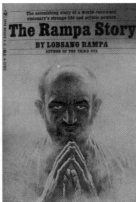 

Idealised portraits of Rampa from covers of paperback editions of his books.

8.
The Legacy

It is possible that if T. Lobsang Rampa had written only *The Third Eye* and had then disappeared from view without being exposed as Cyril Hoskin, his book may well have remained popular and controversial to this day. It would certainly have been derided by anyone who had the knowledge and experience of either Tibet and/or Buddhism to recognise that it was a complete fiction, but the majority of readers might rather have been baffled, wanting to know more about the possibilities suggested by the foreign-sounding author. There is something fundamental in our psyche that seems to hope there are still secrets and mysteries to be discovered, even if common sense tells us that yetis, guardian cats and gilded, mummified gods are unlikely to have existed. Some, of course, will always take such claims at face value.

As I have written earlier, *The Third Eye* is a well-written and lively book, but the newspaper revelations that it was written by Hoskin did the author's reputation severe damage. In the popular perception, he is now thought of as a plumber himself and

Characters of Questionable Faith

commentators continually append an unnecessary 's' to his name and call him 'Hoskins', as the *Daily Mail* and *Express* first did. At the time of the exposé, the story that he was living in an implied *ménage à trois* with Sheelagh Rouse added a sordid aspect to his imposture. When asked to account for himself, Hoskin/Kuan/Rampa offered an explanation so audacious that only those who were really determined to believe in his authenticity could accept it. For everyone else, the additional information about astral-travelling lamas, repeated falls from trees and blinking owls, sounded absurd. But what drove nails repeatedly into the coffin of Rampa's reputation was the publication of each of his successive books with their ever-wilder claims.

In *Cave of the Ancients* (1963), for example, Rampa tells of an expedition of high lamas into the Himalayas where they find 'instruments preserved intact since the days of Atlantis. Among them is a projector with which the monks are able to see how Atlantis was destroyed by its own warring inhabitants:

> Above the ruins towered a strangely evil-looking red cloud, roughly in the shape of a mushroom miles high.[1]

In other books Rampa explains that the Earth is hollow, and tells us we are watched over by the Gardeners of Earth. Even in the 1950s astronomers were aware that planets such as Venus could not support any kind of life, and Rampa's grasp of such scientific concepts as anti-matter are quite laughable.

However, through the 1950s and 1960s Rampa's books resonated with many in the New Age, countercultural, 'mind body and spirit' movements. At the time Rampa was writing *The Third Eye*, Gerald Heard and Aldous Huxley were in America experimenting with mescaline which, it was believed, had the potential to 'enlarge Man's mind'[2] by allowing anyone to see

---

[1] Rampa, *Cave of the Ancients*, 93.
[2] Quoted from the title of an essay by Gerald Heard, 'Can This Drug [LSD] Enlarge Man's Mind?', *Psychedelic Review* 1, no. 1, June 1963.

The Legacy

beyond their ego. Huxley's *The Doors of Perception*, published in 1954, suggested that to expand the mind one needed only take a drug, rather than undergo a fantastical surgical operation.[1]

This was a time when many Westerners were exploring Eastern mysticism in both direct and diluted forms; Heard and Huxley, for example, became Vedantists, a group centred on Swami Prabhavananda, and a decade later, famously, The Beatles would look for enlightenment with their guru Maharishi Mahesh Yogi. John Lennon would sing 'turn off your mind, relax, float downstream',[2] a direct quote from *The Psychedelic Experience*,[3] based on the *Tibetan Book of the Dead*, while Bob Dylan was probably referring to Rampa when he sang, 'If he needs a third eye, he just grows it.[4]

The little known psychedelic band The Dovers released 'The Third Eye' in April 1966, now considered to be 'one of the earliest attempts at reproducing the LSD experience on record':[5]

> Unlocked by the key
> And now I am free
> Magic curtains of green and blue lights pass by
> Moon and sky.

Elsewhere in the musical psychedelic scene, Stacy Sutherland said of fellow band mate, Tommy Hall, from cult band The

---

[1] It should be noted that Rampa was against the use of drugs: 'One of the major dislikes in my life is drugs' (Rampa, *The Rampa Story*, 96); 'Drugs and other forms of getting out of the physical body are truly harmful, they cause harm to the Overself' (Rampa, *You— Forever*, 73).

[2] 'Tomorrow Never Knows' by the Beatles, 1966.

[3] *The Psychedelic Experience* by Timothy Leary, Ralph Metzner & Richard Alpert.

[4] 'Can You Please Crawl Out Your Window?' by Bob Dylan, 1965.

[5] 'The Dovers open their Third Eye' by Jon Savage, *The Guardian*, 4th October 2010.

Thirteenth Floor Elevators, that when he wrote the lyric 'Leave Your Body Behind':

> He believed that, actually, probably still does. Don't know that he ever did levitate, he felt like he was. He believed in astral projection and studied it quite a bit at the time. . . . he read philosophy by people like, if you remember Lobsang Rampa, who wrote *The Third Eye* . . . and several other books?[1]

Alongside counter-cultural liberation, there was underlying tension caused by the Cold War, and Rampa's stories of UFOs also resonated with popular interest, although he usually insisted they were positive manifestations of extraterrestrial interest in humankind. He was able to mention them as an almost everyday occurrence:

> The day we landed in Buenos Aires a U.F.O. came in and actually alighted at the main airport. It stayed for several minutes at the end of a runway, and then took off at fantastic speed. . . . this U.F.O. landing is the subject of an Argentinean Government Report. . . . This world is under observation, but we need not be upset by that.[2]

Like many of his claims, it is difficult to find corroboration; it is a shame that in this instance Rampa did not have one of his many cameras with him! However, not everyone in the New Age/alternative/counter-cultural communities was impressed by Rampa. In 1973, Gordon Creighton, editor of *Flying Saucer Review* wrote that 'a former editor of *FSR* [Gray Barker] had displayed an incredible degree of gullibility'[3] by publishing Rampa's accounts of his travels to Venus in a flying saucer,

---

[1] From an audio tape interview for which many details are lacking, transcribed by Patrick Lundborg, 2002, published at: slidemachine.livejournal.com, 30th May 2011.

[2] Rampa, *Beyond the Tenth* (London: Corgi, 1969), 91.

[3] 'The Tibetan Connection' by Gordon Creighton, *Flying Saucer Review*, vol 19 no 6, 1973. See also vol 38 no 4, 1993.

The Legacy

calling Rampa 'a liar'. Almost exactly twenty years later, Creighton was still editing *Flying Saucer Review* and felt that he had to write almost the same editorial once again, presumably because there were still readers who believed Rampa's claims.

Rampa's books continued to sell into the 1970s—an era in which Erich von Däniken's books of pseudo-history, pseudo-archaeology, and pseudo-science were bestsellers, shelved alongside books by Lyall Watson, with garish reprints of occult texts and books about Ley Lines. It was a heady mix of the spiritual and science fiction that can look quite naïve today, but it can be argued that it continues in more sophisticated forms in contemporary conspiracy theories.

A few books have been written taking Rampa seriously, the earliest of which was Dana Howard's *The Strange Case of T. Lobsang Rampa*, 1958. Howard was obviously in sympathy with Rampa, and it is known that the two corresponded. She cites other examples of people whose bodies have been taken over, such as an American Marine, Calvin Girvin, who apparently became the vehicle for an extraterrestrial, and she also uses the book to discuss her own experiences, which can be found in her other books such as *My Flight to Venus* (1954). However, she doesn't seem *entirely* convinced by Rampa. When discussing his dealings with publishers, she writes:

> After a few words they would know that basically Rampa is an Englishman. He didn't try to hoax the public in this regard.[1]

which is not quite correct. She seems to be relatively open-minded about the possibility of imposture, writing:

> True knowledge is not always sense knowledge. True knowledge is spiritual. . . .[2]

[1] Howard, *The Strange Case of T. Lobsang Rampa*, 27.
[2] *ditto*, 40 *et seq.*

And when discussing Hoskin being taken over by the 'ghost' of a Tibetan lama:

> It might take years for full 'possession' to become completely manifest over another personality. In the meantime, it would become necessary on the physical plane to invent a whole chain of falsehoods to sustain the real truth.

More recently, Pierre Baribeau has written *Les chandelles de Lobsang Rampa* (2014), which uses the blurb: 'Physical reality as we think we know it is an illusion created by the mind. Recognizing this truth is the first step toward liberation from the flesh.'

One of the best and most accurate summations of Lobsang Rampa's career is Karen Mutton's *T. Lobsang Rampa, New Age Trailblazer* which was printed over two issues of the magazine *Nexus* in 2006. The first instalment is clear-minded and even-handed, but the second is more difficult to recommend. In it, Mutton finds recently published news reports and books which she contends support many of the outlandish claims made by Rampa about extraterrestrials, giants, Atlantis, UFOs, underground civilisations, a hollow earth etc. Mutton's article found the perfect home at *Nexus,* an 'alternative news magazine' that discusses geo-politics, alternative health, the supernatural and the unexplained, as well as publishing articles about freedom of speech and related issues. Considering its remit of considering nothing off-limits, it only promotes conspiracy theories and propaganda with a far-right bias.

Today there are websites and Facebook pages dedicated to Rampa, but it is difficult to know how frequently they are visited. He continues to find an audience through poorly produced, self-published books online, and in *My Visit to Agharta* there may even be fake texts on offer.

Christopher Fowler wrote in *The Book of Forgotten Authors* that *The Third Eye* was published at a time of 'wibbly-wobbly . . . quasi-mysticism' and describes it as 'post-war dipsy-doodlism'

The Legacy

for 'intellectually inert seekers of easy enlightenment'.[1] This is harsh, but difficult to dispute.

Discussing Rampa's appeal, Sarah Penicka wrote in 'The Lama of Suburbia':

> Rampa's books are, however, not particularly scholarly: his thoughts are sometimes disordered, he never quotes references and refers to texts extremely rarely. . . . He presented esotericism with simplicity and his books as a reasonably complete source of knowledge, requiring readers to undertake no further study.[2]

Penicka quotes Agehananda Bharati's low opinion of Rampa's readers as a:

> '. . . depressing crowd of partly well-meaning, totally uninformed, and seemingly uninformable votaries' who have an 'extreme dislike of hard theological, scriptural, commentatorial argument, a dislike that characterizes all followers of the neo-Hindu-Buddhist, and the pseudo-Asian movements of a millennial type'.[3]

However, not all readers of Rampa have necessarily been gullible fools. Some, like Michael Dillon, derived unexpected benefit from Rampa's questionable teachings. In *Prisoners of Shangri-La,* Donald S. Lopez, Jr., points out that when discussing Rampa with other Tibetologists and Buddhologists in Europe, he found that many of them had read about Tibet for the first time in *The Third Eye*:

> For some it was a fascination with the world Rampa described that had led them to become professional scholars of Tibet.[4]

---

[1] Fowler, *The Book of Forgotten Authors*, 278 and 280.
[2] Penicka, 'Lobsang Rampa: The Lama of Suburbia', 120, *et seq.*
[3] Bharati, 'Fictitious Tibet'.
[4] Lopez, *Prisoners of Shangri-La*, 112.

Characters of Questionable Faith

Rampa has not just had an awkward relationship with authors and literary critics, but also the Buddhist religious establishment. For example, when Alain Stanké, wrote to the Dalai Lama to ask for his opinion of Rampa's identity, the Dalai Lama's deputy secretary replied:

> I wish to inform you that we do not place credence in the books written by the so-called Dr T. Lobsang Rampa. His works are highly imaginative and fictional in nature. I hope this answers your question.[1]

Letter from the Secretary to the Dalai Lama to Alain Stanké.

Rampa's response to Alain Stanké was that the Dalai Lama *himself* had never said Rampa was inauthentic:

> Everyone knows that high-ranking people have a large number of secretaries . . . who . . . are authorized to write what they

---

[1] Stanké, *Rampa: Imposteur ou initié?*, 134, *et seq.* (My translation.) In a 1982 letter from a Special Assistant to the Dalain Lama (Tendzin Choegyal) to Luis Manuel Da Luz Aparicio, Rampa is called an 'imposter'. (Published on Facebook 25th January 2021.)

The Legacy

consider opportune . . . I know full well that one of the secretaries of the Dalai Lama does not have me in his heart. . . . A well-known American writer went to see the Dalai Lama in India, and he returned with a message assuring me that when Tibet was liberated, the Dalai Lama would welcome me to the Potala.

Having insisted that Stanké should not explicitly put those words into the mouth of the Dalai Lama, he insisted,

. . . consider what was said by his secretaries as suspicious. You don't know their motives. I might know them.

This late-career answer to criticism was remarkably similar to his response to Macrae's reader of a pre-publication copy of *The Third Eye*, whom Rampa said he knew and who had professional reasons for attacking his book. Many of his followers have followed the same pattern: trust only those who reinforce Rampa's claims, and throw suspicion on anyone who doesn't.

Unfortunately for Rampa, others had thought to ask the same questions. The German magazine *Der Stern* reported, with pictures:

The older brother of the ruling Dalai Lama, Lobsang (left), and the monk minister of the last Tibetan Government, Rampa (right), are among those calling the man who pretends to be the reincarnation of a noble lama an impostor.

Characters of Questionable Faith

In 1964/1965, Arnaud Desjardins, a French television director who filmed lamas in exile in India, reported the words of Tenzin Gyatso, 14th Dalai Lama, regarding Rampa's first book:

> 'Whenever you have the opportunity, point out that *The Third Eye* by Lobsang Rampa is not a factual document, but a fiction by a Western author.'[1]

There is also the report of Alfonso Caycedo (founder of Sophrology, a mental well-being practice), who met the Dalai Lama in the mid-1960s. He asked him about Lobsang Rampa and *The Third Eye*:

> His Holiness and the interpreter both had a hearty laugh which disconcerted me a little. After a while, His Holiness continued.
> His Holiness: It is absolutely wrong. The conception of the third eye is there, but his description is all false.[2]

In *La Liberté* in 1984 Jean-François Mayer discussed Rampa and mentioned that one of his supporters had suggested, 'why not ask the Dalai Lama himself'?

> 'It has been done' replies an editor, W Ledauc, who quotes the humorous remarks of the Dalai Lama during his last visit to Switzerland:
> 'Lobsang Rampa never set foot in a Tibetan monastery, nor did he come to Tibet. This does not detract from the romantic value of his work. I have to thank him, he gave us a lot of publicity.'[3]

Lobsang Rampa has refused to go away. Just what should we make of the fact that in the Russian city of Kemerovo, at a road

---

[1] Lenoir, 238. My translation.
[2] Caycedo, *India of Yogis*, 229.
[3] Mayer, *La Liberté*, 23-24 June 1984, 16. (My translation.)

The Legacy

junction at the end of 'Орбита' Square, there is a monument to him by the Moscow sculptor Dmitry Vladimirovich Kukkolos? It was apparently commissioned by a local businessman, who knew the Rampa story well-enough to ask for Mrs Fifi Greywhiskers to be included.

Russian Rampa monument by Dmitry Vladimirovich Kukkolos.

One of the more imaginative attempts to perpetuate the Rampa story online has been the publication of a photo of the 13th Dalai Lama with his entourage in 1910, taken from the *Sphere* magazine, with the claim that the gentleman on the far right of the picture looks uncannily like Rampa.

Portrait of the 13th Dalai Lama, India, 1910. (When reproduced by enthusiasts, an erroneous date of 1890 is usually supplied.)[1]

[1] From *The Sphere*, 19th March 1910.

Characters of Questionable Faith

It has often been asked whether Rampa's imaginative and inaccurate way of looking at the world really does anyone any harm. Agehananda Bharati believes so in his essay 'Fictitious Tibet':

> Buddhism, Hinduism, and the other genuine traditions of the East are misrepresented, and that an image of Tibet is created, and perpetuated, which cannot but be harmful to the future interface between Tibetan culture and the West.[1]

Dr Gilbert has argued that Rampa's writing has been a danger to Tibet:

> . . . the sheer silliness of Rampa's books enables China to claim that only what *they* say is actually the truth, and to deny any legitimacy to other, genuine accounts of Chinese occupation and oppression . . .[2]

Donald S. Lopez Jr has reported that after reading Rampa's *The Third Eye*, his students have asked him some reasonable questions:

> 'Did monks really eat communally and in silence while the Scriptures were read aloud?' 'If a monk violated the eightfold path, was he punished by having to lie motionless face down across the door of the temple for a full day, without food or drink?' 'Are the priests in Tibet vegetarian?' 'Did priests really only ride white horses?' 'Were horses really only ridden every other day?' 'Did acolytes really wear white robes?' 'Did cats really guard the temple jewels?'[3]

Lopez had to report:

> The answer to each of these questions was no.

---

[1] 'Bharati, 'Fictitious Tibet'.
[2] Gilbert, 'Beyond the Lost Horizon', 3.
[3] Lopez, *Prisoners of Shangri-La*, 104, *et seq.*

The Legacy

One understands the confusion of Lopez's students, but even professionals can be taken in. Rampa's assertion that Tibetan temple jewels were guarded by cats was, ludicrous as it seems, reported as ethnographic evidence by F. Sierksma in *Tibet's Terrifying Deities: Sex and Aggression in Religious Acculturation*:

> In the Land of Snows a servant was required to address his master's cat as follows: 'Would honourable Puss Puss deign to come and drink this unworthy milk.' [1]

The Third Eye would appear to have had an effect on comic artists as much as it has on authors of fiction. It was one of several books read by the Belgian cartoonist Hergé in preparation for *Tintin in Tibet* which was serialised weekly from September 1958 to November 1959 in *Tintin* magazine, and published as a book in 1960. Hergé read about the abominable snowman in a number of sources, but his levitating monks may come direct from Rampa.

A frame illustrating a levitating monk in *Tintin in Tibet* by Hergé.

[1] Sierksma, *Tibet's Terrifying Deities*, 107.

Characters of Questionable Faith

The Third Eye would also seem to have influenced Steve Ditko's Marvel Comics character Doctor Strange, who first appeared in July 1963's *Strange Tales* #110.

The Third Eye has since been a big influence on the acclaimed graphic novel by Alejandro Jodorowsky, *The White Lama* (2000). It is set in late nineteenth-century Tibet when, after the Grand Lama dies, an orphan of white explorers is chosen as his reincarnation. It is possible to view it as Western cultural appropriation of Tibet (a charge that can be levelled at Rampa), not least because it perpetuates certain Western stereotypes, some of which were created by Rampa himself. For example, Jodorowsky borrows Rampa's idea of monks adept at martial arts, and also monks flying in kites (both ideas being original to Rampa).

The White Lama by Alejandro Jodorowsky, illustrated by Georges Bess.

Befuddling gullible students and even academics is not necessarily the worst crime in the world. Rather more serious, and tragic, is the story of Kenneth Butler, a seventeen year old from Brighton who was reported in the British *Daily Mirror* in February 1966 as having electrocuted himself while attempting an 'Astral trip to the Past' based on his reading of Rampa's book *You—Forever*. At the inquest Rampa was quoted:

The Legacy

A person in good health who meets a violent end has his 'batteries fully charged', and so the etheric is at full strength. With the death of the body the etheric becomes detached and floats away.[1]

Rampa later commented:

. . . a young man committed suicide and one of my books— *Secrets of the Aura*[2]—was found with him. . . . I challenged the slanderers—as I now challenge you to show me where, in any of my books, I have advocated suicide. On the contrary, I condemn it.[3]

Unfortunately, another tragedy occurred, in Boucherville, Quebec, in November 1972, when a young student shot one of his teachers, then a friend, before killing himself. According to Stanké once again, 'Rampa's book *Les Secrets de l'Aura* was mentioned as being at the origin of the suicide's madness.'[4] For all of the author's faults, it is difficult not to attribute Butler's death to the young man's foolishness, and the Boucherville deaths to something other than the student's belief in Rampa's teachings.

The Sri-Lankan *Sunday Times* reported on how Rampa's version of Buddhism (which allows followers to 'travel to other planets, levitate and contact flying saucers') had unfortunate results:

Some 20 years ago a young man in Germany was rushed to hospital after he used a knife to try to open his 'third eye'. Fortunately he survived but the newspapers were full of reports saying that this was a 'Buddhist practice'.[5]

---

[1] Rampa, *You—Forever*, p.31.
[2] A re-issue of [*You—Forever*].
[3] Stanké, *Rampa: Imposteur ou initié?*, 146. (My translation.)
[4] Reported in Stanké, *Rampa: Imposteur ou initié?*, footnote 1, 146.
[5] 'Blind faith in the third eye', *Sunday Times* (Sri Lanka), 27th May 2018. I haven't managed to track down the original story.

Photograph of T. Lobsang Rampa in later life.

9.
Conclusion

In person, Cyril Henry Hoskin does seem to have impressed many (although not all) who met him. Sheelagh Rouse wrote that on first meeting him she experienced a sensation like 'receiving an enormous electric shock',[1] Warburg wrote that his 'eyes were strange, large, luminous, penetrating . . . He seemed a man not to be trifled with',[2] and Newby wrote that 'Altogether the whole feeling the Lama gave me was one of great power and although it might sound imaginative, I could not help thinking of Rasputin and how difficult it had been for his assassins to kill him'.[3] Alain Stanké wrote, 'I have the very clear feeling of finding myself in the presence of a tender and good being. . . . One of those men from whom we have a lot to learn.[4] Warburg,

---

[1] Sheelagh Rouse, *Twenty-Five Years with T. Lobsang Rampa*, 13.
[2] Warburg, *All Authors Are Equal*, 224-6.
[3] Newby, *A Traveller's Life*, 179-180.
[4] Stanké, *Rampa: Imposteur ou initié?*, 21. (My translation.)

Conclusion

Rouse, Dillon and Stanké all specifically mentioned that he seemed to have psychic powers. However, even those who attested to Rampa's charisma, even his supernatural insights, were not all convinced that he was really a Tibetan lama.

 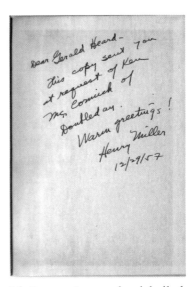

Left, Henry Miller's correspondence with Rampa in a packet labelled 'Do not open until after my death'. Right: the front free endpaper of a first edition of *The Third Eye* inscribed from Miller to Gerald Heard.

Henry Miller had a habit of falling for unlikely New Age stories, having believed at one time that a UFO invasion was imminent, and having been taken in by, among others, Blavatsky, L. Ron Hubbard, Kahlil Gibran and Sri Ramakrishna. From 1958 to 1960 he corresponded with Rampa, but later realised he had been fooled. However, he was never too dispirited by this tendency of his to be duped, writing:

> Any theory, any idea, any speculation can augment the zest for life so long as one does not make the mistake of thinking that he is getting somewhere.[1]

[1] Miller, *Stand Still Like the Hummingbird*, New Directions, 1962, 82.

Characters of Questionable Faith

It is easy to simply dismiss Rampa as a hoaxer or a charlatan, and to view his claims as a joke. Early in his career he was caught out in a fundamental lie and for many people it is therefore reasonable to suspect everything else he claimed, especially when his assertions became increasingly wild. The question that comes to mind is, did Lobsang Rampa *knowingly* create a fiction about his life, or did he really *believe* what he said had happened to him? It is an impossible question to answer, and one major difficulty in making a fair assessment is that Rampa only made public his story of transmigration *after* he had been exposed as Cyril Henry Hoskin. Neither Charles Gibbs-Smith, Cyrus Brooks, Frederic Warburg nor Elliott Macrae heard the story until after the exposé. It is *possible* he would have offered this information later without any prompting, but it looks suspiciously like a tale put together over a few days in Howth in February 1958 when the world's press were at his door, demanding explanations.

What is more interesting than Cyril Hoskin simply being a hoaxer is the clear evidence to show he was adopting an alternative persona as early as February 1948, albeit as 'Kuansuo'. One good reason for wanting to discard the history of Cyril Hoskin was disillusionment after several decades of moving between various unfulfilling means of employment, which may have included the collapse of the dress shop business, and then his trouble in finding any employment at all. In *The Rampa Story* and even more so in *As It Was!*, the character of Hoskin is described as unhappy and Rampa says Hoskin was considering suicide.[1] It is difficult to know to what degree this is a fiction, but it may well suggest an underlying unhappiness with his life. Creating a whole new personality may have been very tempting.

But why a Tibetan lama? Hoskin was obviously interested in Tibet and Buddhism, and had a certain amount of secondhand knowledge. It took approximately seven years to *finesse* the story that made such an impact on Cyrus Brooks at the A.M.

---

[1] Rampa, *As It Was!*, 155.

Conclusion

Heath literary agency, during which time he seems to have impressed some people more than others.

There is every reason to assume that Sheelagh Rouse was convinced by Rampa. When she first met him, he had already assumed the character of Dr Kuan, and it is possible that the first time she ever heard the name Cyril Hoskin was when Hugh Medlicott first talked to her and Mrs Kuan in Ireland. Rouse may well have denied that Dr Kuan was Hoskin before being confronted with evidence, and it was unfortunate that a flustered Mrs Kuan told Medlicott, 'He is not a Tibetan' and that the book was 'fiction'. It sounds like the household required time to get their story straight, so that Kuan, from his sick bed, could insist that 'for very special reasons the identity of the Tibetan author cannot be revealed'.

That a consistent and elaborate explanation of events was required may well have come as a surprise to Rouse, but circumstances were forcing her to take sides, and she decided she could only choose one. This may be why she backed up the Kuans, claiming, 'I have seen the real Dr Kuan but I will not tell you where he is.'

What Rouse thought of the transmigration story when it was first told to her, she does not say.[1] As for inconsistencies in her recollections, the heightened emotion of the time would explain why she was so angry and recalls accusations of 'lurid orgies'.[2] Rampa himself, recalls being accused of such things, although I have not been able to find evidence of any direct accusations.[3]

As for Sarah Hoskin, who was to become Sanya Ku'an just a few years after her marriage to Cyril Hoskin, and who later adopted the name Mama San Ra'ab Rampa, did she really believe that her husband's body had been taken over by a Tibetan lama?

---

[1] Late in life, Rouse said she could not explain the transmigration, saying, 'I understand that I can't understand.' *Out There Radio*, 2021.

[2] Rouse, *Grace*, 25.

[3] In Rampa, *As It Was!*, 178, Rampa wrote that he was accused of, 'black magic rites in the bottom of the house, that I had a secret temple; that I was guilty of all manner of sex orgies, etcetera.'

Characters of Questionable Faith

Or was she complicit in the imposture? She certainly embraced her part in the story from very early on, albeit that she couldn't quite get her story straight in Howth when the press were at their most insistent. Thereafter, in life and in her own books, she kept the transmigration story going.

It must also be noted that after the press stories first appeared, until his dying day, Tuesday Lobsang Rampa never seems to have relented in playing the part that he had created, even if there were elements of his appearance, behaviour and accent that made clear his physical Devonian origins. It may seem odd that T. Lobsang Rampa, the Tibetan lama, had perfect and often loving recall of his 'host's' pre-transmigration life, but Rampa had an explanation for that; he was able to access it via the Akashic Record.

Frederic Warburg considered:

> K., I feel tolerably sure, believed in some sense in his lama-hood, believed he was in fact the lama who had entered the body of Cyril Henry Hoskins [sic]. Pathological, perhaps, but it was this belief that made his book one of the most readable and successful of any I have published. *The Third Eye* was the product of faith, of love for Buddhism as he understood it, a religion as far away from the sordid materialism he sensed around him, as the lowland counties of southern England from the sparkling peaks and glittering domes and palaces of holy Lhasa. All the best counterfeiters surely loved their work.[1]

One of the biggest stumbling blocks faced by Cyril Hoskin in becoming Lobsang Rampa was his relatively humble and mundane beginnings as the son of a plumber from Plympton. If he had been Tibetan, especially if he had come from a suitable religious background, then his claims of transmigration might have been treated with more respect. As Donald Lopez points out, a far more fantastic case of consciousness transference can be found in Tibetan literature in the biography of Marpa, whose

---

[1] Warburg, *All Authors Are Equal*, 245.

Conclusion

son, Darmadoday is meant to have fractured his skull in an accident and, because no recently deceased corpse was available, transferred his consciousness into the body of a recently dead pigeon. He then flew across the Himalayas to India to a dead thirteen-year-old brahman boy into which the bird transferred its consciousness. The boy then arose from his funeral pyre just in time, and became the great yogin Tipupa. As Lopez comments, 'Compared to this a Tibetan taking over the body of an unemployed Englishman seems rather mundane.'[1]

Rightly, we treat sincere religious beliefs with respect, although it does not mean we necessarily have to accept them as factual. It is reasonable to ask if Rampa's story is written-off not just because it is too alternative and left-field, but because certain important details were only supplied when awkward questions were asked. However, all belief systems that require 'faith' rather than empirical proof for legitimacy are open to exploitation by charismatics intending to deceive.

My own opinion is that Rampa's fascination with Tibet was so strong, and his disillusionment with his own life so profound, that he sought refuge in a *persona* that was not his own. It was a persona that he strove to legitimise, and for a time after the publication of *The Third Eye* he succeeded. When the press started asking awkward questions he felt he had to 'double-down' on his assertions because he had recently gained so much and did not want to lose it. And, after repeating his story time and time again, refining and polishing it, he was probably unable to entirely differentiate between fact and fiction. He may have really believed he had wisdom to impart and that he could 'light a candle' in the darkness. To reinforce this, there were many people writing to Rampa to say how useful his writing, teaching and insight had been to them.

It has been argued that another approach might be taken to Rampa. In a thesis entitled *Relire T. Lobsang Rampa: Analysis of a modern myth*, Karl-Stéphan Bouthillette argues that rather

---

[1] Lopez, *Prisoners of Shangri-La*, 105.

Characters of Questionable Faith

than debate Rampa's authenticity and the reality of his writing, we might want to consider the contribution he has made to New Age thinking. He quotes André Couture: 'The New Age, as a religious movement . . . is unfolding before our eyes, right now', and says it would be a shame not to seize the opportunity to study it.

The following chapter attempts to do just this, although, I would like to conclude it is likely that at the end of each day, Rampa must have gone to sleep knowing that his origins were in Plympton, Devon, rather than Tibet.

Lobsang Rampa, June, 1970.

T. Lobsang Rampa and the New Age

It is difficult to define the New Age movement of the twentieth century and do justice to all the different and eclectic philosophies that it encompassed at various times. It can be defined as a very loose grouping-together of non-traditional spiritual beliefs and practices, but it often went further than this, encompassing a willingness to explore a wide range of ideas 'at the frontiers of knowledge and experience'.[1]

Daren Kemp in *New Age: A Guide* (2004) wrote: 'One of the few things on which all scholars agree concerning New Age is that it is difficult to define. Often, the definition given actually reflects the background of the scholar giving the definition.' In my own case, I admit that I am heavily influenced by the tatty paperbacks that used to be shelved in the New Age section in

---

[1] From the title page of *Unexplained Mysteries of the World*, PG Tips, 1989.

bookshops of the 1970s and 1980s; books that ranged from alternative religions, through self-help therapies, to a consideration of the existence of the Loch Ness monster.

It should be acknowledged that much in the New Age drew from an understanding of existing traditions which were often reconsidered and recombined alongside modern developments in psychology and science. It is less often admitted that there was also a large input from showmen, frauds and the science fiction community. The problem is the sheer number of different, quite diverse philosophies that the term New Age can encompass.

In America, New Age studies now finds it convenient to use the example of the Esalen Institute in Big Sur, California as a means of showing how various New Age practices and beliefs could be successfully brought together, but this tends to give prominence to those that are often (although not always) the least controversial and perhaps the most popular today. It is a rather tidy and parochial view of the New Age that roots it to the 1970s, and tends to ignore more fringe ideas, removing from the record a great deal that has largely fallen out of fashion.

I would argue that the New Age movement can be traced all the way back to Madame Blavatsky's Theosophical Society, founded in 1875. This was an attempt to bring together spiritual thinking from both the Eastern and Western traditions and while it has never been mainstream, it has always been influential. It has paved the way for combining a myriad of long-established religious doctrines so that, for example, certain contemporary Christian sects now embrace concepts such as reincarnation.

The fact that Blavatsky was accused in her own day of plagiarising other writers, as well as of offering fraudulent evidence, has never concerned her followers who view this simply as a backlash from the Christian establishment as well as from materialists and sceptics. As often happens when unorthodox ideas are espoused, followers manage to take criticism as validation of those ideas: *they attack us only because they are afraid we know the truth!* This has happened throughout the New Age from

T. Lobsang Rampa and the New Age

Blavatsky, through to Wilhelm Reich and his belief in 'orgone' energy, to contemporary conspiracy theories.

There are those who are sympathetic to New Age beliefs with more considered views, who argue that while mistakes may have been made when new ideas have been proposed, and perhaps some proponents have even acted without honest intentions, there is still a basis of truth in that which has been revealed, or that the truth can somehow be discerned despite fraud and imposture. This is *almost* to adopt the modern, scientific method of enquiry which requires the creation of an hypothesis which is tested and analysed, after which the original idea is adjusted or discarded based on the results. In this way the work of Gurdjieff, Ouspensky, Freud, Jung, Reich, Pavlov, Maslow and many others have been seriously considered and different aspects of their work have been embraced, discarded, developed or synthesised. Naturally, people will gravitate toward those ideas with which they are personally sympathetic, and which resonate with their own life experiences. Few embrace or practice even the most unlikely New Age ideas without a degree of 'enquiry', although there is not always a willingness to seriously consider negative evidence. Adopting any aspect of the twentieth-century New Age becomes a matter of faith analogous to that required for a belief in traditional religions.

It can also be argued that the New Age movement garners more respect now than previously simply because it has been around for long enough to have become established. There would appear to be a generally increased respect today for those individuals who espouse *personal* spiritual beliefs, rather than subscribing to traditional, orthodox religions. Very often these beliefs are underpinned by an almost 'pick and mix' selection of ideas taken from a wide range of historically and spiritually disparate sources, but today this appears to be considered much less unreasonable.

The more 'orthodox' histories of the New Age add to the work of Gurdjieff, Freud, Jung, etc, the mind-altering experi-

Characters of Questionable Faith

ences of drug experimentation in the 1960s.[1] The New Age has also embraced the spiritual beliefs and practices of hitherto marginalised indigenous peoples, as well as, at the other end of the spectrum, cutting-edge science. It has gone down scientifically questionable paths of 'visualisation' to treat cancer, morphic resonance, quantum selves, crystals, and therapies involving spirits, angels and shamen. There are symbiotic relationships between Earth mysteries, alternative archaeology, paganism and Ufology. In attempting to reconnect with a romantically presumed lost wisdom, practices such as Druidism and Witchcraft have been imaginatively recreated.

If in the second half of the twentieth century there was much to be considered by those seeking spiritual enlightenment, and a willingness to explore ideas that even then appeared outlandish and unlikely, they were also likely to be promoted in mainstream media purely for the purposes of entertainment. (One of the most obvious examples being the deforming of cutlery by the power of the mind on prime-time television chat shows.) Although much of this would appear to be quite far removed from recognisable New Age practices such as Yoga, Gestalt Therapy, etc, it all used the same pseudo-spiritual and pseudo-scientific language, often reliant on the power of the minds of adepts, teachers or gurus to reveal the 'truth' that ordinary people could not see; psychics could not only bend forks, but could undertake remote viewing and use other arcane methods such as astral travel to account for that which science had dismissed. These unverifiable sources sought to explain everything from the Bermuda Triangle to UFOs, from the supposed mystic power of pyramids to the curious Nazca lines in Peru.

Unexplained mysteries of all descriptions are pertinent to the New Age because aspects of the movement were employed to explain them. Additionally, many New Age claims were underpinned by the presentation of the apparently lost wisdom from

---

[1] Although this has its genesis in the experiments of Gerald Heard and Aldous Huxley in previous decades.

T. Lobsang Rampa and the New Age

not just exotic or ancient cultures, but from such unverifiable sources as Atlantis, and even extraterrestrials. Unfortunately, it is difficult to objectively discuss any of this with adherants whose information is based on mystical revelation, although ideas such as telekinesis and mind reading ought to be scientifically verifiable.

Into this heady mix of these more or less plausible esoteric ideas we must add the writings of T. Lobsang Rampa. Rampa not only borrowed heavily from the New Age movement and the zeitgeist of the time, but through his books he actively contributed to it.[1] Not only did he popularise many of the concepts of the movement, but he enhanced and embellished others, and of course, his most obvious contribution the discussion was his concept of a phyical 'Third Eye'. This resonated with a long-held suspicion that we do not see the world as it is, that,

> If the *doors of perception* were *cleansed* every thing would appear to man as it is . . .[2]

It is difficult to measure exactly how influential Rampa was, but he was noticeably in the vanguard when presenting his ideas. Take the idea of levitation, for example; in Hinduism, Buddhism and Christian teachings this is usually a by-product or manifestation of divinity, but in *The Third Eye* it is presented as a skill that anyone can learn, requiring only marginally more practice than that required to ride a bicycle. (Levitation is, perhaps, a lesser skill compared to that of invisibility, which

---

[1] His books were, at one time, everywhere. See, for example, *Marley and Me* by Don Taylor (Barricade Books, 1995, 178), where Bob Marley, the great Reggae pioneer, crosses an airport lounge in 1978 and casually picks up an unnamed book by Rampa.

[2] This quote from William Blake's *The Marriage of Heaven and Hell* was used by Aldous Huxley for the title of his 1954 autobiographical *The Doors of Perception* which describes his psychedelic experience under the influence of mescaline in May 1953.

Characters of Questionable Faith

Rampa modesty admitted he failed to master.) Not long after Rampa wrote about learning how to levitate, Maharishi Mahesh Yogi began claiming that those who assiduously practiced transcendental meditation could also learn the skill of levitation (albeit that 'yogic flying' is better described as bouncing).

Rampa with prayer wheels and a crystal, from a mail order catalogue selling his books and various meditation aids [c. late 1970].

Rampa also made many aware of the concept of astral travel; a controlled departure from the physical human body so that the subject can travel throughout the astral plane, giving access to distant locations (including Venus), times and even dimensions. The idea had occurred in many cultures, and enabling the subject to claim experiences and knowledge that would not have been otherwise possible, but once again, Rampa popularised the concept.

The Third Eye, was in many ways a part of the zeitgeist. For example, although the existence of the 'Yeti' had been rumoured and was even adopted into Tibetan Buddhism, Rampa just happened to write about the Abominable Snowman at the time the West was overcome with popular 'yeti-mania'. While attempting to scale Mount Everest in 1951, Eric Shipton had taken photographs of a number of what appeared to be large footprints in the snow, and in 1953, Sir Edmund Hillary and Tenzing Norgay also reported seeing oversized footprints. In

T. Lobsang Rampa and the New Age

1954 there was even a *Daily Mail* 'Snowman' Expedition. Rampa was able to satisfy public interest by describing them from personal observation.

From very early in his writing, Rampa insisted that his life's work was to photograph the human 'aura'. Again, many would have first read about the idea in Rampa's books. It was to become an important part in some alternative medicines, as it is argued by those who claim they can perceive it that the colouration of the aura can play a significant part in understanding illness. In 1939 Kirlian photography was meant to have captured the aura, although the wider scientific community said it did no such thing, and Rampa himself agreed. As far as I am aware, Rampa never managed to capture an aura on film.

Another obvious manifestation of the 1950s zeitgeist in the Western world was an interest in UFOs, or the 'chariots of the gods', as Rampa called them, a phrase that turns up in Classical literature and the Bible, but was made most famous in 1968 by Erich von Däniken. Rampa discussed UFOs and telepathic communication with aliens in the same offhand way that he was able to declare that the island of Ireland is a fragment of lost Atlantis. Rampa confidently branched out into pseudoscience when explaining that the earth is hollow, something that was last discussed in the mid-nineteenth century by John Cleves Symmes Jr. and J.N. Reynolds, by which time the idea had already been discredited and was no longer a scientifically viable hypothesis.

For all that Rampa's books were derided by critics, he found followers for whom no claim seemed to be too unbelievable. Rampa even felt confident in explaining an alternative history of planet Earth, writing:

> In the days of long, long ago earth was a very different place. It revolved much nearer the sun, and in the opposite direction, and there was another planet nearby, a twin of the earth.[1]

---

[1] Rampa, *Doctor from Lhasa*, 173.

Characters of Questionable Faith

He was happy to accept all manner of ideas that run counter to accepted science and which make his books read like fantasy or science fiction. He was happy to discuss clairvoyance, etheric doubles, poltergeists, psychometry, telepathy and teleportation. Numerology, he explained, leant itself to 'quackery' and one

> . . . should only go to a numerologist who has an established reputation because some of the back-street practitioners merely want your money, they do not want to help you as well.[1]

He warned that others, such as mediums, should also be approached with care because not all have the abilities they claim.

It is a sign of confidence in your abilities when you feel able to make predictions which will eventually be empirically tested. Rampa wrote:

> In the year 2004 there will be a tremendous war between China and Russia in space. On Earth, people will huddle in deep shelters and many shall be saved. More lands shall sink and more shall rise. . . .
>
> In the year 2008 or so the Russians and the Chinese will settle their differences under the stimulus of a much greater thing. From far out in space, from beyond this whole system, will come people, humans, who will come here and want to settle on this Earth.[2]

It is to the frustration of literal-minded rationalists that when presented with the failure of an apparently straightforward test of prediction, followers find convoluted reasons and excuses to justify their belief in the prophet. (Please see my essay on the Brotherhood of the Cross and Star.)

Just as several experts on Tibet who disapproved of Rampa nevertheless admitted their interest in Tibet was inspired by his

---

[1] Rampa, *Wisdom of the Ancients*, 91.
[2] Rampa, *Chapters of Life*, 135.

books, so did many more 'lay' readers first learn about Tibet through Rampa's writing. Additionally, he introduced several million readers to a vast range of traditional and New Age concepts, and they would then have then gone on to other sources of information to learn more.

Bibliography

Books by T. Lobsang Rampa:

The Third Eye, Secker & Warburg (London), 1956.
ditto, Doubleday (New York), 1958.
Doctor from Lhasa, Souvenir Press (London), 1959.
ditto, Saucerian Press (Clarksburg, W. VA.), 1959.
ditto, Corgi Books/Transworld Publishers (London), 1960 (pbk).
ditto, Bantam Books (New York), 1968 (pbk).
The Rampa Story, Souvenir Press (London), 1960.
ditto, Bantam Books (New York), 1968 (pbk).
Cave of the Ancients, Corgi (London), 1963 (pbk).
ditto, Ballantine (New York), 1965 (pbk).
Living with the Lama, Corgi (London), 1964 (pbk).
You—Forever, Corgi (London), 1965 (pbk).
ditto, Pageant Press (New York), 1966.
Wisdom of the Ancients, Corgi (London), 1965 (pbk).
ditto, Award Books (New York), 1965 (pbk).
The Saffron Robe, Corgi (London), 1966 (pbk).
ditto, Pageant Press (New York), 1966.
ditto, Bantam Books (New York), 1970 (pbk).
My Visit to Venus, Saucerian Press (Clarksburg, W. VA.),
    [c.1959] (reprinted 1988).
Chapters of Life, Corgi (London), 1967 (pbk).
Beyond the Tenth, Corgi (London), 1969 (pbk).
Feeding the Flame, Corgi (London), 1971 (pbk).
The Hermit, Corgi (London), 1971 (pbk).
The Thirteenth Candle, Corgi (London), 1972 (pbk).
Candlelight, Corgi (London), 1973 (pbk).
Twilight, Corgi (London), 1975 (pbk).
As It Was!, Corgi (London), 1976 (pbk).
I Believe, Corgi (London), 1976 (pbk).
Three Lives, Corgi (London), 1977 (pbk).
Tibetan Sage, Corgi (London), 1980 (pbk).

see also
My Visit to Agharta, Inner Light Publications, 2003.

Magazine articles by T. Lobsang Rampa:

'Saucers over Tibet', *Flying Saucer Review*, March-April, 1957.
ditto, *Flying Saucers* (the 'Official Quarterly Journal' of 'Civilian
   Saucer Investigation', N.Z.), Vol 05 No 01 1957.
ditto, *Saucerian Bulletin*, April 1958, Vol 3 No 1.
'Flying into Space', *Flying Saucer Review*, May-June, 1957.
ditto, *Saucerian Bulletin* #19, October 1958, Vol 3 No 4.

Recordings

The Power of Prayer, Saucerian Records, 1967. Side 1: 'The
   Lama's Story' (The Lamas tells of his persecutions in the
   Western World). Side 2: 'The Power of Prayer'.
Meditation, A Touchstones Ltd, 1969.

Other Works Consulted

Anand, Dibyesh, *Geopolitical Exotica, Tibet in Western Imagination*, University of Minesota Press, 2007.

Bharati, Agehananda: 'Fictitious Tibet: The Origin and Persistence of Rampaism', Tibet Society Bulletin, Vol. 7, 1974.

Blavatsky, H.P., *The Secret Doctrine*, Vols I and II, 1893.

Bleiler, E.F., *The Guide to Supernatural Fiction*, Kent State University Press, 1983.

Bouthillette, Karl-Stéphan, *Relire T. Lobsang Rampa: Analysis of a modern myth*, thesis presented to the Faculty of Graduate Studies of Laval University, 2011.

Brauen, Martin, *Dreamworld Tibet: Western Illusions*, Weatherhill, 2004.

Buckley, Michael, *Eccentric Explorers*, CrazyHorse Press, 2008.

Caycedo, Alfonso, *India of Yogis*, National Publishing House, 1966.

Das, Sarat Chandra, *Journey to Lhasa and Central Tibet*, John Murray, 1902.

Dillon, Michael (Lobzang Jivaka), *Out of the Ordinary: A Life of Gender and Spiritual Transitions*, Fordham University Press, 2017.

Eaton, Barry, *Radio Out There*, March, 2021. Barry Eaton interviews Karen Mutton, who, in turn, interviews Sheelagh Rouse.

Evans, Christopher, *Cults of Unreason*, Harrap, 1973.

Fowler, Christopher *The Book of Forgotten Authors*, Riverrun, 2018.

Gilbert, Martin, *Never Despair: Winston Churchill 1945-1965*, Heinemann, 1988.

Gilbert, Dr. Robert A., ' "Beyond the Lost Horizon": Tibet, the Masters and Shangri La as imagined in popular fiction', a lecture given to the Theosophical History Conference, 2016.

T. Lobsang Rampa Bibliography

Harrer, Heinrich, *Seven Years in Tibet*, Rupert Hart-Davis, 1953.

Harrer, Heinrich, 'My Seven Years in Tibet,' *The Geographical Journal*, Vol. 120, No. 2, June, 1954.

Harrer, Heinrich, *Beyond Seven Years in Tibet*, Labyrinth Press, 2007.

Howard, Dana, *The Strange Case of T. Lobsang Rampa*, Llewellyn Publications, 1958.

Jackson, Roger and Wm. E. Ashley, *Henry Miller: A Personal Archive*, 1994.

Lenoir, Frédéric, *La rencontre du bouddhisme et de l'Occident*, Paris, Fayard, 1999.

Lopez, Donald S., Jr., *Prisoners of Shangri-La: Tibetan Buddhism and the West*, University of Chicago Press, 1998.

Lopez, Donald S., Jr., 'The Mystery of the Three-Eyed Lama', *Tricycle: The Buddhist Review*, Winter 1998.

Martin, James, *Calgary: The Unknown City*, Arsenal Pulp Press, 2001.

Maxwell, Pat, *Stories Behind My News Pictures*, Choice Publishing, 2010.

Mayer, Jean-François, 'Quand l'Occident se passionne pour un Tibet imaginaire . . . La supercherie du faux lama Lobsang Rampa', *La Liberté*, Fribourg, 23-24 June 1984.

Michie, David, the blog posts 'A Few Words on Lobsang Rampa' and 'The enduring fascination with Lobsang Rampa', at *The Dalai Lama's Cat: Buddhist compassion in action*, 30th March, 2018.

Miller, Henry, *Stand Still Like the Hummingbird*, New Directions, 1962.

Mutton, Karen, *T. Lobsang Rampa: New Age Trailblazer*, extracted from *Nexus* (Australia), Volume 13, Numbers 2 and 3, February-March/April-May 2006.

Newby, Eric, *A Traveller's Life*, Collins, 1982.

Penicka, Sarah, 'Lobsang Rampa: The Lama of Suburbia', in *On A Panegyrical Note: Studies in Honour of Garry W. Trompf*, eds Victoria Barker and Frances di Lauro, Sydney Studies in Religion, 2007.

Rampa, Mama San Ra'ab, *Pussywillow*, Corgi, 1976.
ditto, *Tigerlily*, Corgi, 1978.
ditto, *Autumn Lady*, Corgi, 1980.
Rickard, Bob, 'HOAX! T. Lobsang Rampa', *Fortean Times*, June/July 1992.
Rouse, Sheelagh, *Twenty-Five Years with T. Lobsang Rampa*, self published, 2005.
Rouse, Sheelagh, *Grace: The World of Rampa*, self published, 2007.
Sierksma, F., *Tibet's Terrifying Deities: Sex and Aggression in Religious Acculturation*, Moulton and Company, 1996.
Snow Lion Newsletter, Autumn, 1991.
Stanké, Alain, *Rampa: Imposteur ou initié?*, Éditions internationales Alain Stanké, Ltée, 1980. [Translations from the text are mine.]
Waddell, Laurence Austine, *Lhasa and its Mysteries,* John Murray, 1905.
Warburg, Frederick: *All Authors Are Equal*, Hutchinson, 1973.

Academic Collections
'Ken McCormick collection of Doubleday and Company, inc., records, 1882-1992', Manuscript Division, Library of Congress, Washington DC.
Henry Miller Collection, Box 46, Folder 11, University of California Library Special Collections, Los Angeles, CA.

Appendix 1

The Burgess Report

CYRIL HENRY HOSKIN
BIOGRAPHICAL DETAILS

Born 8th April, 1910, at Plympton, St Maurice, Devonshire, England.

Father—Joseph Henry Hoskin, Master Plumber (born 1878 in Plymouth).

Mother—Eva Hoskin (name before marriage—Martin).

Sister—Dorothy Winifred Hoskin, born 21st March, 1905, Plympton, St Maurice, Devonshire. This sister is now married to the Rev Illingsworth-Butler, rector of Linby, Nottinghamshire.

Hoskin's father kept a plumber's shop in the Ridgeway, Plympton, Devon. He attended Plympton village school. Left at the age of 15.

He was always a delicate child. He never did any work after leaving school, except to potter around his father's shop, supposed to be helping his father. He was a very odd child. People considered him a complete crank. He was always experimenting with electrical things and insects. As a child he never played with other children. He was considered by people who knew him to be a spoilt child. As a teenager he helped in his father's shop occasionally, but would lay in bed for days at a time and was considered lazy.

The mother sold the property in Plympton and took Cyril to live at the married daughter's house. In 1940 the mother and Cyril left Annesley and went to live at 13, Warwick Avenue, London, W.2. Hoskin was then employed by a Surgical Goods Manufacturing Company and described as a Works Manager.

Later in 1940, he obtained a job as a Correspondence Clerk for a London firm offering education by correspondence courses. As a result of bombing, this firm moved to Weybridge, Surrey, and Hoskin went there, living in a flat provided by the Company.

On 13th August, 1940, he married Sarah Anne Pattinson, a nurse at a Richmond hospital. She is a native of Cumberland.

During his time with the Correspondence firm at Weybridge, he became more and more peculiar in his manner, and among many strange things he did was:—(1) he used to take his cat out for walks on a lead (2) during this period he began to call himself Kuan-suo and he had all the hair shaved off his head.

He left his firm in September, 1948. After which he lived in rooms near Weybridge for some months and then went to South London where he was subsequently seen carrying on business of sorts as a photographer. His activities between 1950 and 1954 are somewhat vague, but he was seen by one person who knew him and said that he was 'A Criminal and Accident Photographer'. He next appears living in Bayswater in 1954 calling himself Dr KUAN-SUO and is about to write *The Third Eye*. Until he went to live in Dublin there is no evidence of his ever having left the British Isles.

A copy of the report was given by Hugh Richardson to Donald S. Lopez, Jr, who reprinted it in full in his book, Prisoners of Shangri-La: Tibetan Buddhism and the West, *University of Chicago Press, 1998.*

Appendix 2

Daily Mail, 1st February 1958

The Mayfair wife speaks for bogus Lama
by Hugh Medlicott

The man accepted by thousands as the Tibetan Lama of *The Third Eye* has been exposed as a brilliant hoaxer.

He is no Lama from Tibet. He is a plumber's son from Plympton, Devon—plain Mr Cyril Henry Hoskins.

At his cliff-top villa near Dublin, he and his wife live as Dr and Mrs Kuan with 27-year-old Mrs Sheelagh Rouse, once a gay member of West End Society.

She is one of his many followers who believe in his oriental and clairvoyant powers—produced, he has claimed, by a brain operation which gave him a 'third eye'.

Mrs Rouse, wife of an Old Etonian Lloyd's broker, has been presented to the Queen at a Buckingham Palace tea party.

Her children

Now she helps Mrs Hoskins to answer a world-wide flood of letters from people seeking advice.

Since helping in his work she has placed her two eldest children, Fenella, seven, and Jarvis, five, in a boarding school.

Her year-old son, Khanda, is with her mother–in-law at Woking, Surrey.

As Lobsang Rampa, Mr Hoskins is the author of the best-seller *The Third Eye*, either published or about to be published in 12 countries.

Characters of Questionable Faith

As Dr Kuan-suo, or under his favourite alias of Dr Kuan, he reads the stars and gives advice on spiritual and health problems for a fee.

His book, written under the dateline 'The year of the Wood Sheep,' begins:

'I am a Tibetan, one of the few who have reached this strange western world . . .'

'A fiction'

His wife, who was a State Registered Nurse at a Richmond hospital when they married on April 13, 1940, told me:

'The book is fiction. He had tried to get a number of jobs without success. We had to have money to live.

'So he was persuaded to write the book. We depend upon its sale for money.'

Now he has been exposed as one of the biggest hoaxers of the century by Mr Clifford Burgess, a Liverpool private detective.

Mr Burgess said last night in a London hotel that he had been instructed by a group of Tibetan scholars to make the investigation.

In three weeks he and his pretty 19-year-old assistant, Miss Sheila Briant of Hoylake, Cheshire, have travelled more than 3,000 miles.

They have interviewed scores of people and taken statements running into thousands of words about 'Dr Kuan.'

His 'ordeal'

'It has been a long and difficult job,' said Mr Burgess, 'but I am glad I have been able to help in the exposure of this man who claimed he was a Tibetan Lama.'

The claim of Dr Kuan has been made in the greatest detail in his book.

On the dustcover he describes how, at the age of seven, he entered a lamasery and the Dalai Lama decreed that his exceptional clairvoyant powers should be enhanced by a surgical operation known as 'the opening of the third eye'.

148

Appendix 2: *Daily Mail,* 1st February 1958

In the book he explains the 17-day long ordeal which gave him the third eye.

But Cyril Henry Hoskins has never been to Tibet. He has never had a brain operation. He is a sick man with heart trouble and other ailments.

The Third Eye says: 'The construction and grammar of this book leave much to be desired, but I have never had a formal lesson in the English language.

'My "school of English" was a Japanese prison camp, where I learned the language as best I could from English and American women prisoner patients . . .

'Some of my statements, so I am told, may not be believed . . . That is your privilege but Tibet is a country unknown to the rest of the world.'

These are some of the claims he makes:

THAT after he left Tibet he fought with the Chinese Nationalist Forces against Japan and was taken prisoner.

THAT he has a medical degree from Chungking University and was in charge of English and American women in a displaced prisoners' camp where he performed major operations.

THAT after the first A-bomb dropped on Japan he escaped in a fishing boat to Korea and made his way to Britain by way of Moscow and New York.

THAT he has flown in a flying saucer and is the son of a prince of Tibet.

The incense

These are the facts:

He is 47, the son of a master plumber, Joseph Henry Hoskins.

After leaving school he helped his father until he died in 1937, then went with his mother to live in Nottinghamshire.

He worked for a firm of surgical instrument manufacturers then left and became a clerk with a correspondence school of engineering.

There he shaved his head, grew a beard and changed his name to Dr Kuan-suo.

To the managing director he wrote a rhyme which ended:

'You may wonder why I go on so, but will you please remember I am Kuan-suo.'

Now with his wife and blonde Mrs Rouse, daughter of Mr John Isherwood, paper mill owner of New Mills, Derbyshire, he lives at Howth, near Dublin.

Dr Kuan was too ill to see me when I called at the white-and-green villa overlooking the island of Ireland's Eye.

His wife, her greying hair tied in a bun and a wooden Eastern medallion around her neck, invited me into the house with its sweet scent of incense.

There in a room with a wooden Eastern statuette on the mantelpiece and an Oriental brass table in the centre, she and Mrs Rouse at first denied that Dr Kuan was Cyril Henry Hoskins.

Mrs Rouse said: 'He was a great man. He has wonderful powers.'

Then they told me he adopted the name of Kuan to hide the identity of the real Dr Kuan, who wrote the book and lives in fear of Communism.

Madame Kuan said: 'He will not tell anyone who the real Dr Kuan is. He will sacrifice everything to protect him.'

Mrs Rouse added: 'We were prepared for snoopers to come and pry out the facts. I have seen the real Dr Kuan but I will not tell you where he is.'

Then Madame Kuan telephoned me and said: 'I've got to tell you. This will hurt him very much.'

'My conscience'

'He is not a Tibetan. That is his photograph on the cover of the book. He has written another one on the same lines.'

From his sick bed Mr Hoskins sent me a message maintaining the authenticity of the book.

It said: 'This story is true but for very special reasons the identity of the Tibetan author cannot be revealed. I have never bedraggled anyone in my life, no matter what the cost.

Appendix 2: *Daily Mail,* 1st February 1958

'I shall not bedraggle anyone now. I have almost no chance of life. This shock is reducing it even more.

'I must be guided by my conscience in what to do. My life has been hard and bitter and I consider that in this other blow of publicity I am doing what is right.'

Mrs Rouse's husband, John, an ex-Regular Army officer who lives in Kensington W. said at his City office last night:

'I know the stories that are circulating about Lobsang Rampa, but I believe none of them and I do not want to discuss them.

'I have known him for two and a half years and I am convinced he is thoroughly genuine.

'He has been a guest in my home, a good friend of my wife and myself, and I am quite sure he is no phoney.'

'She believes'

Mrs Rouse's mother, Mrs Margery Isherwood, said:

'She has told me he is a brilliant surgeon and she believes implicitly that he belongs to a high-ranking Tibetan family.

'She believes he has wonderful mystic powers.'

Mr Hoskins's 80-year-old mother is living with his sister, Mrs Winifred Illingworth-Butler, wife of the Rector of Linby, Nottinghamshire.

Mrs Illingworth-Butler said: 'I know nothing about it.' Her husband added: 'We have not heard from him for a long time.'

His agent, Mr Brooks of Mayfair, W1, said: 'I am surprised. He possesses extraordinary powers of telepathy. He has given me proof on a number of occasions.'

Mr F.J. Warburg, director of the firm who published the book said: 'I am very surprised. I thought he was Chinese.

'We were not sure ourselves about the book and sent it to 20 people who all gave different opinions.

Foreword

'In the first edition we printed a Foreword in which we said we could not check the authenticity of the facts and left it up to the reader to judge. It is published as a non-fiction work.'

Here are the views of three experts on Tibet who have read the book.

Dr D.L. Snellgrove, of London University. 'I am of the opinion it's not authentic.'

Mr Hugh Richardson, of St Andrews, Fife, who was in charge of a British trade mission in Tibet for seven years: 'It's quite obvious it's not written by a Tibetan.'

Mr Marco Pallis, author and Himalayan explorer: 'To anyone who has been there, the book proves itself to be false.'

Already the book has sold 60,000 copies in Britain, 85,000 in Germany, 27,000 in Norway and 50,000 in France.

Appendix 3

Daily Mail, 3rd February 1958

The Mail, first with the News of the Third Eye Hoaxer,
Continue the Story

The Bogus Lama speaks from his sick-bed
His wife praises him

by Hugh Medlicott

The hoaxer known as a Tibetan lama, but who is really plain Mr
Hoskins, defended himself last night. Haltingly he made a
statement on a tape recorder from his sick bed in his cliff-top
villa overlooking Dublin Bay. Frequently he had to rest to gain
strength for another sentence.

He denied that he had ever taken any money for giving
advice to people about their health and spiritual problems.

He maintained that his book *The Third Eye*, already
published, and another about to be published are true.

Afterwards he issued a statement, through his wife, about *The
Third Eye*. In his book he describes how an operation gave him a
third eye producing clairvoyant powers.

'Wonderful'

His wife told me: 'He was asked to write the book. At first he
did not want to do it.

'He did what he thought was right. He's trying to do something good in the world. He's a very wonderful man.'

She said he was willing to have the book investigated and says
'anyone can analyse it.'

But he was not prepared to be questioned himself about it. 'He is much too ill to see anyone.'

She said her husband's second book is called *Medical Lama*—'a follow-on of *The Third Eye*.'

The plump, grey-haired woman asked me not to call on her husband again as my aura was penetrating the house and making him ill.

Too ill

He has coronary thrombosis and his doctor has signed a letter saying he is too ill to see visitors.

His full name is Cyril Henry Hoskins. He is a plumber's son from Plympton but he uses the names of—

Lobsang Rampa, the name in his book.

Dr Kuan-Suo or alternatively just Dr Kuan.

Despite his claims 47-year-old Hoskins has never been to Tibet, is not a lama, and has never had a brain operation. The Eire police say he is a British citizen.

He and his wife and Mrs Sheelagh Rouse, 27-year-old wife of a London broker rented the house, 12 miles from Dublin, from a sea-going doctor so that Dr Kuan could have quiet for his meditations.

At first they only had half the house, and in his desire for solitude, Dr Kuan persuaded the other occupants to leave.

Then he realised he would be seen in his garden by passers-by and when clambering up and down the cliffs beneath his house. He had an 8ft-high concrete wall built.

Gave bicycles

What kind of life did he lead?

He seldom went down on the harbour before his illness. When he did he wore a dark grey suit, dark overcoat and a Homburg hat. At home he wore the loose-fitting robes with coils of religious beads of a lama.

The few people who have met him say he is quiet and kindly. He gave new bicycles to two of Mr Edgar McLoughlin's sons

Appendix 3: *Daily Mail*, 3rd February 1958

who used to take him newspapers from the sea front shop up the hill.

He offered education in an academy in Texas to other children. Their parents refused the offer.

He was exposed as a hoaxer by Mr Clifford Burgess, a Liverpool private detective who was instructed by Tibetan scholars to make the investigation.

Since helping with his work, Mrs Sheelagh Rouse has placed her two elder children, Fenella, seven and Jarvis, five, in a boarding school. Her year-old son Khanda is with her mother-in-law in Surrey.

Nuisance

Mr Frederic Warburg, director of the firm who published *The Third Eye*, said last night: 'We certainly did not ask the Lama—as I prefer to call him—to write the book.

'In fact, I believe it was offered to another publisher before we saw it.

'It is true that he said frequently what a nuisance it was having to write it.'

Mr Warburg said his firm was not handling a second manuscript, recently completed by Hoskins.

UNDER A BLUE ROBE I SAW HIS BIG FEET
By Daily Mail Reporter

Television producer John Irwin told last night of a meeting with Lobsang Rampa soon after his book *The Third Eye* was published. He said: 'No normally intelligent person could meet him and believe he was Tibetan or Chinese. He was thoroughly Western.

'He is over 6ft tall, bald, and clean-shaven.

'He came to tea with me after I had written to his publishers and after the stars, he said, had indicated the day on which he should call.

Characters of Questionable Faith

'He was wearing a saffron cloak and a blue skirt under which I could see brown woollen socks and sandals on very large feet. He had a West Country accent and I could see this pale man was not a lama.

'Almost every sentence he spoke was prefaced with "In my Country".'

Fantastic

'He talked a lot about my aura and said he saw colours which suggested tranquillity. I had clairvoyant powers he said, which could best be used with a crystal ball.

'He seemed to be a gentleman, but harmless and lonely and completely lost in the fantastic role he had set himself.

'He was a sad man and, while I am sure he has no magic powers or strange knowledge, if he did write this book he has remarkable powers of imagination.'

Mr Irwin has written, directed and produced hundreds of radio and TV programmes. He is a former BBC man and produced ATV's Question during its four-year run.

Appendix 4

Daily Express, 3rd February 1958

I regard myself as the Lama's daughter and I am here of my own free will, says former Mayfair hostess

The FULL truth about the bogus Lama

Express staff reporter

A former Mayfair hostess, now secretary to the author of *The Third Eye*, the book published by Secker & Warburg which is said to have hoaxed the literary world, announced last night: 'I regard myself as the Lama's daughter.'

A private detective says that the Lama, Dr Kuan, is Cyril Henry Hoskins, a plumber's son from Plympton, Devon.

His blonde secretary, 27-year-old Mrs Sheelagh Rouse, who is with the Lama at Howth, eight miles from Dublin, her blue eyes direct and steady, added: 'I am here of my own free will.'

Mrs Rouse, mother of three small children, is estranged from her husband, an Old Etonian Lloyd's broker. 'There is no hope of a reconciliation,' she said. 'It is all over. Someone employed a private detective to discredit the Lama and win me back.'

The Lama—he claims that he has been possessed by a Tibetan monk—said from his sick bed, 'I saw this girl's marriage breaking up. I wanted to help.'

Twisting her hands nervously Mrs Rouse added: 'I never want to see my parents again. I have found peace with the Lama and his wife.'

Characters of Questionable Faith

Mrs Rouse's husband John is now in London with the three children—Fenella, aged seven, Jarvis five, and 12-month-old baby daughter Khanda.

Doctor's Certificate

The dimly-lit villa overlooking Dublin Bay is the focal point of controversy. The issue: Is the Lama a hoaxer?

'Yes'—says Liverpool detective Clifford Burgess.

And Tibetan scholars, writers and explorers say that the Lama's book is not true.

Last night Lama Hoskins, who says that a brain operation gave him the powers that make 'the third eye' told me:--

'I am too ill to go to hospital. I have a very serious disease.' And his grey-haired wife Sanya produced a doctor's certificate saying he was too ill for visitors.

Then the Lama said: 'I have taken no money from the hundreds of people who write to me. Why should I? My book is a best seller.'

It has been published in 12 countries. So far it has brought him £20,000 in royalties.

Appendix 5

Daily Express 4th February 1958

The Three-Eyed Lama Once Sold Corsets

The 'Third Eye' Lama, 47-year-old Cyril Henry Hoskins, a plumber's son who is said to have hoaxed the world with his 'autobiography', was once a character in a street of London 'characters'.

Four years ago he and his wife ran shops in Kensington's Church street.

The lama—known as Dr Kuan—and his wife sold books, antiques, corsets, and women's clothes.

They were there for about a year and lived in a furnished flat off Ladbrooke-grove with their two Siamese kittens.

It was in 1953 that the 'mysterious man from the East' took over the business. His grey-haired wife Sanya said she was a State registered nurse before her marriage.

They claimed that they had a wealthy backer in Manchester.

Dr Kuan enthralled his neighbours with tales of his past.

His Claims

He said he had entered a Tibetan monastery at the age of seven for training as a medical missionary. He claimed to be a Doctor of Science, Doctor of Medicine, Master of Arts and to have a civil engineering degree. 'I was at Chungking University,' he said.

When they left, Dr Kuan said he and his wife might go to America. They sold their business and left no forwarding address.

'We thought we had seen the last of them,' said a neighbour last night.

Characters of Questionable Faith

But the Kuans returned to the district. At the end of 1956 they telephoned friends saying they had taken a flat in Bayswater. And the doctor gave away some copies of his book, *The Third Eye*, in which he claims to have been 'possessed' by a Tibetan monk.

The Brotherhood of the Cross and Star

Olumba Olumba Obu (1918-?),
'The Sole Spiritual Head of the Universe'.

The Brotherhood of the Cross and Star

One day in the early 1990s, out of the blue, I received a phone call from an old school friend, Danny Goring, and I am sure our conversation began with an exchange of the usual niceties. However, he very quickly said he wanted me to know he had decided to embrace Christianity, to which I admitted my surprise.

Danny and I had kept in touch after school, during our time at university while I was in Sheffield and he was in Newcastle. When I relocated to Lewes in East Sussex with my partner, Rosalie, in 1991, it was great to discover that Danny and his family had also moved there. We saw a great deal of them all; with his brother, George, Danny was making music, and they ran a shop together for a time. I also helped their mother, Rosemary, publish a book of her poetry.

While at school, Danny and I had written songs together, and we had often discussed religion, especially alternative religions and beliefs. One book I remember discussing at length was Aldous Huxley's *The Doors of Perception*, and we wrote a song together called 'Greenpinkamber' (Danny's title) about what we might see if we could perceive the world 'as it really is'. It was as much a song about drug-taking (through reading about hallucinogenic substances—I, for one, had no first-hand experience), as it was about perceptions of reality. I believed that in our explorations Danny thought the same way that I did—that all these alternative routes to enlightenment were fascinating, even if often far-fetched. It appears that we were not so aligned in our thinking, after all.

When I told Danny that I was surprised he had decided to become a Christian, he asked me why. He pointed out that he had been on a quest and had finally found what he sought in

The Brotherhood of the Cross and Star

God. When I said I was still searching, he asked me, quite reasonably, if the quest wasn't more important to me than the attainment of it.

I don't think my first question for Danny was quite so perceptive. I asked why, after all the alternatives he had considered, he had decided upon Christianity? Apart from anything else, it was the religion of our parents, whose beliefs we had always questioned. What I had overlooked was the fact that Danny's mother and father, Rosemary and Jeremy, were far from being conventional Christians. I remember some great conversations about politics and religion around the kitchen table at the Gorings' house when they lived in Rushlake Green, and his parents were always open-minded and thoughtful, especially when I remember how uninformed and gauche my comments would have been. They were so undogmatic that it was only much later that I realised they were Unitarians. Another of Danny's brothers, Charlie, became a Church of England vicar, but I could never take him seriously after one Sunday when he had lost his dog collar and made a replacement out of an old margarine tub.

I asked Danny to take me through the basics of his new belief. I asked if he thought that a man called Jesus had once walked the Earth and had performed the miracles ascribed to him in the Bible. Danny replied,

'I don't just believe in Christ; I've met him.'

Danny's story goes back to 1990, not long after he had graduated from university, when his brother, George, told him about the Brotherhood of the Cross and Star (B.C.S.), a church he had come across while living in London. The organisation (they don't like being called a church, and say they are 'a way of life') has always been based in Nigeria, founded by the 'exotic-sounding'[1] Olumba Olumba Obu.

---

[1] Danny's description, from his blog post 'Love is the Answer', 10th June 2020.

The Brotherhood of the Cross and Star

In August 1990, Danny and George travelled to Calabar, Nigeria, and they met Obu personally, and he impressed them both. Later, their mother and father also went out to Nigeria, apparently very sceptical, but they were similarly convinced that Obu was not just a great religious teacher; they, too, believed that his pronouncements were the word of God, expressed by Christ who had come to Earth again. And what was more, this physical incarnation of Christ was, unlike the previous manifestation, immortal.

I have to admit I found all this difficult to accept, but none of the Gorings at this time were interested in evangelising and it did not affect our friendship. They had been reassured that 'all would be well'. When Danny and George released a 7" single themselves, 'Here Comes Love', I bought a copy and asked what they were doing by way of publicity and promotion. They said that was in the hands of the Lord, although the holy A&R department did not prove particularly helpful.

At this time, all I really knew about the Brotherhood was what Danny told me: that it had been founded by Olumba Olumba Obu, who had been born in a poor village (Biakpan) in Cross River State, Nigeria, in 1918. He had left his village for Calabar and eventually set up his organisation at 34 Ambo Street, which remains the base of the church to this day. I had no reason to doubt Danny's claim that the Brotherhood did very useful charitable work in Nigeria, and that their headquarters had been a place of refuge for many people of different religious denominations during troubled times in Nigeria. The Brotherhood claimed to have over a million members, and the Gorings told me that there was not only a bethel in London, but in various capital cities worldwide.

In 1993, Rosalie and I moved into the Sussex countryside, and during our time there, Danny and George also lived nearby in Warbleton and in Horam. They still made no overt attempt to evangelise, even when, in about 1994, we were invited to a 'Love Feast' in the grounds of Lewes Castle. On a fine summer evening, various friends of the Gorings joined with members of the Brotherhood, most of whom had come down from London.

The Brotherhood of the Cross and Star

The members of the church all wore 'soutains', or long white robes. Fruit was served (the Brotherhood insists on vegetarianism), and we were all circled three times for some reason to do with spiritual cleansing (we didn't feel inclined to take offence). The music was lively and religious, but the only song that was memorable was a traditional folk song, sung by Rosemary Goring. To us outsiders it all seemed colourful, loving and non-threatening.

I talked about The Brotherhood with Danny at various times, but it wasn't until one day in 1995/6 that he asked if he could come to see me, bringing a friend from the Brotherhood called Gabriel. Danny said that he hadn't been able to adequately explain the teachings of Obu, but a more experienced, long-time member ought to be able to answer all my questions and relieve me of any doubts. It was obvious that they hoped to convert me and we had a long discussion that I rather relished, although, as the afternoon wore on, Rosalie would become less sanguine about their presence in our house.

I was told again, in no uncertain terms, that Olumba Olumba Obu was Christ reincarnated. When I asked Gabriel upon what authority they believed this, he said unequivocally that Obu had made it clear to his followers that he was Christ, although he didn't like to admit this directly because he was far too humble. This humility was, in itself, apparently an assurance that he had to be Christ. (An argument that has always reminded me of a scene in Monty Python's *Life of Brian*.)

I was told that Obu had performed verifiable miracles (mainly healing), and had made precise predictions that had come true. They told stories of people from around the world who had experienced visions of Obu, even though he never left his headquarters in Calabar.

It was also asserted by Gabriel and Danny, very solemnly, that Obu was immortal. I had already worked out that their Leader had to be seventy-seven years old at that time, but they said my calculation was meaningless because he could never die.

I remember pressing them on the immortality claim, suggesting that if Obu passed away the next day, would they try to

166

The Brotherhood of the Cross and Star

suggest that he had been immortal in a spiritual, rather than a physical sense. But no, they insisted on physical immortality. Apologising for my crassness and pedantry, I asked them whether the physical death of Obu would prove he was not what he claimed to be. After continually side-stepping the question by saying it was a meaningless scenario, I eventually browbeat them into agreeing that his physical death would be a problem for them, but only because they considered such a test would soon be irrelevant; Obu had apparently come back to Earth for the express purpose of saving from physical destruction and eternal damnation all those who embraced him. The world was about to end . . .

And they insisted that the end of the world was not to be at some unspecified time in the future—they said that everything we knew would be physically destroyed the moment the world's clocks clicked over to the year 2000. I was asked if, for the sake of my own comfort for just a few more years, I was willing to pay such a heavy, eternal penalty? The Brotherhood was, essentially, a millenarian movement.

It seemed to me the first and most obvious question was, what about those who had not heard of Obu? Would genuinely kind, loving people die and be sent to Hell because they had been so unfortunate as not to have ever heard of Obu?

Gabriel was unconcerned; the whole world had time to make an informed decision. He explained that with its million members worldwide, the Brotherhood had time to tell absolutely everyone about Obu before the Day of Judgment, and they could either accept him as Christ, or deny him, as they wished. If they decided on the latter course, they would perish.

I apologised again for my crassness, but asked if the physical survival of the world in the year 2000 would also mean that everything they had been told by Obu had been false. Again they tried to assure me it would never be an issue, and that my insisting on an empirical test was unspiritual and pointless. But they eventually deigned to descend to my materialist level for long enough to agree that it could, in theory be seen as a test of Obu and everything that he preached. I was pleased that we

The Brotherhood of the Cross and Star

would all have a means of assessing Obu's claims, even if my doubts were viewed as being rather insulting.

I have focussed on the believed-immortality of Obu and the end of the world prediction because it seemed to be a big part of the persuasion process. However, I must also state that Danny and Gabriel did also both spend a lot of time talking about peace and love and the wonderful things that the Brotherhood did, not just for their followers, but also for their neighbours in Calabar. They were certain, they said, that if I went to Nigeria with them I would be persuaded of their cause. They offered me a free plane flight to meet Obu, and I asked if it would be a return ticket. No, Gabriel said, it need only be one-way because, he was confident, once I had met Obu, I would never want to leave Nigeria.

When the two representatives of the Brotherhood finally went away, I felt that there had been an interesting battle, albeit one that had ended in stalemate and could not be resolved until the year 2000. Rosalie, though, was horrified by Danny and Gabriel. As she pointed out, they were guests in our house and they had done everything possible to persuade me to go off to Africa on my own, leaving her and our son, Tim, born only a year before. Quite reasonably, she suggested that they should never step over our threshold again.[1]

It was, perhaps, a year or two later that Danny and I had a chance to properly talk about our discussion with Gabriel. I asked how the plan to tell everyone in the world about the forthcoming Armageddon was proceeding, and I received the concession that although Brotherhood members might not be able to tell absolutely everybody on Earth in person, one to one, the Spirit of Obu would be 'revealed' to everyone in good time.

---

[1] When I reminded Danny of this a few years later, he denied that a one-way ticket to Nigeria had ever been offered to me. He did admit, though, that they had only attempted to convert me on that occasion, not Rosalie.

The Brotherhood of the Cross and Star

I conceded that this was an expedient spiritual solution to an overwhelming problem, and wished them luck with it.

I was also given continued assurances in the build-up to the year 2000, that physical annihilation of the world was still expected. I clearly recall asking again, if the world does not end, does that mean that Obu is not who he says he is? Danny reluctantly agreed that Obu had set himself the ultimate test of Messiah-hood, but he was confident Obu would pass. I said that the elderly Obu would have to make it to the year 2000 first, but I was assured, once again, that he could never die, physically or spiritually. On one of those occasions we were in the Warble-in-Tun pub, and I clearly remember saying to Danny, 'Let's have a bet on this; if the world doesn't end, then you owe me a pint.' I should state that Danny was confident in agreeing to the wager.

In January 2000, Danny and I talked on the phone. The first thing I said was, 'You owe me a pint.' He was slightly embarrassed, although not as embarrassed as I thought he should be. He explained that the first year from Christ's birth would have been called year one, so that exactly two thousand years later it would be 2001 (not 2000)! It appeared that Obu, the incarnation of Christ himself, had made a basic error in his maths calculation, and there was, in fact, a year to go before the end of the world. I have to admit that I didn't know whether to laugh or be annoyed.

Of course, I had to phone Danny again the following January. In 2001 I reminded him of the bet and told him he still owed me a pint. He disagreed, and I pointed out that, quite clearly, the world had not ended. He replied,

'Hasn't it? *It has for those with eyes to see. . . .*'

Apparently the world had moved into a new millennium and for members of the Brotherhood it had altered completely and irrevocably. Apparently, what had happened was astounding. Was I so blind that I could not have noticed?

I reminded Danny that on various occasions he had promised no less than the total physical destruction of the whole planet— annihilation on a global scale that would be painfully obvious to every man, woman and child (who had not embraced Obu).

The Brotherhood of the Cross and Star

'And that,' said Danny, 'is exactly what has taken place.'

It was now explained to me that Obu had never said the world would be destroyed for non-believers. His followers, it appeared, were at fault, not Obu, because they had misunderstood and misinterpreted his teachings. It didn't help, I was told, that Obu always preached in his native Efik language, which would be translated into Nigerian English, and errors would probably have been made.

When I asked why Christ himself had allowed his followers to make such a mistake, I never received a straight answer, and I still have not received one to this day. I was told that Obu could not possibly be wrong, ever. I asked whether they still believed he was physically immortal, and I was assured that he was still going strong at eighty-one.

It struck me that if I was going to discuss the Brotherhood further with the Gorings, I would need to know more, and by this time, the Brotherhood had embraced the internet and were publishing Obu's sermons ('The Everlasting Gospel') online. I did read several of them, although, personally, I find them rambling and overlong. They were also a little odd at times, although the central message has always been one of peace and love. Now there was also the proclamation that we (well, *they*) had entered a new spiritual era.

I did learn a certain amount, although by this time Obu seemed to have handed over the leadership of the Brotherhood to his son, Rowland, and a lot of what I could find on other websites seemed to be about almighty rows that had taken place between Rowland and the Brotherhood's bishops. It didn't help that the church also had its enemies in Nigeria and I had to treat some of the stories told about them (often by Christians of other denominations) with some scepticism.

What spurred me to look deeper into the life of Olumba Olumba Obu was the way an old friend for whom I still have the greatest respect was willing to find excuses for behaviour which struck me as fundamentally flawed at best, and at worst duplicitous.

An early photograph of Olumba Olumba Obu.

Olumba Olumba Obu

To write about Olumba Olumba Obu, the founder of the 'New Religious Movement' the Brotherhood of the Cross and Star, is difficult without relying heavily on information given by Obu himself in his own writings, and also on material provided by the Brotherhood and its followers. There is little reason to doubt the basic facts of his life, although the many and various stories of healing and miracles cannot be independently verified as they are usually single testimonies of individual followers about supernatural events. There is a lack of potentially useful information about some periods of Obu's life, although it is reasonable to suppose these were not necessarily relevant to either Obu's personal position as Leader of the Brotherhood, or to the development of the Brotherhood itself. The reason for the scant information about his early life, according to G.I.S. Amadi in his essay 'Purity and Power', is partly,

The Brotherhood of the Cross and Star

'. . . ignorance, and partly in order to support the notion of deity.'[1]

The one really major lacuna in Obu's biography is actually his death (or otherwise); a subject upon which the Brotherhood is singularly unhelpful. There are parallels between the way that Obu's life has been represented by his followers and the way that biographies have been written by other religious organisations promoting the exceptional achievements of their leaders. Impartiality is always difficult, but sometimes there is no attempt at impartiality, particularly when it suits biographers to promote a particular agenda, in this case the 'divinity' of Olumba Olumba Obu.

Obu appears to have been born in the village of Biakpan near Calabar in Cross River State, Eastern Nigeria, in 1918. He, himself, insists it was no coincidence that it was at the time of a worldwide influenza epidemic, which he says was the working of the Holy Spirit to cleanse the world of its evil inhabitants (which was a harsh judgement when epidemics do not make informed moral decisions on who to kill and who to spare). Obu argued that the influenza year was symbolic of his own role as purifier and deliverer of the world from its many ills.

It is said that his birth was foreseen by Prophetess Otemegan Otumesin and Prophet Enu Enu Nkpa.

The story that has grown up around Obu is that he never went to school, received no theological training, and was never a part of any established church. This suggests that his knowledge of the Bible was, perhaps, a supernatural manifestation of his divinity. However, Obu *does* appear to have attended school, although only to receive a very basic education, perhaps for the first two or three years of primary school. He told one journalist:

---

[1] G.I.S. Amadi, 'Purity and Power', Ph.D. dissertation, University of Nigeria, 1982, p. 208.

Olumba Olumba Obu

I have never attended any theological institute but I went to school as a child.[1]

It is claimed that he was conscious of a calling at an early age.

The first words that I spoke three years after I was born were: 'Call me Teacher, Master, Etubom . . . I am the universal Teacher I have come to reveal my Father to the world.'[2]

An alternative version is:

But his sense of mission emerged early: when he was only five he said to his father: 'Call me Teacher'. The first people he taught were the children with whom he played and went to school.[3]

Obu recalled:

I was enlightened by the Father about the people in the World and their state of sins when I was five years old.[4]

He also said:

I was not yet five years when I knew all things.'[5]

Obu was presumably to a degree self-educated, not least in theological maters, although his parents were both Presbyterians and his immediate background was therefore Christian. Their own faith was far from usual in Biakpan, where the majority would have followed traditional Nigerian religions.

---

[1] Ray Ekpu in an interview with Obu, *BCS Journal,* No. 2, 1983, p. 102.
[2] Olumba Olumba Obu, 'I Am That I Am', ooo-bcs.org/i-am-that-i-am/
[3] Sister Rosemary Goring, 'Brotherhood for Beginners' (http://freespace.virgin.net/dolly.daniels/BOOKS/bcsintro.htm)
[4] OOO, *Prophets' Handbook*, 1965, p.12.
[5] OOO, *Our Lord Jesus Christ the Alpha and Omega*, n.d., p. 45.

The Brotherhood of the Cross and Star

Obu invariably preached in the Efik language, but in later life he could also converse very well in English. (One assumes that he never proof-read his sermons, published in English as 'The Everlasting Gospel'.)

Aged eight he went to Calabar, working as an apprentice to his uncle, Kanu Mba in the textile trade. Ten years later, in 1936, he set up his own stall in Calabar market and was initially successful in business. He is meant to have spent his spare time teaching and healing, and his business apparently only failed because he was too generous to customers and refused to pursue debts. He is said to have become a full time preacher and healer in 1944, aged twenty-six. At this time he married, and began to invite people to his home for Bible study meetings, initially at No. 8 Eton Street.

The movement that would become the Brotherhood of the Cross and Star appears to have come into official existence in 1956, when Obu formally registered with the Federal Government. Originally, his prayer group was called 'Ekuk' meaning 'Holy Circle', and they were also called the 'Prayer Band' before becoming 'Christ's Universal Spiritual School of Practical Christianity', a name that is often still sustained, even after they finally became known as the Brotherhood of the Cross and Star. (Some members say that the Brotherhood came into existence with the birth of Obu, while others, including Obu himself, say it has been in existence since the birth of Adam.)

> Brother E.B. Eye, one of the original members of the brotherhood, said, 'The first day the Father performed baptism was two days to 8th August 1958. He did baptism twice: I think it was on the 6th and 7th. Then in the evening of August 8th he asked everybody to wear white. That was the first outing and the Father moved the entire Brotherhood from Eton Street to 26 Mbukpa Road that night. People talked but what could they do, and as far as I can remember there were no attacks—members just marched peacefully with the Father leading the line.'[1]

[1] https://reachouttrust.org/brotherhood-of-the-cross-and-star/

Olumba Olumba Obu

The above suggests that there existed hostility toward Olumba's initiatives, and this seems to have come primarily from members of established, missionary churches. (This hostility took especially serious form when coordinated violence was directed towards Brotherhood members in 1977.)

The new building at 26 Mbukpa Rd soon proved too small, and land at 34 Ambo St was bought and new buildings were erected; a healing home, an elementary school, a guest house, an assembly hall with a public address system, and offices with a printing press and bookstore. Further buildings have been added over the years, and this address is still the headquarters of the Brotherhood.

The Brotherhood has always centred on Obu, 'The Sole Spiritual Head' of the organisation (and 'the Universe'), as well as its physical 'Leader'. He has various interchangeable titles suggesting the veneration in which he has been held by members. Although Brotherhood beliefs are based on traditional Christianity, members' understanding of the Bible and the words and actions of God, Christ and the Holy Ghost are interpreted exclusively through Obu, whose teachings are often far from orthodox. Obu argued that until he began to preach God's word, the Bible had always been adulterated:

> From the time of Adam to the time of Christ, the Gospel that people received was borrowed. This is the first time that mankind is receiving teaching directly from God himself [i.e. through Obu]. The teaching of Moses was adulterated; that is why it includes the burning of candles and the counting of rosary beads. Our Lord Jesus Christ in His own (first) advent went to the Church, therefore his teachings were slightly adulterated.[1]

Although many Brotherhood doctrines are based on the Judaic-Christian tradition, other beliefs take elements from

---

[1] OOO, *August Pentecostal Assembly Weekly Gospels*, vol 1: The Spirit of God (n.d.), p. 62.

The Brotherhood of the Cross and Star

different religions and cultures. (The central Brotherhood teaching is 'Love', and it is only fair to the movement that this should be stressed.) Obu dismissed the Old Testament, and explained that the only part of the New Testament that he considered relevant was the Book of Revelation, because it described the time in which he and his followers were now living:

> Although you may look at the books (sic) of the revelation as a very small pamphlet, our duty is essentially found therein.[1]

It is contended by Obu's disciples that the whole Bible had been altered to make it fit with other belief systems, which is why Brotherhood members are able to reconcile their version of Christianity with, for example, ideas of reincarnation. Fundamentally for the Brotherhood, God is in everything, but God has also previously and explicitly manifested directly as human beings; Adam, Enoch, Noah, Melchizedek, Moses, Eljah and Jesus. Although it is rarely said in public, the belief of his members is that God has manifested for the eighth and final time as Olumba Olumba Obu.

There are some apparent inconsistencies in Obu's teachings about these manifestations of God; in 'The Revelation of the Holy Spirit', Obu said:

> Adam never saw God. Melchizedek never saw God. Noah Never saw God. None of them saw God except our Lord Jesus Christ, the only begotten son of God, who was with the Father, and who is the Father.[2]

According to Obu, each of the incarnations of God had a specific assignment, and came to Earth under a new name when a new task was required. This appears to be a syncretisation of the Hindu doctrine of the periodic incarnations of Gods

---

[1] OOO, *The Everlasting Gospel: Pentecostal Special Message to the Entire World*, vol. 1 (1980).

[2] OOO, *Christmas Pentecostal Assembly Weekly Gospels*, vol 1.

176

Olumba Olumba Obu

(Avatara), but more likely derives from the tradition in many African religions which embrace reincarnation.

One of Obu's more unorthodox beliefs was that Jesus was flawed:

> You have heard he was taken into the desert to be tempted. There was no physical personality that took him there, but it was the sinful flesh in him as a human being . . . Any person born of a woman must have the imperfect flesh, and similarly, Christ had to undergo the same process.[1]

Furthermore, Christ showed his imperfection through racial discrimination toward the Syrophenician woman and was far from omnipotent, having confined his activities to a few locations around Palestine. Obu was obviously superior:

> Was Jesus omnipresent? He did the work as a Son, only to be seen when he moved from place to place. But in my case, I am seen everywhere lavishly at the same second, while I am here.[2]

Christ showed his failings through anger (throwing over the tables of the money-changers in the temple) and poor judgement (turning water into wine).[3] Obu taught:

> Both John the Baptist and our Lord Jesus Christ came . . . and yet could not practice the Word of God.[4]

Further, Christ cursed the cities of Bethsaida and Chorazin, and called woe down upon those who refused to listen to him, whereas, Obu asked:

---

[1] *BCS Journal*, No. 2, 1983, p.52.
[2] OOO, *The Supernatural Teacher*, Book 1, 1979. See also *The Supernatural Teacher* Book 3, p.49.
[3] OOO quoted in S.A. Kevin, *The Universal Love*, n.d., p. 61.
[4] See E.B. Eyo, *New Heaven and New Earth*, n.d., p. 91.

The Brotherhood of the Cross and Star

Have I ever suspended any member or have I ever cursed any person?[1]

Obu taught that Jesus 'fell' during his first existence as Adam, 'causing the death of the world',[2] and in accordance with Karma came back to pay for the sin of his previous life: 'to hang on the tree to save the world'. Having thus paid for that sin, Jesus had reincarnated for the last time, as Obu, now spiritually perfect.

Obu pointed out that attempting to address God using any of his previous names would mean you would not be heard—a supplicant would have to use his current appellation:

> Therefore, if you shout on Jehova now, you will receive no help. God is not known by that name now. . . . For instance, this is no time for the God of Abraham, Isaac and Jacob. This is no time for the God of Israel.[3]

If Jesus is no longer the current name of God,[4] the clear implication, although Obu was often reluctant to say it aloud, was that the current name is Olumba Olumba Obu.

When Friday Michael Mbon wrote his excellent dissertation on the Brotherhood (University of Ottawa, 1986) he pointed out that:

> Of those members of the BCS interviewed in the course of this research, over eighty-five percent believed that Obu was God in Human form. . . . Indeed, not only do members believe that their leader is God, they actually address him by divine appellations.[5]

---

[1] OOO, *August Pentecostal Assembly Weekly Gospels*, vol 1: 'The Spirit of God'.

[2] OOO, *The Light of the World*, Vol XII, 1971, p. 23, *et seq.*

[3] OOO quoted in S.A. Kevin, *The Universal Love*, n.d., pp. 21-22

[4] *Sunday Concord*, Lagos, 1st January 1984, p.8.

[5] Friday Michael Mbon: *Brotherhood of the Cross and Star: A Sociological Case Study of New Religious Movements in Contemporary Africa*, 1986, p. 158.

Olumba Olumba Obu

Obu would usually deny in public that he was God, despite the clear inference of his many pronouncements, and his followers likewise often deny this to non-members of the Brotherhood. Mbon noted that Obu, however, had never been known to reprimand anyone for calling him by divine names. Obu's answer was:

> Why should I stop them? Have I stopped those who call me devilish names such as 'Satan', 'Lucifer', 'Beelzebub', 'Ekpinoi' and all the rest? My members call me what I am to each of them. How can I stop that? What I am to them, what they see in me, that's exactly what they call me. That is part of their religious experience and I cannot interfere with anybody's religious experience.[1]

Mbon writes:

> Having said that, Obu went on to narrate how John the Baptist had once sent his disciples to find out from Jesus whether he (Jesus) was the Christ, the Messiah; and how Jesus, instead of directly affirming his Messiahship on this particular occasion, sent back John's disciples to their master with the words, 'Go tell your master what you have seen.'[2]

In this instance, Obu made a direct inference that he and Christ were the same, while disingenuously refusing to confirm it. Mbon calls this 'calculated silence' and refers to Amadi's term 'seeming ambiguity'. There is a very good reason for this. Even though Obu published a booklet entitled *I am not God but Olumba Olumba Obu*, which ought to be unambiguous, there exists an official document that reveals why Obu refuses to

---

[1] Mbon's personal interview with Obu, 11th October 1980, reported in his *Brotherhood of the Cross and Star: A Sociological Case Study*, p. 159.

[2] Mbon, *Brotherhood of the Cross and Star: A Sociological Case Study*, p. 160.

The Brotherhood of the Cross and Star

make a public statement. To the Spiritual Council of Churches he reported in 1981:

> The words we speak do not bring in as many converts as our behaviour. Someone who does not shout that Leader O. O. Obu is God but shows love, convinces me more than the one who proclaims his deity but steals and fornicates and of course these very people finally call the Leader a devil. [The booklet] 'I am not God but Olumba Olumba Obu' has opened the way to many people to come in. Those who swore they would never come in to worship read this booklet, saw the truth in it and have come in to worship God . . .[1]

Of course, the above only explicitly states that Obu was aware that being called God turned away possible converts, and though it might have been sensible or cynical (depending on your position), it is not in itself an admittance of his belief in his Messiahship. However, there are other documents going back to the 1980s that are a clear admission.

It must be remembered that members of the Brotherhood wear white robes, but Olumba Olumba Obu wore a scarlet robe. In 'The Secret Name and the Garment Dipped in Blood', Obu asked to whom this quote from the Book of Revelation referred: 'And he was clothed with a vesture dipped in blood: and his name is called The Word of God'. He answered himself:

> This portion proves beyond all reasonable doubts that the revelation of Leader O.O. Obu was foretold before the foundation of the world. Christ was not clothed in a garment dipped in blood. When the people of the world ask you where the name of leader O.O. Obu is written in the Bible, refer him to this prophetic statement.[2]

Obu claimed:

---

[1] BCS, Spiritual Council of Churches minutes, April 25, 1981, p.7.
[2] OOO, *The Supernatural Teacher*, Book 1, page 1.

Olumba Olumba Obu

With that red garment on me, I am omnipresent, omnipotent, and omniscient.[1]

And:

My garment reveals my deity . . . One that is 'mighty to save' and . . . clothed in red garment . . . is no other than the Leader O.O. Obu. Having known about this new name and the truth surrounding it, why do you continue to express doubts? In the whole world it is the name of leader O.O. Obu alone that is mighty to save. It is the only name that all God's creation, including angels, spirits, demons, mermaids, thunder, air, fishes, animals, trees, etc bow to. . . . Leader Olumba Olumba Obu had existed before the world was formed.[2]

He also wrote:

Anybody who doubts the deity of the Leader, let him practice the teachings that are in the Brotherhood of the Cross and Star, then he will realise whether the word is from man or from God. . . . I am the sole and ultimate controller and it is for this cause that I come so that I will show the wisdom of truth in practice.[3]

Despite direct statements to the contrary, arguments over semantics and downright deceit, it is obvious that Olumba Olumba Obu not only believed that he was God reincarnated for the final time, but he encouraged this belief among his followers.

But why would decent intelligent and loving members of the Brotherhood often be so happy to keep quiet about the divinity of their Leader? Surely they had a duty to tell the world? After all, they claim that 'the Brotherhood of the Cross and Star is

---

[1] OOO, *The Supernatural Teacher*, Book 1, page 3.
[2] OOO, *The Supernatural Teacher*, Book 1, page 11.
[3] OOO, *August Pentecostal assembly Weekly Gospels*, 3&4 (1981), pp. 76. 102; cf. BCS Journal, No. 2, 1983, p. 58.

today the last hope for mankind'.[1] Members who believe Obu is God, or Christ come again, say that he refuses to be drawn because he does not want to provoke the actions that caused Christ to be crucified. (It could reasonably be argued that their belief in Obu's immortality should save him from actual death.)

But nobody within the Brotherhood has been in a position to argue or debate with Obu. Although there is a significant hierarchy within the church (and there is a liberal use of titles issued), and presumably Obu is happy to delegate certain responsibilities, he insisted that he was not in any way to be questioned. To an Extraordinary Meeting of Leader's Representatives he said:

> Those who cannot obey me can go and build their own organisations—not Brotherhood.[2]

And in public he pronounced:

> No one in Brotherhood . . . has the right to suggest, dictate or advise the Leader . . . When you are blind, how then can you show me what to do? In fact this was the first instruction that I received from my Father.[3]

However, all the semantics and obfuscation now appear to have gone out of the window. In an article in the Nigerian *Sun* newspaper in May 2022 it was stated that at a press conference a Brotherhood spokesman had said:

> 'Olumba Olumba Obu is the Ancient of Days that was to come and who has come, the personified comforter, the Spirit of the Truth and God the Father who has manifested in human form in fulfilment of the scriptures.'

---

[1] *Sunday Concord* (Lagos), 1 January 1984, p. 10.
[2] BCS, *Extraordinary Meeting of Leader's Representatives*, held Jun 26 1967, pp. 10-11
[3] OOO, *The Light of the World*, Vol XV (n.d.) p. 8.

Olumba Olumba Obu

That would seem to be an unequivocal and official declaration that Obu was God. Nobody seems to want to deny this now, not even Obu himself, because he appears to no longer be available for comment.

If Obu was God reincarnated on Earth in a line of succession that included Jesus, a Leader who could not be questioned and was, in his own words, 'omnipresent, omnipotent, and omniscient', what could followers do but believe him when he suggested that the world was coming to an end in the year 2000?

Brotherhood members now argue that the predictions made by Obu were only for a new age which could be joyfully embraced by those with the spiritual understanding to accept it.[1] But this is not what they were teaching in the last decade of the twentieth century. The excuse given for anticipating physical Armageddon for the entire planet was a simple misunderstanding of Obu's meaning. If it was possible to ask Obu today why he allowed his followers to misunderstand him, no doubt he would use a similar argument to the one employed when asked why he didn't correct his followers when they called him God or Christ, 'Why should I stop them?' This was presumably 'part of their religious experience'. It is curious that a 'Teacher', as he was first meant to have declared himself aged three or five years old, should decide that it was not his place to instruct them in such apparently important matters.

As is often the case with the Brotherhood, members today point to pronouncements made by Obu about the year 2000 which might have various interpretations, or even appear unambiguously suggestive that the year would herald a changeover to a hitherto unsuspected Edenic existence ('for those who have eyes to see'). Certainly, there is little in the record to overtly

---

[1] Essentially, BCS moved from being a 'millenarianism' movement (believing in a cataclysmic and destructive event in 2000), to a 'millennialism' movement (believing in a more peaceful arrival of fundamental change).

The Brotherhood of the Cross and Star

suggest the total physical destruction of the planet by fire that his disciples promised unbelievers. However, there is enough evidence to suggest that Obu was making specific predictions that have blatantly not come to pass. Obu wrote:

> In 2001, we shall pass into a new generation, the generation of the reign of Jehovah and His Christ where only righteousness dwells. That generation will not admit any bit of sin. There will no more be any class distinction between men and women, children and adults, white or black. All will be united into one-ness in love. [1]

which would have been wonderful, if it had happened. He further wrote:

> From 2001 onward whoever does not possess this love will never be allowed to marry, work, or do anything to earn a living. He will never succeed in any undertaking. There will be great punishment to sinners if ever they will be allowed to remain. Such punishment and sufferings which have never existed before the foundations of the world were laid.[2]

If any sinners remain, and I would suggest that many do, it is not obvious what great punishments may have occurred.

> All what people have endeavoured to do from the beginning of the world will end in 1999. The reign of our Lord Jesus Christ begins fully in 2001 to fulfil his words (in Matt. 19:28). . . . From 2001, all different governments of the world will surren-der their governments to our Lord Jesus Christ. After the year 1999 there will be no Army, Navy, Air Force, Police, Law courts, Judges, Magistrates and Lawyers will no longer exist. All

---

[1] OOO, 'A Special Message from Leader Olumba Olumba Obu: Towards a New Generation', *Daily Times* (Lagos), 15th February 1985, p. 11.

[2] 'The Supreme Leader in 2001 Years' by Olumba Olumba Obu, from *The Everlasting Gospel*.

Olumba Olumba Obu

carnal laws will be revoked, and only 'love one another' will reign supreme.[1]

Also:

In this new age, the circle of incarnations and reincarnations shall be stopped. Hence, no birth, no transition, no pains, sorrows, poverty, lamentation. We shall all attain the Christ consciousness which has eluded us as of this period of time. . . . the perishable body has been completely transformed into an imperishable body.

Man shall not be afraid of the animals nor shall he ever treat his brother with contempt. The skies, seas, fire, ants, etc would do each other no more harm. Nations shall fight wars no more as we shall exist in a spiritual state with bodies adaptable to the plane of perfection.[2]

Brotherhood members now talk of these predictions as having been 'spiritual' and 'symbolic', and that they should not be taken literally, which was exactly how they took them at the end of the twentieth century. No doubt they can feel satisfied, on a spiritual plane, that:

. . . members of the brotherhood of the Cross and Star will rule over the whole universe.[3]

They may also have not noticed that in the new spiritual era, the Biakpan dialect would be the lingua franca of the whole world. 'BCS teaches that this was the language used by God to communicate with Adam and Eve. . . . (and) to be the Word of God.'[4] In anticipation of this, in 1985 Apostle E.K. Ukpat published *Biakpan: Emon Anneyeng (The New World Language)*.

[1] 'The Supreme Leader in 2001 Years' by Olumba Olumba Obu, from *The Everlasting Gospel.*
[2] O.E. Akpan, *Life After Death and the Mastery of Life*, n.d., p.82.
[3] OOO, *December Pentecostal Assembly Weekly Gospels*, No. 4, 1980, p. 73.
[4] G.I.S. Amadi, 'Purity and Power', p. 391.

The Brotherhood of the Cross and Star

It does not seem unreasonable to judge somebody who claims to be omnipresent, omnipotent, and omniscient by the quality of their predictions, and by the standards of many observers, Olumba Olumba Obu appears to have fallen short of the mark.

Millenialist movements first came to prominance from the late nineteenth century through to the end of the twentieth when there was a flurry of expectation. The Jehovah's Witnesses previously prophesied that the end of the world would take place in 1878, 1881, 1914, 1918 and 1925, and seem to have taken those setbacks in their stride, although after they prophesied Armageddon again for 1975, the society's leadership were forced to issue an apology. When we entered the new millennium without any of the appreciable apocalyptic changes predicted, the response of millenarians ranged from acceptance to denial, and the Brotherhood must fit the second category. The world has ended and been replaced with another—but only for members of the Brotherhood. If that seems to outsiders to be a rather ineffectual apocalypse, especially given everything that they had been previously promised, then there was another test of Olumba Olumba Obu that he would have appeared to have failed; that of immortality.

There is little in the record to suggest that Obu himself claimed to be immortal, although, in a spiritual sense it might have been taken for granted if he had been God reincarnated. Also, it would be of little relevance whether he, to all appearances an ordinary man, could never physically die when, *after* the new millennium, there would be no death for anybody, because the perishable body would have been 'completely transformed into an imperishable body'.[1] Obu's immortality, however, is something that has always been insisted on, and is still claimed for him now. And Brotherhood members still state that his is a physical, not just a spiritual immortality.

---

[1] Ref 1 Corinthians 15:53

Olumba Olumba Obu

Unfortunately, Olumba Olumba Obu has not been seen in public since before 2003. If he were alive today, he would be one hundred and seven years old, which is not impossible, but would be unlikely. When asked, Brotherhood members refuse to admit that he may have passed away. As is often the case with the Brotherhood, there is what appears to be needless obfuscation.

Olumba Olumba Obu preaching in Calabar.

'Rowland' son of Olumba Olumba Obu,
who is now called 'Olumba Olumba Obu'.

The Succession

What does not help understanding of the Brotherhood is that in 2000 Obu apparently transferred leadership of the B.C.S. to his eldest son, Rowland, who is now known, confusingly, as 'King of Kings and Lord of Lords, His Holiness Olumba Olumba Obu'. The names of Obu senior and Obu Junior are now somewhat interchangeable, which might imply, perhaps, a spiritual and physical succession of some kind, but in 2020 a Brotherhood spokesman, Christ Shepherd Edet Archibong, stated that although Obu senior was no longer seen in public, he was alive and well. Essentially there are now meant to be two 'sole' spiritual heads of the Universe.

Unfortunately the succession did not go smoothly, despite all appearances in official Brotherhood literature and on their website.

Jeremy Goring told me:

The Succession

> . . . those who didn't like it [the succession] departed and set up a rival organisation.[1]

which seems a slight understatement of events. Under the headline 'Bishops Fight Olumba', *Newswatch* in 2002 reported that Obu had been dragged to a police station, which was journalistic hyperbole because he seems to have actually been driven there by his son 'in a Nissan Quest car'. This was:

> . . . the first time he would step out of the sect's premises in 53 years. . . . News quickly spread around that the man who many believed was long dead or gone blind was in the police station. A large crowd was said to have gathered outside the police station to catch a glimpse of the man. The police later issued a statement denying responsibility for that exposure of Olumba, whom many saw as humiliating. The bishops' faction also denied responsibility for the action.[2]

Four Brotherhood bishops[3] claimed Rowland had introduced:

> 'unwholesome' practices and teachings in the church. They also said Rowland now answers [to the name] Olumba Olumba Obu, which he is not.

> . . . The bishops, who spoke to *Newswatch* said the children of Olumba have now taken divine titles that are unscriptural. For instance, Rowland is now said to answer 'king of kings and lord of lords' while Ibum answers 'Queen Mother'. Ajah, one of Olumba's daughters has the title 'Supreme Mother' while another called Onoghen is addressed as 'Blessed Mother'.

---

[1] Reply (Mar 27 2014, 3:56 pm) to 'Changing the World' by Danny Goring, 7 December 2013. dannygoring.wordpress.com
[2] *Newswatch*, Volume 36 No 9, 2nd September 2002.
[3] Cyrinus O. Akpan, Asukwo Ekanem, Okpalla Williams and Matthew Ejedawe.

The Brotherhood of the Cross and Star

Ekanem claimed Rowland had introduced animal sacrifices into the sect's practices, which was denied. It was reported:

> The polarisation of the Brotherhood membership resulted in violent clashes between Rowland's supporters and those of Ibum and the bishops. Machetes and other dangerous weapons were freely used in the fights, which took place within the 34 Ambo Street, Calabar premises of the sect and the surrounding Streets. Many people were wounded, with some spending several weeks receiving treatment in hospitals.

The crisis appeared to have split the Brotherhood into two camps, although this is not obvious to outside observers. There would be arguments over account books and property, resulting in court cases.[1] In 2006 the Brotherhood family and Leadership were in dispute in America, not over the spiritual nature of the succession, but the legal ownership of property.

In 2008 a law suit was filed in the Federal High Court of Nigeria by Helen Johnson Udo *aka* Queen Mother against the registered Trustees of the Brotherhood, which was officially headed by 'His Holiness Olumba Olumba Obu'. She was restrained from interfering in the Brotherhood and appealed against the judgment. She appealed again in 2011 for a reversal of the judgment, and finally the High Court ruled against her in 2021.

The Brotherhood issued a press release after the judgment against the Queen Mother, signed by Christ Shepherd Edet Archibong who concluded that by their decision the supreme court had affirmed:

---

[1] This was especially embarrassing when Obu had predicted that after 1999, 'There will be no . . . Law courts, Judges, Magistrates and Lawyers will no longer exist.' His daughter, Ajah Obu, did have the grace to say to a journalist, 'This is one of the things my father has preached: No one should take anyone to court.'

The Succession

> . . . the divine position occupied by His Holiness Olumba Olumba Obu as the Executive Chairman and Head of Administration and indeed Leader of the BCS Worldwide.[1]

But which Olumba Olumba Obu was referred to? Outside of the Brotherhood, most interested observers have had to conclude that the man born in 1918 has probably died. One former follower, Pastor Lovina Amangala Iburene of The Truth Ministry/The True Lovers of Christ, World Charity Ministry, Lagos, told *News Express* that he died in 2003:

> Olumba gave up the ghost and was secretly buried . . . He died in the night. . . . I was informed by an insider.[2]

Unfortunately, the above is not authoritative, but the date is one that has been widely shared.

Of course, members of the Brotherhood who sincerely believe in Obu as a deity do not need 'proof' of his physical immortality. No doubt the Brotherhood would argue it would be insensitive and crass to wheel him out so as to convince unbelievers, but it doesn't seem too much to ask them to clarify this point, especially as Obu is meant to be a 'Teacher'.

It is surprising that the Brotherhood doesn't simply tweak their story a little and argue that immortality was never a claim Obu made for himself, and that being with us 'spiritually' is good enough. After all, one of the beliefs of many traditional African religions which has been incorporated into the Brotherhood is the idea that the dead are still alive among the living. Obu taught that the 'living-dead' are still members of Brotherhood congregations and participate actively in services:

> Do you know that all those people whom you declare dead long time ago are still here? They go to morning and evening prayers and are washing (sic), and doing every bit of thing.

[1] *The Will* (Nigeria), 16th November 2021.
[2] *News Express*, quoted at *Information Nigeria*, 23rd November 2014.

During Pentecostal Assembly all of them attend. They take part in all activities.[1]

But no, the Brotherhood insists Obu Sr is still physically alive. One can only assume that his son's authority might not be as certain if it was revealed to followers that his father was no longer alive. The succession has not been without struggles, but Obu Jr does not seem to have his father's ability to overcome the demolition of one of the certain foundations upon which The Brotherhood of the Cross and Star was built.

---

[1] OOO, *The Supernatural Teacher*, book 4, p. 151. See also The *Supernatural Teacher*, Book 2, p. 74 and *Our Lord Jesus Christ the Alpha and Omega*, pp. 46, 51-52.

Russell vs The Gorings

In 2013 Danny Goring published online the latest in a series of blog posts about the Brotherhood, 'Changing the World'. I replied, because on Facebook Danny had just been saying that he was following the teachings of Jesus Christ, and I pointed out that this had not been an accurate statement: he was following Christ's words 'as interpreted by a man called Olumba Olumba Obu', a man who prophesied that everyone would have heard that he was an incarnation of God by the year 2000, at which time the world would end. A friend of Danny's from the Brotherhood, Nkor, replied, quoting Obu:

'We do not rejoice . . . in position'

and I pointed out that this was odd coming from a man who delighted in the title 'Sole Spiritual Head of the Universe'. Danny's father, Jeremy, had published a very interesting 'Testimony' in which he had criticised evangelism in the USA 'where the proclamation of the gospel goes unashamedly hand in hand with the cult of personality', and I suggested there was very little difference when the 'charismatic personality at the head of the Brotherhood allows you all to think that he is Christ'.

I called the Brotherhood a 'cult' at the time, and received a reply from Jeremy stating that:

> If you really think that Danny (and other family members) had succumbed to the blandishments of such an organisation then you are not the intelligent person I thought you to be.

I apologised for using the word cult, but gave my reasons for being concerned about old friends. I also wrote that neither he nor Danny had addressed my point about the millennial prophecy, and pointed out that to claim Obu had been misinterpreted was to turn a blind eye to his gospel, 'The Reign of Love by

The Brotherhood of the Cross and Star

2000 AD', which made his prophesy quite clear. I pointed out that Obu's claimed superiority to Christ, and the politics surrounding the succession of Rowland (and the assumption of his father's name), caused me concern. I wrote:

> It is a great shame that those who disagree with the man you follow are condemned by him to be cast 'into a lake of fire burning with brimstone'. Are those the words of a loving Christ?

I then received a reply from somebody called Shalom, who pointed out that my impression of Obu was erroneous because,

> He emphatically discouraged His members from calling Him Christ, Jesus, or God.

I was then told what a fine man Obu is, leading by example, never forcing anyone to worship him. I was also told that Obu had never said the world would come to an end but, rather, 'something spectacular will happen'.

> So my dear brother Ray, forget who Olumba is, or isn't, Love ye one another that is the golden rule of this age of the Holy Spirit.

To be fair to Shalom, the above description is a severe précis of his message. I didn't quite know whether it was worth engaging.

Jeremy then wrote to say:

> I am impressed by your extensive researches into BCS, but you need to be aware of the unreliability of some of the source material, and that the 'gospel' I had mentioned was 'addressed primarily to the people sitting in front of him'.

Jeremy added:

Russell vs The Gorings

And the prophecy proved to be true. Early in 2001, a few weeks into the new Millennium, an important event took place in the hall. The Leader crowned his eldest son (who had originally been named Olumba Olumba Obu but who had—to avoid confusion—been known as Roland) as 'King of Kings', and those who didn't like it departed and set up a rival organisation. For those in Calabar and for hundreds of thousands of others this was indeed the end of an era.

Danny then pointed out that I had not answered Shalom, and quoted, 'The more you look, the less you see!'

I replied to Shalom, asking him if he believed Olumba was Christ, Jesus or God? Because Danny had written, 'Our job is just to give you the information' I pointed out I was asking for specific information:

> Do you believe Olumba is Christ, Jesus, or God?
> Why did he allow you to be mistaken for so long about the end of the world?
> Is Olumba, the man born in 1918, still physically alive?

Danny replied:

> Anyway, to answer your questions. Olumba is not Jesus. Who is Jesus? There are many people in Spain and South America today bearing that name. Jesus of Nazareth was the man who was crucified on the cross of Calvary but the Spirit which raised him from the dead is eternal. Is he Christ? Depends what you mean by Christ. Christ means 'anointed one'. Everyone who has received the baptism of the Holy Spirit is 'christened' or anointed. Is he God? Depends what you mean by God. Jesus told us that 'God is a spirit, and they that worship him must worship him in spirit and in truth' (John 4:24) He further said that 'I and my Father are one' indicating that God the Father (spirit) and God the son (son of man) are one. Of course all this may not mean much to you if you do not believe the words of Jesus Christ as then there is no common reference point (as you mentioned in your response to Shalom). If however you do believe his words then you would understand that there is no

such thing as death because he conquered death and assumed authority in all planes of manifest. As I told you on Facebook, Leader Olumba Olumba Obu is very much around, if you can receive this.

Finally, looking back now and reflecting on the issue I'm quite clear that no one in BCS was misled over the millennium/end of the world. When the Father made his pronouncement about the end of the world no one in BCS anticipated what he had in mind. It is a spiritual language. 2000 was simply the beginning of the end of the 'world', a spiritual system based on the lower nature and characterised by the traits I mention in the above post. It did not mean the physical destruction of the planet. After all, you must have heard the saying 'world without end'? Love was indeed enthroned in 2001 when the Holy Father revealed the One who had come to rule in fulfilment of the book of Revelation 11:19-16. But that's another story . . .

This was not the end of our discussion, but in further posts we did not succeed in getting any further forwards. I did have a long telephone conversation with Jeremy one evening, and he was adamant that any millennialist prophecy for the destruction of the world was as a result of *my* faulty understanding at the time and *my* poor memory now. He insisted that Obu Senior was still alive and well, despite the fact that nobody had seen him in public since 2003.

Sadly, Jeremy Goring died in 2023, aged ninety-three. He was an intelligent and caring man for whom I had great respect, even if we managed to disagree profoundly about the Brotherhood. He had been made an Archbishop in the Brotherhood, and in December 2023 he was declared a Saint by Olumba Olumba Obu.[1]

In 2006 Brotherhood claimed its membership had grown from a million before the beginning of the new millennium to ten million members, although, as the *Los Angeles Times*

---

[1] For the sake of accuracy, this was Olumba Olumba Obu, Jr (formerly known as Rowland).

Russell vs The Gorings

reported, this is 'a figure that could not be independently verified'.[1]

Unfortunately, a great deal about the Brotherhood cannot be independently verified, which will be the case all the time the organisation refuses to answer direct questions and prefers to reinterpret the past to fit the ever-evolving new narrative.

---

[1] *Los Angeles Times*, 7th June 2006.

Addendum

Is the Brotherhood of the Cross and Star a cult?

The word 'cult' is an emotive one, and certainly not a description that members of the Brotherhood recognise. (Then again, not many cults do thus self-identify.) There is no single agreed definition of 'cult' in this context, but there are certain recurring characteristics of cults, such as leadership by a single charismatic individual who espouses unorthodox or novel beliefs, and whose word cannot be questioned. Recognising this as an aspect of the Brotherhood does not necessarily mean that a cult has been identified, because other items on the 'cult checklist' must also be addressed. I would suggest that the single most important characteristic of a cult is the inability of members to leave without fear of persecution. When basic human rights are denied, not necessarily by physical means, but through psychological and coercive control, then red flags should appear. However, 'soft' manipulation of membership of groups can take various forms, and many established churches can be accused of doing just this.

It is not just cults that promote the belief that they are special and that those outside the community are wrong, but cults tend to reinforce not simply an 'us and them' attitude, but are often hostile to those outside. As an outsider to the Brotherhood, I have never felt any hostility from Danny; indeed, he has welcomed my questions and willingly engaged in discussion. Naturally, most religions would prefer members not to question their beliefs, aims or actions, and they encourage an adherence to organisational hierarchy, but few actively attempt to isolate members from friends and relations outside the church. The Brotherhood has been adept at exerting what looks to me like soft influence by offering members employment, honorific titles, and even by encouraging them to marry within the church. However, it should be recognised that such isolation happens to a degree in any such organisation when loyalties and commitments are altered by membership. And as for the ease with which an organisation can be left by members, it is worth considering so many other relationships that we form during our lives, whether they are family, workplace, or social groups. In all of these there is the potential for us to experience individual characters, practices, etc., that make us uncomfortable, and at an extreme may be downright exploitative. Removing ourselves from the situation may often mean denying ourselves access to much else that is positive, including valued relationships.

During my researches, I came across Timothy Wyllie's memoir, *Love Sex Fear Death: The Inside Story of the Process Church of the Final Judgement* (Feral House 2009/22).[1] Wyllie is honest about the problems of having been in a cult; the real privations and unreasonable demands it made upon him and other members, but he also offers some explanation of why the Process Church attracted members in the first place. What struck me most was a 2016 *Dangerous Minds* interview in which Wyllie admitted that if he was to live his life again, knowing what he knows now, he might still join the Process Church. His reason for so doing would be that, despite the very real problems of being in the cult, he learned a great deal that would not have otherwise been made known to him.

Pointing out that there were apparently positive aspects of membership of the Process Church is not to in any way defend cultish practices in any organisation. But to understand cults it has to be recognised that they must offer some attraction to

---

[1] The Process Church of the Final Judgment (also known as the Process Church) was a British religious group founded in 1966 by Mary Ann MacLean and Robert de Grimston who first met as members of the Church of Scientology. Thrown out of the Church in 1962, they briefly ran a Scientology splinter group called 'Compulsions Analysis' before setting up The Process Church, and were popularly considered Satanists.

The Brotherhood of the Cross and Star

potential followers, and people have to find some benefits to membership, if only initially. Cults do not always retain members purely because they have been brain-washed into staying, or because leaving can be made to seem impossible.

To return to the Brotherhood of the Cross and Star, after some reflection, I do not believe it should be called a cult any more than many other established churches, although I do think *all* churches exist on a continuum scale that suggests a degree of cult-like activity. It is unlikely that insiders and outsiders will ever agree on a particular point to place them.

Works Cited and Consulted

Amadi, Gabriel I.S., 'Purity and Power', Ph.D. dissertation, University of Nigeria, 1982.

Akpan, O.E., *Life After Death and the Mastery of Life*, n.d.

'Brotherhood of the Cross and Star', *BCS Journal*, No. 2, 1983.

ditto, Extraordinary Meeting of Leader's Representatives, held 26th June 1967.

ditto, Spiritual Council of Churches minutes, 25th April 1981.

Edwards, Neil, *Sympathy for the Devil*, 2015 (documentary on the Process Church).

Ekpu, Ray, Interview with Obu, *BCS Journal*, No. 2, 1983.

Eyo, E.B., *New Heaven and New Earth*, n.d.

Goring, Daniel, 'Changing the World', 7th December 2013 dannygoring.wordpress.com

ditto, 'Brotherhood of the Cross and Star—a spiritual reform movement for humanity', 21st April 2019, dannygoring.wordpress.com

ditto, 'Into Africa', 26th December 2019, dannygoring.wordpress.com

ditto, 'Love is the Answer', 10th June 2020, dannygoring.wordpress.com

Goring, Sister R., *Brotherhood for Beginners*, http://freespace.virgin.net/dolly.daniels/BOOKS/bcsintro.htm

Kevin, S.A. *The Universal Love*, n.d.

Mbon, Friday Michael, *Brotherhood of the Cross and Star: A Sociological Case Study of New Religious Movements in Contemporary Africa*, Ph.D. dissertation, University of Ottawa, Canada, 1986.

Obu, Olumba Olumba, *August Pentecostal Assembly Weekly Gospels*, vol 1: The Spirit of God, n.d.

ditto, *August Pentecostal Assembly Weekly Gospels*, 3&4, 1981.

ditto, *December Pentecostal Assembly Weekly Gospels*, No. 4, 1980.

The Brotherhood of the Cross and Star

ditto, *Everlasting Gospel, The: Pentecostal Special Message to the Entire World*, vol. 1 (1980).
ditto, 'I Am That I Am', ooo-bcs.org/i-am-that-i-am/
ditto, *The Light of the World*, Vol XII, 1971.
ditto, *The Light of the World*, Vol XV, n.d.
ditto, *Our Lord Jesus Christ the Alpha and Omega*, n.d.
ditto, *Prophets' Handbook*, 1965.
ditto, *Supernatural Teacher, The,* Books 1-4, 1979.
Wyllie, Timothy, *Love Sex Fear Death: The Inside Story of the Process Church of the Final Judgement*, Feral House, 2009/22.
ditto, *Dangerous Minds* 2016 interview with Wyllie.

Miscellaneous Newspapers
Daily Times (Lagos), 16th February 1985.
Los Angeles Times, 7th June 2006.
Newswatch, Volume 36, No 9, September 2nd 2002.
Sunday Concord, Lagos, 1st January 1984.
Will, The (Nigeria), 16th November 2021.

Miscellaneous Websites
Information Nigeria, 23rd November, 2014.
reachouttrust.org/brotherhood-of-the-cross-and-star

Scientology:
A Question of Personality

L. Ron Hubbard, 1950 (*Los Angeles Daily News*).

Scientology: A Question of Personality

In the summer of 1984 I was walking through The Lanes in Brighton when I was accosted by a young woman with a clipboard. She asked if she could have just a few moments of my time and my natural response was to politely decline and keep on walking. However, she insisted she wasn't trying to sell me anything and that she had only a handful of simple questions to ask. I know I only agreed because it was a bright sunny day and she was very good looking. Later, I realised *all* the young people with clipboards accosting pedestrians in The Lanes were good looking, and they all approached potential interviewees of the opposite sex. (Given Brighton's reputation as the 'Queer Capital' of Britain, this was quite short-sighted of them.)

As promised, the young woman did only ask a few questions, and as she wrote down my answers I was told that my responses were genuinely very interesting. Naturally, I was flattered by this, which was what was intended. The young woman's charm then went into overdrive as she turned on me an incredible smile and suggested I would be a really good subject to take a personality test that she could arrange there and then. She said it would be scientifically analysed while I waited, giving me an objective evaluation of all my strengths and weaknesses. The whole pitch was carefully calculated to appeal to my narcissism as well as to my teenage hormones, and I admit I fell for it. I was invited to follow her up into a large, bright office above an adjacent shop. I was cynical enough to assume there would be a catch of some kind, but I couldn't imagine, at that moment, what it might be.

We sat down, one to one, and the questions she asked did seem relevant to the stated aims of the test, but there were really far too many of them and I quickly regretted agreeing to take part. It would have been embarrassing to back out, though, and the pretty young woman's apparent interest in me meant that I persevered.

Scientology: A Question of Personality

I was assured that the Oxford Capacity Analysis test was well-respected and internationally recognised. Many others who have been foolish enough to put themselves through it have suggested that the results are usually negative, so the person analysed is encouraged to seek the assistance that would then be generously made available, but I remember my results were quite positive. Rather than being told that she could correct deficiencies in my personality, the young woman said that she would personally love it if I would consider learning all about Dianetics; apparently I was a perfect candidate. She said that she and all her good-looking, bright and healthy friends were willing to share techniques and exercises with me that would increase my potential in all areas of my life. I would be able to operate on a higher level of mental capacity for as much as eighteen hours a day with just a little sleep. She and her friends were living proof that it worked!

It might have been quite appealing, but they all reminded me of earnest Jehovah's Witnesses I had met. At this point I felt able to make my excuses and leave. As I went out, I accepted the fat paperback that was given to me.

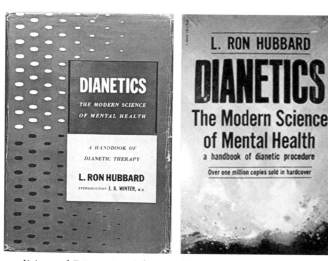

First edition of *Dianetics: The Modern Science of Mental Health*, Hermitage House, New York, 1950, and the paperback given free in 1982, published by Bridge House.

Scientology: A Question of Personality

On the way home, I could make nothing of the book, *Dianetics: The Modern Science of Mental Health*; it seemed to be pseudo-scientific gibberish. When I related my adventure in The Lanes to my parents, they explained that I had met The Scientologists and said I had done well to come away without being brainwashed and dragged into their cult. I was told that Scientologists were dangerous weirdoes who had been involved in all kinds of scandals, but still had a big headquarters just outside East Grinstead.

I initially, wrongly, conflated Scientology with my equally uninformed ideas about Christian Science. This led me to think that they were some kind of Christian sect, albeit a very unorthodox one. It wasn't until I read Christopher Evans' *Cults of Unreason* (1973) that I understood much more. His story of The Church of Scientology was horribly fascinating, albeit that many details were superseded by Russell Miller's biography of L. Ron Hubbard (the founder of Scientology) entitled *Bare-Faced Messiah* (1987). Documentaries about the dangers of Scientology have regularly been broadcast (at least two made by Louis Theroux), which make it difficult for the public today to think of them as anything other than dangerous charlatans. There is an awkward balance required of commentators because, in many respects, the beliefs of Scientologists are laughable (they don't like to discuss this in public, but they believe in 'Xenu', the extraterrestrial ruler of a 'Galactic Confederacy'). Additionally, L. Ron Hubbard's life is so full of obnoxious behaviour, outrageous claims and obvious lies, that one is almost encouraged to laugh at those who are persuaded to join. The amusement Scientology's claims can engender has to be viewed alongside the very real damage that they have obviously done to the lives of many of their followers and their families. One should always endeavour to respect the religious beliefs of others, but it is difficult when a Church and its members have been guilty of such appalling behaviour over the years, some of it resulting in criminal convictions.

In all the exposés of Scientology, observers will point to the author Theodore Sturgeon's statement that Hubbard once told

Scientology: A Question of Personality

the Los Angeles Science Fantasy Society that the only way to make money was to start a religion. Sam Moskowitz also stated in an affidavit during an Eastern Science Fiction Association meeting that Hubbard had said:

> 'You don't get rich writing science fiction. If you want to get rich, you start a religion.'[1]

Others, including the editors Sam Merwin and Lloyd Arthur Eshbach, have exactly the same memories of Hubbard's motivations, although their stories were generally told after Scientology first began to be discredited.

It is impossible to say whether Hubbard was only trying to benefit financially by first creating Dianetics, and later founding the Church of Scientology. The latter was set up after he lost control of much that he had achieved with Dianetics which, in its earliest and simplest form, was simply a fairly harmless 'craze' that made him a great deal of money. The trouble with attributing Hubbard with nothing but brazen financial cynicism is that he was such a narcissistic fantasist that he may have really believed he was making positive scientific advances which would help humanity. Similarly, Scientology fought long and hard to acquire the status of a 'church' and most commentators state that this was primarily for the reason of the tax benefits they could then enjoy. However, there must have also been an element of attempting to legitimise its activities, and many within the movement feel that Scientology *is* a church, even if it appears to be a perversion of the concept to outsiders. It is possible that, to some extent, Hubbard was also a self-deluded altruist, although the horrific ways in which the Church of Scientology has always gone about its business suggests its principal aims have always been power and money, alongside the aggrandisement of Hubbard.

Happily, I do not have any personal horror stories to tell about The Church of Scientology, and my brief brush up against

[1] Sam Moskowitz, 14th April 1993.

Scientology: A Question of Personality

their organisation does not reveal anything new about the unethical lengths to which the church goes to recruit new members. Over many years, investigators and ex-members have put themselves at great risk to unearth evidence of Scientology's activities, because when the church identifies a perceived enemy they are usually considered 'fair game' and the Church argues that they should be punished and harassed using any and all means possible.[1] Their activities have ranged from the horrific to the farcical and, in contrast, their attempt to persuade me of their 'cause' on a Saturday afternoon in Brighton might simply be considered cynical marketing, or even a bit of a joke. (Having told my parents what had happened, I remember we laughed at the idea that there must be at least as many ugly Scientologists who were not allowed to go recruiting.) But everything about the recruitment technique was underhand, and employed almost exactly the same methods as were used in the 1950s; even the test I underwent was unchanged from when it was first written in 1959, and it is still used today. This one small part of their activities is worth examining, even if it is just the tip of the Scientology iceberg, because it should serve as a warning about the methods Scientology apply in *all* aspects of their organisation.

A part of being persuaded to take the Oxford Capacity Analysis test was the assurance that it was well-respected and internationally recognised. The name of the test implied that it must have some academic imprimatur, which it certainly does not. In reality, it is a test the Scientologists devised themselves, and far from being recognised by any reputable psychological organisations, scientology has been accused of misusing their test for their own ends.[2]

---

[1] See Urban, 'Fair Game', 356–389.

[2] Accusations made by both the Australian Anderson Report (1965) and the British Foster Report (1971). Psychologist Rudy Myrvang told *Aftenposten* that the OCA was designed to break down an individual; he described the test as simply a recruitment tool for the organisation.

Scientology: A Question of Personality

The good-looking acolytes in Brighton almost certainly knew that they were misleading people, because they will have been told that the test was created by their outrageously multi-talented leader, the humanitarian L. Ron Hubbard. However, one doesn't have to delve far into the archives to discover that they are lying to themselves about this. The test was actually written by an early Scientologist called Ray Kemp, and the church later credited it to Hubbard so as to add yet another questionable achievement to their founder's long but completely fabricated list of accomplishments.

Ray Kemp and L. Ron Hubbard.

Kemp had been a Royal Navy radar technician before he came under the spell of Scientology, and he certainly had no training in psychology when he devised the test. Hubbard, though, was quite happy for people to assume roles in his organisation based on his assumption that they would most likely have gained any relevant experience in a 'past life'. Later taking credit for the test himself would not be at all uncharacteristic of Hubbard, whose imagination and drive meant that he seemed to believe himself capable of anything he wanted. When, at one point in his history, he felt compelled to command a small fleet of rusty ships, he would make people their captains

Scientology: A Question of Personality

based on their seafaring experience in a past life. Perhaps the most remarkable example of his self-delusion was when he wrote to the US Navy to ask them to send him the medals he had earned during World War Two. When he received only four routine campaign medals, rather than the seventeen medals he was expecting (including a 'Purple Heart'), he simply ignored them, displaying before journalists a range of medals he knew he had never earned, including two that were not even created when he had seen military service.

A photograph of Hubbard's medals, given to *The New Yorker* by the Church of Scientology.

Scientologists have always widely misused the word 'Science', following the lead of Hubbard who invariably attributed his wild claims to the results of extensive research and experience which, like his academic credentials, do not bear any independent scrutiny. There is no way that the word 'scientific' can be attributed to their very questionable personality test because 'science' was never used to create it, and science has never been used to analyse the results. Indeed, Scientologists have no intention of presenting an 'objective' evaluation of their test to the public (even if that was possible). The whole thing is a ploy, as Hubbard himself admitted:

> It has been found that this is a good, reliable method of getting people to come in. The essence of testing procedure is (a) to get the person to do a test and (b) get him or her to come in to

Scientology: A Question of Personality

have it evaluated. From this follows his or her getting processing and training as sold to the person by P&R [Promotion & Registration] at the same time as the evaluation is done.[1]

He added:

Test evaluation is modern, scientific fortune telling.[2]

Having taken the member of the public through the test, the so-called 'evaluator' follows a script learned by heart, originally written by another Scientologist, Peter Greene. This is represented as 'a factual scientific analysis'[3] based on the answers given, but it is applied without any reference to the results and comes directly from the official Scientology 'OCA Automatic Evaluation Script'. Usually, problems with the subject's personality are identified and various potential solutions are mentioned, such as undertaking courses in psychology, psychoanalysis, confidence courses, mental exercises, etc. These alternatives are mentioned so as to suggest that the evaluator is being even-handed before suggesting the help of Scientology. However, the alternatives will always be dismissed with the explanation:

. . . . these things had a very limited application and you could get yourself terribly involved in mysteries, expenses and wasted time, before you found any solutions to your difficulties.[4]

The only answer, according to the pre-written script is:

'All across the world today, people are coming to us, to find simpler, more straight forward answers.'[5]

Hubbard made it very clear how people are to be handled:

[1] Hubbard, 'New Testing Promotion Section'.
[2] *ditto.*
[3] Hubbard, 'Evaluation Script'.
[4] *ditto.*
[5] *ditto.*

Scientology: A Question of Personality

The idea is to impinge on the person. The more resistive or argumentative he is, the more the points should be slammed home. Look him straight in the eye and let him know, 'That is the way it is'. Proceed with evaluation on the low points, column by column. Make a decisive statement about each. If the subject agrees—says, 'That's right', or 'That describes me all right', or similar—leave it immediately. You have impinged. If he argues or protests, don't insist. You simply are not talking on his reality level. Re-phrase your statement until it is real to him. Stop as soon as you get through. As soon as you get an impingement, look subject in the face and say, with intention, 'Scientology can help you with that' or 'That can be changed with Scientology', or some similar positive statement.[1]

In many cases, Scientologists also add an IQ test to their examination, a test that is of limited, even questionable validity and no relevance. Once again, there a script for how to interpret IQ results, again manipulating the person evaluated so that they accept the assistance of Scientology.

The highly critical 1965 Anderson Report on Scientology in Australia and the 1971 Foster Report in Britain both make fascinating reading on the subject, even though they had no access to the Scientology back-story of Xenu (which I will discuss later). These reports were published as a result of Australian and British government enquiries into the Church of Scientology, and Foster, especially, quoted extensively from Hubbard's own writings to make the point that just about every aspect of the organisation was fraudulent.

One fundamental danger of Scientology discussed by Anderson and Foster was the similarity between the organisation's method of 'processing' and the practices of both brain-washing and hypnosis. Anderson noted:

---

[1] Hubbard, 'Evaluation Script'.

Scientology: A Question of Personality

The astonishing feature of Scientology is that its techniques and propagation resemble very closely those set out in a book entitled *Brain-washing*, advertised and sold by the HASI [Hubbard Association of Scientologists International]. This book purports to be 'A synthesis of the Communist Textbook on Psychopolitics', 'Psychopolitics' being defined as 'the art and science of asserting and maintaining dominion over the thoughts and loyalties of individuals, officers, bureaus and masses, and effecting the conquest of enemy nations through "mental healing".'[1]

The 1965 Anderson Report on Scientology (left) and the Foster Report, 1971 (right).

The Anderson Board noted that despite elaborate alternative claims for its publication history, *Brain-washing* 'bears a startling resemblance to Hubbard's own literary style':

> Whether he is the author, as was suggested by a witness hostile to Scientology, is probably immaterial. What is of some significance is that his organization assiduously sold and distributed this manual. . . . Certainly, a great part of the manual is almost a blue print for the propagation of Scientology.

---

[1] Anderson, *Report*, 112, *et seq.*

Scientology: A Question of Personality

On the subject of hypnosis:

> It is the firm conclusion of this Board that most Scientology and dianetic techniques are those of authoritative hypnosis and as such are dangerous. Hubbard and his adherents strongly protest that his techniques are neither hypnotic nor dangerous. However, the scientific evidence which the Board heard from several expert witnesses of the highest repute and possessed of the highest qualifications in their professions of medicine, psychology, and other sciences—and which was virtually un-challenged—leads to the inescapable conclusion that it is only in name that there is any difference between authoritative hypnosis and most of the techniques of Scientology Many Scientology techniques are in fact hypnotic techniques, and Hubbard has not changed their nature by changing their names. Hubbard seems quite capable of thinking that if he postulates that Scientology techniques are different from hypnotic techniques then they are different.[1]

Neither report suggested that an outright ban on Scientology would be effective, but they both suggested legislation be enacted that would ensure anyone undertaking psychotherapy should be registered, and that would have to include Scientologists (who were undertaking their own form of psychotherapy, albeit under new labels given to them by Hubbard). Psychotherapy in the United Kingdom would become 'a restricted profession open only to those who undergo an appropriate training and are willing to adhere to a proper code of ethics',[2] making the point that Scientology did not meet such criteria.

With reference specifically to the Oxford Capacity Analysis test, the Anderson report noted:

> These IQ and personality tests figure prominently in Scien-tology, and are often used to deceive a person as to his state of

---

[1] Anderson, *Report*, 154.

[2] Introduction to Foster, *Enquiry*, 1971, page v, point 4a, 'My principal recommendations'.

Scientology: A Question of Personality

mental health and to create a feeling of inadequacy and anxiety. The evidence shows that these initial tests are deliberately used to make the individual uncertain and anxious and predispose him to undertake Scientology processing or study on the promise that Scientology techniques can improve some undesirable trait supposed to have been revealed. These tests are conducted by inexperienced persons, who neither understand what they are doing nor appreciate the significance of the results which they obtain.[1]

Anderson also noted that the copyright of the Oxford Capacity Analysis is in Hubbard's name, but that,

> . . . it is a peculiar circumstance that it is one of the very few pieces of written Scientology material which does not prominently carry either his name or the word, 'Scientology'.[2]

The reason for this is simply that they are attempting to present the Oxford Capacity Analysis Test as independent.

In Britain, Foster reported that the Test had been investigated by a Working Party of the British Psychological Society (giving the Working Party's credentials). They were forced to conclude that:

> . . . the Oxford Capacity Analysis is not a genuine personality test; certainly the results as presented bear no relation to any known methods of assessing personality or of scaling test scores. . . . The legend 'produced and edited by the Staff of the Hubbard Association of Scientologists International' which appears on the cover is totally inappropriate to a personality measure—such an instrument is not 'edited', it is developed through painstaking research. The validity of the OCA booklet itself is therefore in doubt.[3]

[1] Anderson, *Report*, 108.
[2] *ditto*, 144.
[3] Foster, *Enquiry*, point 131, 76.

Scientology: A Question of Personality

So why are the Scientologists still using the Oxford Capacity Analysis test, all these years later, when it has been almost universally derided? The obvious answer is that it must be an effective tool for recruitment. But there is another reason why it hasn't been improved or altered in the light of criticism; it is claimed by Scientologists that it was written by Hubbard himself, and if there is a deity in the Church of Scientology, it is Hubbard, and how can one improve the work of a deity?

Following the Personality test, 'auditing' is offered. In the early days of Dianetics, anyone with a copy of Hubbard's book was encouraged to psychoanalyse their family and friends from the comfort of their front room. Auditing has always been a way to get people to consider what has happened in their past that may be negatively affecting their behaviour today. Some very basic and uncontroversial psychoanalytic techniques were offered with novel (and copyrightable) terminology; 'auditing', for example, sounded like modern business-speak, and calling bad memories 'engrams' appeared technical, while removing those engrams to become 'clear' seemed desirable. The later addition of an E-meter into the process, (a basic galvanometer) gave the public not only the idea of added scientific input into the process, but it was something else Hubbard could sell to them.

And advertisment for an early E-meter (or galvanometer) in the *Journal of Scientology*, issue 1-G_0003.

Scientology: A Question of Personality

At each stage of increasing involvement with Scientology, and the subject's apparent development, there are further psychological methods employed to draw the Scientologist deeper into the 'church'. One of the techniques has always been to tell members that as they rise through the hierarchy they will become privy to otherwise hidden knowledge—a technique identified with numerous cults, as well as by occult organisations. The term 'occult' is not necessarily inappropriate because after the Second World War Hubbard became involved with Aleister Crowley's Temple of Thelema through John 'Jack' Whiteside Parsons.[1]

The Sunday Times, 5th October 1969.

[1] Scientologists do not recognise it as a part of Hubbard's biography.

Scientology: A Question of Personality

There is little that is overtly Thelemaic about Scientology today, but Hubbard's 1950s science fiction background looms large over the secret knowledge that is slowly revealed to initiates of Scientology as they climb through the ranks. Before Dianetics and Scientology, Hubbard had been a prolific author of popular science fiction adventures for the 'pulp' magazines, and the unique theology behind Scientology is taken directly from the cheaply produced mass market magazines for which he had written.

Astounding Science Fiction, June 1951, containing Hubbard's first article on Dianetics.

What nobody is told when they first meet a Scientologist offering a free personality test is the story of Xenu. In fact, ordinary Scientologists won't know about this themselves because it is only revealed to very advanced members in OT III from the 'Advanced Technology' doctrines. Lower-level Scientologists are only told that seventy-five million years ago a great catastrophe occurred in our sector of the galaxy, causing profoundly negative effects for everyone ever since. Members of the public might not necessarily be put off if told this, but the full details of Scientology 'theology' are that Xenu had been the ruler of the Galactic Confederacy when the catastrophe occurred. Earth was apparently then known as 'Teegeeack' and was just one of

Scientology: A Question of Personality

seventy-six overpopulated planets with an average population of 178 billion. Life within the Confederacy appears to have been very similar to the recent 1950s with aliens walking around in clothes like ours, using similar cars, trains and boats.

According to Scientology doctrine, Xenu was about to be deposed, so he decided to eliminate the excess population under his control, working with psychiatrists to turn them all into tax inspectors,[1] capturing their souls and sending them off in space-ships[2] to Earth where they were exterminated by Hydrogen bombs lowered into volcanoes before being simultaneously detonated.[3]

If you really want to know about Scientology, you have to stick with this . . .

The many billions of disembodied souls, which Hubbard called thetans, were blown into the air by the explosions and were captured using an 'electronic ribbon', before being sucked into 'vacuum zones' where they were made to watch a 'three-D, super colossal motion picture' for thirty-six days, with images of:

> . . . God, the Devil, Angels, space opera, theatres, helicopters, a constant spinning, a spinning dancer, trains and various scenes very like modern England.[4]

thus implanting misleading data. These 'R6 implants' caused a loss of personal identity and confused thetans clustered into the few remaining bodies that had survived, and apparently they still cling to our bodies today (and are termed 'body thetans'). It just

---

[1] It should be pointed out that, coincidentally, Hubbard hated psychiatrists and tax inspectors.

[2] The spaceships bore an uncanny resemblance to the Douglas DC-8 airplane.

[3] 75 million years ago would take us back to the Campanian Stage in the Upper Cretaceous Series, and there is no evidence of anything so significant in the geological record.

[4] Hubbard, *HCO Bulletin*, 2nd October 1968.

Scientology: A Question of Personality

so happens that only Scientologists can identify and remove them.

The story continues with governmental characters called the Loyal Officers finally overthrowing Xenu and locking him in 'an electronic mountain trap' which may be in the Pyrenees. Teegeeack was thereafter considered a 'prison planet' by the Galactic Confederacy, and has since suffered repeatedly from incursions by alien 'Invader Forces'.

If you would like to know more detail of the Scientology backstory you have the choice of either spending at least £100,000 on a series of Church of Scientology courses, or reading the documentation now freely available on Wikileaks. For Scientologists to progress further along the 'Bridge to Total Freedom', the requirement is an unquestioning belief in Xenu and body thetans.

Hubbard described the devastating effect of Xenu's genocide on Earth (and the other 75 planets which formed the Galactic Confederacy):

> It has since that time been a desert, and it has been the lot of just a handful to try to push its technology up to a level where someone might adventure forward, penetrate the catastrophe, and undo it. We're well on our way to making this occur.[1]

Dianetics and Scientology began to ask much of followers very early on in their history, as Hubbard claimed that the simple 'auditing' gave access to not just memories of early childhood, but to the experience of birth, and even the time spent in the womb. But having penetrated that far back, past lives were then made accessible. Through this process, Hubbard was able to discuss, with great confidence, 'Incident I' for example, which is meant to have occurred four quadrillion years ago.[2] In Incident I an unsuspecting thetan heard a loud snapping noise, saw a

[1] Hubbard, *Ron's Journal 67*.
[2] Wright, *Going Clear*.

221

Scientology: A Question of Personality

flood of luminescence, and then witnessed a chariot followed by a trumpeting cherub.[1] This fantasy, Hubbard insisted, occurred four quadrillion years ago, which is 4 with the addition of 15 zeros. Unfortunately, the universe is believed by most scientists to be only 13.8 billion years old, or 1.8 with the addition of 9 zeros. Unfortunately, presenting such an argument to a Scientologist for whom this is a matter of faith is very difficult. (They will argue, not unreasonably, that our argument is made based on our faith in current, mainstream science.)

It is possible, of course, that the good-looking young woman in the Brighton Lanes might have lured more curious young men like me into a consideration of Scientology if she *had* said she wanted to talk about Xenu and the great catastrophe that occurred in our sector of the galaxy seventy-five million years ago, rather than just offering a free personality test. But I doubt it.

Scientology is probably as well-known for taking any criticism badly, as for any of its other traits. The Foster report pointed out that usually,

> The reactions of individuals and groups to criticism varies from grateful acceptance or amused tolerance, at one end of the scale to a sense of outrage and vindictive counter-attack on the other. Perhaps unfortunately (especially for its adherents) Scientology falls at the hyper-sensitive end of the scale. Judging from the documents, this would seem to have its origin in a personality trait of Mr Hubbard, whose attitude to critics is one of extreme hostility. One can take the view that anyone whose attitude to criticism is such as Mr Hubbard displays in his writings cannot be too surprised if the world treats him with suspicion rather than affection.[2]

---

[1] The incident is described in Operating Thetan level III (OT III), written in 1967.

[2] Foster, *Enquiry*, point 173, 127, *et seq.*

Scientology: A Question of Personality

Scientology vigorously condemned both the Anderson and Foster reports, but it is worth quoting one of Foster's findings:

> It is a frequent complaint of the Scientology leadership that those who have reported adversely upon Scientology in the past leave out of account the evident sincerity of Scientologists' dedication to their cause, its beliefs and its practices. Lest I be accused of the same omission, let me make it plain that I am quite satisfied that the great majority of the *followers* of Scientology are wholly sincere in their beliefs, show single-minded dedication to the subject, spend a great deal of money on it and are deeply convinced that it has proved of great benefit to them. But it is only fair also to make the obvious point that none of this furnishes evidence of the sincerity of the Scientology leadership, whose financial interests are the exact opposite of those of their followers.[1]

Returning to my very limited point about the Oxford Capacity Analysis test, if it is not to be simply an exercise in narcissism, it ought to be undertaken to identify the subject's faults and weaknesses, thus allowing them to take steps to become a better person. In the hands of Scientology, however, it is not the faults of the subject that are revealed, but those of the people who administer the test. Unfortunately, such faults run through the entire DNA of the Church of Scientology, as it is fully aware, and they have no intention of rectifying them. The great majority of the followers of Scientology *might be* wholly sincere in their beliefs, but they appear to sincerely believe that misleading and manipulating people outside the church is entirely reasonable behaviour.

[1] Foster, *Enquiry*, point 168, 120.

References

Anderson, Kevin Victor, Q.C., *Report of the Board of Enquiry into Scientology*, State of Victoria, Australia, 1965.

Evans, Christopher, *Cults of Unreason*, Harrap, 1973.

Foster, John, *Enquiry into the Practice and Effects of Scientology*, Her Majesty's Stationery Office, 1971.

Hubbard, L. Ron, *Dianetics: The Modern Science of Mental Health*, Hermitage House, New York, 1950.

ditto, 'Evaluation Script', HCO Policy Letter of 15th February 1961.

ditto, *HCO Bulletin*, 2nd October 1968.

ditto, 'New Testing Promotion Section', HCO Policy Letter, 28th October 1960.

ditto, *Ron's Journal 67*, a lecture given on 20th September, 1967. Tape #6709C2.

Miller, Russell, *Bare-Faced Messiah*, Michael Joseph, 1987.

Urban, Hugh B., 'Fair Game: Secrecy, Security, and the Church of Scientology in Cold War America', *Journal of the American Academy of Religion*, 74, Oxford University Press, 2006, 356–389.

Wright, Lawrence, *Going Clear: Scientology, Hollywood and the Prison of Belief*, Alfred A. Knopf, 2013.

Thee Temple ov Psychick Youth

Alex Fergusson (left), Genesis P-Orridge (seated) and
Peter Christopherson (right), 1981.
(Photo by Janette Beckman.)

The Temple ov Psychick Youth

Official histories of the band Psychic TV (PTV) have long claimed that it was formed in 1981, jointly, by Genesis P-Orridge (from the experimental/industrial group Throbbing Gristle) and Alex Fergusson (from the punk/experimental band Alternative TV). However, this is to sideline the role of another ex-Throbbing Gristle member, Peter 'Sleazy' Christopherson, who is only acknowledged as joining in 1982, despite the fact that the film/TV aspect of PTV were reliant on his film-making abilities from the start. As Matthew Levi Stevens has pointed out:

> Sleazy founded the video production company, Psychic Television Limited, in March 1981, with himself as director and the address on all the headed stationary being his own in Chiswick. . . . he took the name 'psychic television' from Stephen King's *Salem's Lot* ['. . . I'm not talking about ghosts precisely. I'm talking about a kind of psychic television in three dimensions. Perhaps even something alive. A monster, if you like.']¹

Getting to grips with the myths surrounding PTV begins even with their formation.

The new band played their first live show in the autumn of the same year as a part of a multi-performance event, the 'Final Academy', dedicated to and featuring William Burroughs. Perhaps 'played' is not quite the right term; as *Flowmotion* fanzine reported. After an announcement:

> There is no one on stage, only images on TV screens at each stage side and a larger projection on the screen at the back. Then the voice of Genesis P-Orridge . . . 'As you can see Psychic

¹ Matthew Levi Stevens, private email.

Thee Temple ov Psychick Youth

TV is not a group, is not a band, does not do gigs, who could be on stage, to present what? . . . We feel there has been too much spectacle and entertainment . . . entertainment has no place here. . . . Psychic TV is a name chosen by initiates of the Temple of Psychick Youth to administer the public side of our work . . . None of us can think of any way that standing here on stage messing around with musical instruments and keeping people amused would serve any useful purpose . . .' As an introduction to PTV it couldn't have worked better.[1]

Front and back covers of *Force the Hand of Chance*, 1982.

In November 1982, PTV's debut studio album, *Force the Hand of Chance* was released. The music was credited to Christopherson, Fergusson and P-Orridge, while others who contributed included Marc Almond, Paula P-Orridge, and 'Mr Sebastian' whose mellifluous voice provided the 'Message from the Temple'. Among others acknowledged were 'Geff Rushton and David Tibet of the Temple ov Psychick Youth'.

A single, 'Just Drifting', came out later in 1982, and PTV's follow-up album, *Dreams Less Sweet* was released in 1983, again with Christopherson, Fergusson and P-Orridge at the helm. Once more, among others acknowledged were Rushton and Tibet.

---

[1] *Flowmotion*, # 5, 1982, 16.

The Temple ov Psychic Youth

The tracks on both albums ranged from sentimental love songs ('Just Drifting' and 'Stolen Kisses') to the downright funky ('Ov Power' has been described as 'Aleister Crowley channelled through the body of James Brown'[1]), with all kinds of unsettling and interesting aural collages in between. Because the soundscapes were made up from various sources, ranging from the mundane to the esoteric, it was difficult to pigeonhole PTV beyond the label 'experimental'. Occult and magical sources were obviously a strong inspiration, but there also seemed to be a practical self-help message being pushed. The first album had what appeared to be a voodoo head on the front cover, but Christopherson and P-Orridge featured on the back in the garb of strangely corporate Catholic priests. The free poster showed them again, in austere black and white, and parents must have wondered what on earth was going on if they found their teenager had pinned it to their bedroom wall.

Genesis P-Orridge and Peter Christopherson.

Nobody who bought the first two albums could have failed to miss the references to Thee Temple ov Psychick Youth (TOPY),

[1] Reynolds, Simon, *Rip It Up and Start Again*, p. 475.

Thee Temple ov Psychick Youth

which was mentioned on the album sleeves, as well as underpinning the track 'Message from the Temple'. However, it was not clear among the multiple layers of audio, visual and written references what was intended to be taken seriously in PTV's world and what might be ironic. From the outside, it was not obvious whether TOPY was simply a novel way of presenting a fan club.

For those who received TOPY's 'bulletins', it seemed at first to be a lively and thriving community of misfits and dropouts who appreciated a home-made counter-cultural scene that encompassed music, art, magic and jewellery. Personally, it was the self-improvement message that put me off; there was too much discussion of discipline and taking personal responsibility so as to enable empowerment and change for it to sound like much fun. Apart from this, the initial vibe did not otherwise appear to be much different from various other political and musical collectives looking to negotiate a way through the polarised Thatcherite 1980s. The occult ideas were picturesque and interesting and had a counterpart in the idealistic political messages of other bands like punks Crass,[1] who also championed alternative lifestyle possibilities. Even TOPY's requests for donations were not outrageous; after all, the photocopied bulletins were made up without even the benefit of a long-arm stapler. When members were told that mailings were bankrolled by just three or four individuals, and 'No one at T.O.P.Y. receives wages',[2] who would mind playing a benefit gig for TOPY (and thus gaining a little esoteric kudos by association)?[3]

---

[1] Like Crass, TOPY had a hippy ethos at its heart which seemed to go against the prevailing alternative punk culture.

[2] 'TOPY Finance', TOPY Newsletter c. 1987, p. 11.

[3] Later fundraising was for a 'Big House' project—a communal Temple ov Psychick Youth house that was to be bought, preferably in a remote, rural location, where members would be able to live and work communally. This aim was unrealised, and while the funds disappeared, it is unlikely they amounted to much, although the money was sent in good faith by people who often had very little.

The Temple ov Psychic Youth

*

At least a decade of context is required for any understanding of the creation of either PTV or TOPY. P-Orridge had been born in 1950 and was a child at the time of the 1960s culture and counter-cultures he so admired. He set up his first 'collective', called 'Worm' in 1967 while still at school, and he was a part of various artistic endeavours while in Hull and London. In late 1969, back in Hull, he set up COUM Transmissions, an avant-garde artistic and musical troupe that explored, deconstructed and re-presented art in various media. They intentionally courted controversy, most obviously through sexuality.

COUM Transmissions, 1969-1978.

By 1975, P-Orridge's energies were also directed into the band Throbbing Gristle (TG) with Chris Carter, Peter Christopherson and Cosey Fanni Tutti. The intention was to continue to be experimental and confrontational, while operating more within a recognised form of popular culture. This did create a larger audience, although success was critical rather than commercial. P-Orridge's major 'achievement' at this time, in terms of publicity and exposure, was COUM's 1976 Prostitution show which enabled the newspapers to gleefully report details of how shocking and depraved they were. Because they were in receipt of Arts Council grants, the show was debated in Parliament, where P-Orridge and Tutti were described as 'wreckers of civilisation',[1] which will have pleased them both.

Always resistant to definition (although they are credited with the creation of the 'Industrial' music genre), Throbbing Gristle have sometimes been suggested as an alternative and more radical path to Punk, which appeared at the same time. The only thing they really had in common was confrontation; Punk was a popular positive force that put basic rock and roll back into the hands of anyone who wanted to play a guitar, whereas TG seemed mainly to inspire musicians who wanted to explore aural boundaries. TG were influential, but disbanded in June 1981 because, according to Tutti, she and P-Orridge split as a couple.

When P-Orridge put together a new project with Fergusson and Christopherson, PTV was a direct progression from Throbbing Gristle in its continued use of the Burroughsian 'cut-up' method, through which material is randomly generated and is either a source of inspiration, or presented as finished art in its own right. The title of the first PTV album, *Force the Hand of Chance,* acknowledged this.

P-Orridge's counter-cultural hippy background can also be detected in his request to Williams Burroughs for an introduction to Brion Gysin at this time. With Ian Sommerville, Gysin had co-created the 'Dreamachine', a rotating cylinder with holes, lit from within by a lightbulb, which was meant to induce a hypnagogic state (somewhere between waking and sleeping) and an altered perception of reality. A Dreamachine would be used often in PTV and TOPY events and rituals.

In some ways, experiments to induce altered states of consciousness would find a more comfortable fit when PTV later embraced acid house music.[2] For now, though, the big philoso-

---

[1] Comment attributed to M.P. Nicholas Fairbairn.
[2] P-Orridge would try to claim he had invented Acid House Music but, rather, they appropriated what came out of Chicago and the Haçienda in Manchester.

The Temple ov Psychic Youth

phical shift between TG and PTV would be in embracing the possibilities of magical practices through both Chaos Magick and Sexual Magic. In *England's Hidden Reverse*, David Keenan was quoting P-Orridge when he wrote:

> PTV was originally conceived as a 'para military occult group' designed to rejuvenate 'the arena of magic'.[1]

With Christopherson, P-Orridge had written the first drafts of *Thee Grey Book*, intended as an instruction manual for Psychick Youth, 'a compendium of techniques for usurping control logics and recovering the mastery of the self.'[2] In defining an organisation that was in many ways as odd and difficult to describe as its music, the magical underpinning was significantly shaped by the input of David Tibet and Geff Rushton (later renamed John Balance). Balance stated:

> 'We all chipped in a lot of stuff to that . . . Tibet and I would formulate stuff which we'd report back to Genesis.'[3]

Throbbing Gristle considered themselves cultural terrorists, attacking the establishment and the social status quo, while insisting that individuals should embrace and celebrate their own autonomy. This time, however, individuals were to gain control through magical processes, and the idea was to instigate 'Esoterrorism',[4] an assault on all the same targets as before, but by occult means. It was an interesting idea, although, from the outside, it was difficult to see how serious it was. When juxtaposed with the sound of trim-phones, and the track on *Themes*, 'The Mad Organist' (which sounded like the aural equivalent of the children's television show Michael Bentine's *Potty Time*) one

---

[1] Keenan, *England's Hidden Reverse*, p. 38.
[2] *ibid.*, p. 31.
[3] *ibid.*, p. 41.
[4] A term used by P-Orridge in his essay collection *Esoterrorism, Selected Essays 1980-1988*, UV Press, 1989.

Thee Temple ov Psychick Youth

might have been forgiven for assuming it was all just an elaborate hoax. After all, Mr Sebastian seductively suggested:

> Clean out the trappings and debris of compromise, of what you've been told is reasonable for a person in your circumstances. Be clear in admitting your real desires. Discard all irrelevancies. Ask yourself, who you want as friends, if you need or want to work, what you want to eat . . .[1]

not long after P-Orridge had been singing, 'Stolen kisses, fa-fa-fa-fa-faa.'

The occult ideas were interesting and different. Crowley was a big influence on Tibet, and hence on TOPY. Tibet borrowed from various aspects of the Hermetic Order of the Golden Dawn and the Ordo Templi Orientis, so that Victorian interests were fused with aspects of psychedelia and postmodern ideas of Chaos Magick. P-Orridge himself admitted the influence of the Process Church of the Final Judgement and collected a number of their magazines and other publications. The Process Church had been set up in 1966, and courted controversy in the late 1960s, before succeeding in becoming notorious through association with the Manson Family murders in 1969. (An association that was almost entirely created by the media.) The Temple had different intentions to the Process Church which (despite coming from a Scientology background) also had a distinctly hippy background, albeit with Gothic trappings. Apart from general cult-like practices, there were various aesthetic similarities, not least in the presentation of TPY and Process publications and the importance of their symbol. The Process church used a swastika-like 'P-Sign', while TOPY adopted a 'psychic cross'.

---

[1] Message from the Temple, *Force the Hand of Chance*, 1982.

The Temple ov Psychic Youth

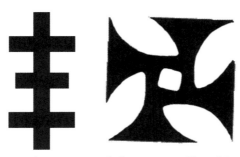

TOPY's 'psychic cross' and the Process Church's 'P-Sign'.

The sexual side of TOPY was very much based on the ideas of the occult artist Austin Osman Spare, and was introduced largely through Balance. In sexual magic, the idea is that the orgasm has power, and if the combined sexual energy of the TOPY membership could be harnessed, it might potentially have huge power at its disposal. However, as Kat, Tibet's girlfriend was later to tell Keenan:

> [Tibet's] favourite line is, 'if all these magicians are so great and powerful why are they all so broke and don't have girlfriends?'[1]

Arguably, it was in Psychic TV's more experimental videos, rather than in their music, that they were really pushing at boundaries and flirting with extremes, but they were not the only ones attempting this. Art students all over the country were watching the films of Kenneth Anger and were emulating Derek Jarman, using newly accessible and relatively cheap video equipment. P-Orridge is meant to have claimed at one point, 'Psychic TV is a video group who does music, unlike a music group which makes music videos'.[2]

PTV created some reasonably standard music videos to accompany the records they released, but other video was far

---

[1] Keenan, *England's Hidden Reverse*, p. 305.
[2] Original quote not found, although it is frequently attributed to P-Orridge.

more experimental. There was something about the fuzzy, low-fidelity quality of the medium that suited Psychic TV's activities, resulting in messy, disturbing footage that invited viewers to interpret meaning for themselves. By creating transgressive and sometimes brutal imagery, they claimed association with the darker side of human nature, including occult and cultish imagery and iconography.

Much of this was projected at gigs and events, although tapes were available through mail order direct from TOPY in the early 1980s. A compilation of all the material to date, *First Transmission*, was only meant to be for fans who had bought all of their ever-increasing output of albums, although copies were shared around. On databases it is given a release date of 1982, and has a duration of four hours in length, although the video tape I saw at the time had been edited down to one hour and I remember seeing only the more conventional music videos.

P-Orridge and Tibet.

The Temple ov Psychic Youth

The idea of creating a cult obviously appealed to P-Orridge, although he would claim he was setting up an 'anti-cult',[1] saying that TOPY was formed of 'only leaders, and not followers'.[2] Under the auspices of art and employing irony at every turn, anything could be discussed, presented and even acted out, and any negative reaction was obviously the result of small-mindedness or ignorance, as well as a lack of a sense of humour. (After all, Neil Andrew Megson calling himself 'P-Orridge' was funny and self-deprecating.) For those who find fascination in dark extremes, why not flirt with the imagery of Charles Manson? Surely, shaved heads, pigtails, tattoos and piercings create a sense of belonging—they are not 'uniform' of any kind?

Psychic TV band photo, featuring Charles Manson t-shirts.

With a diversity of countercultures thriving in late 1970s/ early 1980s Britain, adding militant, occult ideas into the mix seemed reasonable for an experimental art project which

---

[1] *Thee Psychick Bible*, p. 418.
[2] 'Letter to Jean-Pierre Turmel', *Thee Psychick Bible*, p. 32.

employed parody. Genesis would claim that membership of TOPY climbed, at its peak, to 10,000 members, but this was more myth-making; at its height, TOPY membership never rose above 400 paid-up members.

Left to right: Peter Christopherson, John Balance, Caresse as a baby, Paula P-Orridge, Alex Fergusson, Genesis P-Orridge.

*

It is always interesting when, after a movement is created by a group of like-minded people, schisms appear. The first prominent member of the TOPY family to leave was David Tibet, which might seem strange when many of the occult underpinnings of its philosophy came from his studies in magic and his knowledge of occult orders and societies. He said:

> 'At one point I felt that Genesis and I were quite close friends but that relationship disintegrated . . . I think his character changed. Why, I don't know.'[1]

Tibet told me, several years ago, that he began to find everything about TOPY uncomfortable; just one example was that he didn't know if the jiffy bag that would come through the letterbox addressed to Thee Temple would contain the menstrual

---

[1] Keenan, *England's Hidden Reverse*, p. 46.

The Temple ov Psychic Youth

blood of an acolyte, or the proceeds from a TOPY benefit gig (which might be several hundred pounds in used fivers). The tipping point was when P-Orridge began passing off Tibet's work as his own.

Tibet went on to form his own band Current 93. In 1983 Christopherson and John Balance also left to form Coil. As far as the outside world was concerned, Psychic TV was just changing and evolving as most bands do, losing members and gaining new ones. I finally got to see Psychic TV play live in 1986 following the release of the singles 'Roman P' (1984) and 'Godstar' (1985) when Psychic TV had taken a different direction. Fusing 1960s nostalgia with contemporary dance music, their new 'hyperdelic' sound wasn't defying convention so much as simply adding 'Jive Bunny' beats to sixties pastiches, creating something quite brittle and two dimensional (although it sounded more impressive live than on record). References to Charles Manson[1] gave it a bit of an edge, perhaps, but the Beach Boys vocals were close enough to the originals that they may have been samples. It didn't help my personal perception of P-Orridge that I should have seen PTV at the intimate Take Two Club in Attercliffe, Sheffield, but late in the day, Marcus Reynolds, who ran the club, was persuaded by P-Orridge that he should move the gig to the Leadmill. This involved the promoter in huge expense, but ticket sales were poor, and P-Orridge knew that Marcus had lost a great deal of money, but he still threw cash into the small crowd (and thus into Marcus's face).

PTV was at its most likely to descend into self-parody in 1989 with the release of 'Joy' which included the founder of the Church of Satan, Anton LaVey, reciting the Lord's Prayer backwards. Anyone would have thought PTV was trying far too hard to court publicity with the over-excitable tabloids. P-Orridge was aware of the controversy caused by the Process Church when they appeared to be Satanists (although their neo-Gnostic

---

[1] 'Roman P.' was Roman Polanski, whose wife Sharon Tate had been killed by followers of Manson.

Thee Temple ov Psychick Youth

philosophy was actually giving equal prominence to Christ and Satan, and suggested that they should be reconciled).

It was in about 1990 that I took an interest in the Temple again. I had just bought their reprint of Crowley's *The Stratagem*, having previously been unable to afford their publication of Austin Osman Spare's *The Starlit Mire*. I was talking enthusiastically about the book to Jane Howden from the Sheffield band Cosa Nostra, and she expressed disenchantment with TOPY, saying her band had played a couple of benefit gigs for the Temple, but sending bundles of cash down to an address in Brighton filled her with disquiet; she really had no idea what TOPY would be doing with it. (I am not sure she was ever a paid-up member of the Temple, but she was one hell of a bass player.)

Jane was echoing the concerns of many associated with TOPY at the time, but few outside the Temple took any interest in what still looked simply like arguments about a fan club. After all, Psychic TV continued to make records and to tour, and later, in 1992 the shit would really hit the fan and TOPY's internal organisational problems would become seriously eclipsed.

*

With reference to his original contributions to TOPY, Balance said:

> Everything had to be reported back to [P-Orridge], nothing was allowed outside the net. It was really draconian.'[1]

Balance also remembered:

> I read the right signs, did the right things, i.e. pretended to be in awe, submissive and pale. . . . [TOPY] draws in willing victims . . . I found things getting too autocratic and one-lined for my liking.

[1] Keenan, *England's Hidden Reverse*, p.41.

The Temple ov Psychic Youth

It's funny, charisma goes a long way and when you're young and excited and things are happening and when you are obviously causing a sensation in some way you stick with it. David saw through it first.[1]

David Tibet told Keenan:

I thought TOPY was a really good way to disseminate interesting information on interesting areas that people may not have thought about . . . I was very unnerved when it seemed to be becoming a cult. I wasn't happy with any of the directions the project was moving in.[2]

Peter Christopherson stated:

[TOPY became a] horrible sort of manifestation ... a cult with a leader, whose followers did whatever [P-Orridge] said.[3]

P-Orridge had always been fascinated by cults, and almost as soon as he had set up TOPY he was able to start acting like a cult leader, albeit claiming that he was being ironic. Any community has the potential to take on aspects of a cult by creating a dependence on that community by those who feel they have something to lose by leaving. It doesn't only happen within religions, but is often associated with organisations that have a charismatic leader and a hierarchy—both of which fit with TOPY.

To be considered a cult, TOPY would have to have dedicated followers who would sacrifice everything for the cause, as well as apostates who flee, scarred by their experience. In *England's Hidden Reverse* David Keenan perpetuated the idea of fanatical followers by quoting P-Orridge in describing Ossian Brown (for example) as 'the perfect warrior priest',[4] who 'submerged him-

[1] Keenan, *England's Hidden Reverse*, p. 46.
[2] *ibid.*, p. 46.
[3] *ibid.*, p. 64.
[4] Keenan, *England's Hidden Reverse*, p. 217.

Thee Temple ov Psychick Youth

self totally and set up a 'ritual house'[1] in Brighton, known for its rigorous, ascetic practices. These sorts of claims are simple manipulation, conferring followers with a status with which P-Orridge calculated they would be flattered into agreeing, thus adding to the construction of an image of TOPY and P-Orridge himself that he wanted others to help promote.

Brown is an interesting example. He was a TOPY member in his mid to late teens, and he remembered his relationship with P-Orridge as 'parental in a bizarre way'.[2] But P-Orridge had the ability to become a 'tyrant, [with] lots of lectures and screaming fits . . . everything had to be in its right place, at the right time'.[3] Rather than fleeing from a cult, it is clear that Brown simply became disillusionsed and left.

Due to an international fan base for PTV, TOPY had become an international organisation, so a degree of management structure was understandable. 'Stations' were set up in other countries, which made sense, but an artificial hierarchy was also instituted which designated members a Ratio of One to Five. It was meant to be possible for ordinary members to ascend through the Ratios through their devotion to the cause. It might have been considered post-modern and ironic by some, but TOPY also began enforcing excommunication if disciples violated 'privacy', 'trust', or were found guilty of 'theft from the community, both material and intellectual'.[4]

P-Orridge was working his way through the checklist of requirements for the definition 'cult'. Balance noted that P-Orridge's own personal interests were adopted as the official party line without question, and if members did not follow this, then they found themselves ostracized. Balance remembered that TOPY intentionally followed the practices of Jim Jones, the Process Church, and other such cults as a kind of 'cultural

---

[1] *ibid.*, p. 217
[2] *ibid.*, p. 217.
[3] *ibid.*, p. 218.
[4] *Thee Psychick Bible*, p. 468.

camouflage'.[1] By copying them, the cult of TOPY became a 'self-fulfilling prophecy'.

Brown recalled the paranoid atmosphere within the TOPY community, which included 'destructive mind games, bullying techniques, and pecking orders . . . there was a mob mentality [when] someone would fall out of favour and a pack would form, and slowly they'd get pushed out of the circle'[2] towards permanent excommunication.

Balance and Christopherson both said they were horrified by the unquestioning obedience exhibited by some acolytes; something P-Orridge did not discourage. They recalled that those who gravitated toward the Temple were often emotionally damaged and vulnerable before they even entered the fold. And their fervour was frightening, with 'a psychological need for being told what to do, no matter what the consequences would have been'.[3]

As Dan Siepmann pointed out in his online essay, 'Groupthink and Other Painful Reflections on Thee Temple ov Psychick Youth', P-Orridge has come to be idolised in certain spheres for having lived life at the cutting-edge of culture. But Siepmann points out that in very few of the eulogies printed since P-Orridge's death in 2020 has anyone mentioned that he had a history of being violent and manipulative. Take, for example, the experiences of Cosey Fanni Tutti. In her memoir, *Art Sex Music* (Faber & Faber, 2018), Tutti wrote about the psychological and physical abuse inflicted by P-Orridge during her time with him as a part of COUM Transmissions and TG, as well as his sexual coercion and other manipulative activities. When published, these accusations were not actually refuted by P-Orridge, who simply replied, 'whatever sells a book, sells a

---

[1] 'Groupthink and Other Painful Reflections on Thee Temple ov Psychick Youth' by Dan Siepmann, 27th September 2019, et seq.

[2] Keenan, *England's Hidden Reverse*, p. 218.

[3] 'Coil: Lust's Dark Exit', Electric Dark Space, 1991. Interview by Olav Hagen.

Thee Temple ov Psychick Youth

book'.[1] Paula P-Orridge, his wife, later reported that Tutti had asked her if she would confirm Genesis's behaviour if he tried to sue her over the comments.[2]

Tutti wrote that P-Orridge:

> . . . placed himself in a guru-like position . . . he could never be wrong.[3]

Another collaborator on COUM Transmissions, Ian Evetts (Spydeee Gasmantell) recalled that P-Orridge 'just wanted followers, not people to contribute', [4] and Greg 'Foxtrot Echo' Taylor thought that P-Orridge's talent was in his 'capacity to charm and coerce those in h/er[5] orbit'.

P-Orridge had always been a clever manipulator. In the 1980s and 1990s TOPY's opponents were the establishment. Anyone living a countercultural or eccentric lifestyle was fair game for the media, so TOPY could always be considered the underdogs. As Dan Siepmann pointed out,

> Early adopters of P-Orridge revivalism include a few mid-to-late '00s books and magazine profiles (e.g., Simon Reynolds' *Rip It Up and Start Again* and David Stubbs' essay in *The Wire*). . . . But after 2015, journalist, fan, and artist adoration for P-Orridge and TOPY surged. Reverent features spread like wildfire in a variety of publications, such as the *New Yorker*, *SPIN*, *The Guardian*, *i-D* (1 and 2), *Tiny Mix Tapes*, *The Quietus*,

---

[1] *New York Times*, 9th November 2018.

[2] 'Surviving Genesis', Alaura O'Dell (Paula P-Orridge) talking to Alan Rider, Outsideleftmusic, outsidleft.com.

[3] Tutti, *Art Sex Music*, p. 82.

[4] 'Groupthink and Other Painful Reflections on Thee Temple ov Psychick Youth' by Dan Siepmann, 27th September 2019, et seq.

[5] P-Orridge adopted gender neutral pronouns with the 'Pandrogeny Project' with his partner, with whom he underwent body modifications so they would resemble one another, after which they identified as a single pandrogynous being named 'Breyer P-Orridge'. She pronouns will be used to relate to P-Orridge after the 'Project'.

The Temple ov Psychic Youth

Pitchfork, *PopMatters*, *Vice Media* verticals both active and extinct, *self-titled*, HERO, *Dazed*, *CVLT Nation*, *CLRVYNT*, local alternative weeklies, and even putatively authoritative sources such as AllMusic.com. Even my own academic writing joins this bandwagon.'[1]

All the above ignored the darker side of P-Orridge's character and activities. Commentators often overlook what happened within TOPY because it often appears to be simply an extension of the band, and Psychic TV continued making records, and Genesis P-Orridge moved on to other projects which can be seen, reasonably, as further progressions of interests he had always espoused. Few realise how and why TOPY imploded and had to be wound up.

Somehow, P-Orridge sought to blend into a smooth emulsion the contradictory ideas that members should embrace personal responsibility and celebrate their autonomy, while at the same time:

> ... immerse themselves 100% in devotion to the group ... even at the risk of personal disintegration and mental collapse. Transformation can only occur if the Individual is prepared to sacrifice all they have, including a previous personality, and place in a status quo.[2]

Far from promoting individuality, the ego was meant to be eliminated. To do this, P-Orridge and the TOPY leadership created protocols to destroy individual personality. The best example of this was the insistence that disciples' names should be replaced by 'KALI' for women and 'EDEN' for men, with a following number indicating the order of their arrival into TOPY. In *Thee Psychick Bible* P-Orridge claimed 'the names

---

[1] 'Groupthink and Other Painful Reflections on Thee Temple ov Psychick Youth' by Dan Siepmann, 27th September 2019.
[2] *Thee Psychick Bible*, p. 409.

Thee Temple ov Psychick Youth

were used to give a sense of equality',[1] but in an interview in 2006 he admitted:

> It's also well-known in any study of cults, that another way of controlling people is to remove their previous name and give them one of their own.[2]

As David Keenan wrote, TOPY became just like 'the autocratic religious cults they set out to parody'.[3]

Members were told to give up a proportion of their assets to help fund the Temple's socio-political activities. Back in 1987 they were asked simply to sell a few unwanted records, but later P-Orridge's insistence on a tithe caused dissent, and P-Orridge attributed unrest at this to a 'rebel faction' who were envious of:

> . . . the charisma and respect that tended to be associated with my SELF and . . . the Ratio Five inner circle . . . We seemed to have the more glamorous role, media visibility . . . and I had a nice house and car.[4]

Apparently, the questioning of TOPY authority caused paranoia within Ratio Five, resulting in security measures, leading to further unrest as members called P-Orridge and others higher up the hierarchy 'egocentric and totalitarian'.[5] P-Orridge called detractors a 'wolfpack' who were 'organizing a coup of some kind',[6] although he did concede there were reasons for their anger.

---

[1] *Thee Psychick Bible*, p. 418.
[2] Unedited Transcript of his *Invisible Jukebox* by Alan Licht in *The Wire*, September 2006.
[3] Keenan, *England's Hidden Reverse*, p. 47.
[4] *Thee Psychick Bible*, p. 423.
[5] *ibid.*, p. 425.
[6] *ibid.*, p. 426.

The Temple ov Psychic Youth

In P-Orridge's version of events, 'a small minded and bigoted parochialism'[1] would bring about the disbanding of TOPY. He had a 'purity of motive'[2] and a:

> . . . personal disinterest in the ego glory, but acceptance of it as a necessary cultural phenomenon.[3]

P-Orridge officially dissolved the TOPY network in 1991, although some pushed back against this—notably the North American chapter (TOPYNA), which eventually became autonomous, although not without a great deal of acrimony.

P-Orridge first attempted to point out that TOPY had been:

> . . . voluntarily terminated by its SOURCE . . . in accordance with their original intent. Any person . . . claiming Membership . . . is clearly either a fool or a charlatan. . . . Do not support them in their delusions.[4]

Members of TOPY asked what happened to the 'modern tribal framework'[5] and 'unity ov Purpose'?[6] When argument failed, P-Orridge threatened lawsuits to protect his copyrights and intellectual property, which looked to members as though he was attempting to maximise future commercial opportunities. Rather than a counter-cultural guru, this sounded like the last refuge of the capitalist materialist.

During their arguments TOPYNA wrote to P-Orridge:

> *[TOPY] collapsed after being built on a foundation of untruths and misguided ideals . . . TOPY was the design of ONE*

---

[1] *Thee Psychick Bible*, p. 431.
[2] *ibid.*, p. 425.
[3] *ibid.*, p. 426.
[4] *ibid.*, p. 509.
[5] *Ibid.*, p. 100.
[6] *ibid.*, p. 100.

Thee Temple ov Psychick Youth

person, with a desire to CONTROL a CULT for his own personal pleasure and egotistical growth.[1]

P-Orridge did everything possible to stop TOPYNA from using the Temple's name, symbols and any other branding. His insistence on the disbanding of the whole organisation confirmed the views of many members that it had only ever been about P-Orridge, never about individual liberation, much less the creation of a supportive community.

*

The original TOPY was meant to be a safe place for 'outsiders'. It was awakening sleepwalkers, empowering the powerless and raising the self-esteem of the marginalised. And by becoming a part of that group, members were meant to gain a position of power in society that had hitherto been denied to them. It was a beguiling proposition then, and it is equally appealing today for those that read more rose-tinted accounts of P-Orridge's life.

The Temple was meant to have been in opposition to authoritarian control. TOPYNA exists to this day, and a fundamental part of their painful (re)birth story was a realisation that they had been deceived all along by P-Orridge as the leader of TOPY.

P-Orridge claimed he wanted to follow Burroughs and 'smash the control machine',[2] but rather than destroy the control machine, he seems to have been more interested in creating one of his own.

*

---

[1] Autonomous Individuals Network, 'Statement of Intent' quoted in 'Groupthink and Other Painful Reflections on Thee Temple ov Psychick Youth' by Dan Siepmann, 27th September 2019.

[2] William S. Burroughs, *Dead City Radio*, 1990.

The Temple ov Psychic Youth

Having written the above, it is important to state that there are still many ex-TOPY members who remember their time in the organisation positively. There does seem to be a direct correlation between good memories and the distance from TOPY headquarters at which members found themselves. In different cities, especially those abroad, there was more autonomy for members; a willingness to give a sense of community to outsiders and weirdoes was embraced. And when the Psychic TV bandwagon came to town for gigs, P-Orridge's visits were a welcome distraction from everyday life. P-Orridge's willingness to act as a guru did not always have harmful effects, and even a brief visit to TOPY headquarters in London or Brighton were not necessarily negative experiences. Those who had the most troubling and traumatic experiences tended to be those who remained within the orbit of P-Orridge for any prolonged length of time.

The *Sunday People*, 24th July 1988.

A Note on the Satanic Panic

A big part of Psychic TV's story, and that of P-Orridge, was the 'Satanic Panic' of the early 1990s. It is hard to believe today that anyone took it seriously, but they did. The scare was first created by newspapers in the US, but it was soon reproduced in the UK where the tabloids printed headlines that were barely credible because they were simply untrue. In 1992, Britain's Channel 4 documentary series *Dispatches*[1] fuelled the flames by presenting the Psychic TV video, *First Transmission*, as evidence of Satanic ritual abuse.[2] A woman identified as 'Jennifer Evans' admitted on camera to being coerced into killing one of her own children. It was trailed in the *Observer Magazine* three days before broadcast, in an article headlined 'Video Offers First Evidence of Ritual Abuse' by Eileen Fairweather who reinforced the assertion of presenter Andrew Boyd that it was evidence of Satanic ritual abuse.[3] (The journalist did not disclose that she had also been a researcher working on the program.) A helpline number was given immediately after the documentary.

Despite assertions that all of the tabloid press ran with the story, a more cautious approach was soon being taken. Even the *Observer Magazine* which had backed Boyd's assertions the week before, now reported:

> Far from providing any definitive answers to the question of the existence of large-scale 'Satanic' cults, it is clear that the Channel 4 programme has given rise to still more heated debate,

---

[1] 19th February 1992.
[2] It is unknown whether the makers of *Dispatches* were aware that the video had been partially funded in the 1980s by Channel Four itself.
[3] Eileen Fairweather, 'Video Offers First Evidence of Ritual Abuse,' *Observer Magazine*, 16th February 1992, p. 4.

Thee Temple ov Psychick Youth

with sceptics passionately arguing that the video is evidence not of a Satanic cult but of a bizarre performance art.[1]

However, the allegations still resulted in the P-Orridge household being raided by the police.

Scotland Yard seizes videos and books

David Rose
Home Affairs Correspondent

SCOTLAND Yard's Obscene Publications Squad last week seized books, videos and correspondence from the Brighton home of rock musician Genesis P. Orridge, leader of the sect responsible for a video depicting a bloody 'satanic' ritual.

A Channel 4 *Dispatches* programme last Thursday screened excerpts from the video, in which a naked man is beaten and repeatedly cut with knives, a young woman scarred with another sharp implement and a pregnant woman apparently subjected to an abortion.

The programme, previewed in last week's *Observer*, did not disclose the source of the video at the request of the police. However, it has now emerged that it is the work of Mr Orridge (alias Neil Megson), founder of the rock band Psychick TV and an associated organisation known as Thee Temple ov Psychick Youth, TOPY.

The video begins with an introductory section in which the film director Derek Jarman is shown speaking in front of an occult triple cross. Dubbed over his image is the voice of a tattooist and 'body piercer,' who specialises in fitting rings and studs for nipples and genitals,

known in occult circles as Mr Sebastian.

In the video he delivers a lecture against repression of all kinds, and in favour of the gratification of all desire, however extreme.

Scotland Yard sources say the material seized on a search warrant from Mr Orridge's home filled an entire lorry. The police have not yet begun to sift it, nor have they seen the new videos. Mr Orridge is on holiday in Thailand with his wife, Paula, and their two daughters.

It is understood that a helpline set up after the *Dispatches* programme produced a substantial response. One caller was

a teacher of a girl, 15, who is said to have been offered drugs at TOPY meetings and had explicitly sexual letters from TOPY leaders. She is to be interviewed by police.

Far from providing any definitive answers to the question of the existence of large-scale 'satanic' cults, it is clear that the Channel 4 programme has given rise to still more heated debate, with sceptics passionately arguing that the video is evidence not of a satanic cult but of a bizarre performance art.

Several *Observer* readers have contacted us saying that they saw the video projected at Psy-

The Observer, 23rd February 1992.

The *Dispatches* programme was later wholly discredited, as were all the Satanic abuse stories,[2] but not before a great deal of damage had been done to the reputations and lives of those caught up in them. That P-Orridge, Psychic TV and TOPY had been knowingly courting controversy and outrage did not mean that intelligent investigate journalists should have fallen for what they were pretending to get up to. The P-Orridge family were genuinely adversely affected but, ever the showman, Genesis decided to make the most of it. He has tried claiming that he and his family were deported,[3] but because they had been out of the country at the time the documentary was broadcast and their house was raided, they simply decided not to return to England

[1] David Rose, 'Scotland Yard Seizes Videos and Books After TV Film of "Ritual Satanic Abuse",' *Observer Magazine*, 23rd February 1992, p.11.

[2] *Dispatches*' 'Jennifer Evans' was later identified as an anti-abortion counsellor called Louise Errington.

[3] 'Strange Love', *Radar Magazine*, Jul/Aug 2008.

A Note on the Satanic Panic

(which was reasonable, given the atmosphere of suspicion). P-Orridge then said that they had chosen to go into self-imposed exile in California because they believed it would be impossible to get a fair hearing in England. He may have been correct, but he attempted to turn the situation to his advantage:

> We were now in exile: the first British citizens persona non grata since Quentin Crisp, Oscar Wilde, and Aleister Crowley. Good company.[1]

Moving to America may not have been the first choice of the P-Orridge family, but it was said amongst those that knew Genesis that at this time he was also facing some very uncomfortable investigations from the Inland Revenue. Too many jiffy bags of used fivers had been put through his door and the income never declared. (He would not be the only person to inflate claims of membership of an organisation, and then be asked to account for where the subscriptions had gone.)

Dan Siepmann refers to P-Orridge's 'planned revisionism', claiming his re-telling of the TOPY story was a 'tool for obscuring abuse':

> Case in point: P-Orridge and h/er apologists are all too keen to play up TOPY's 'Satanic Panic' controversy as supposedly emblematic of claims levelled against them by adversaries. In their storytelling, the misrepresentation of TOPY's 'First Transmission' video art tape (as depicting ritual child abuse, leading to the much-ballyhooed Scotland Yard raid on their Brighton compound) demonstrates the lengths to which their antagonists will go to smear and discredit the group. But while this police raid was no doubt in error, and alarming for all involved, Thee Temple subsequently used this event as a smokescreen to conceal their actual offenses.
>
> Obviously, TOPY hid no basement dungeons, or depraved playgrounds of devil worship for the ritual torture of infants, as daytime talk shows of the era were eager to avow. Yet by

[1] P-Orridge, *Nonbinary*, p. 291.

Thee Temple ov Psychick Youth

repeating this flimsy distortion repeatedly, almost gleefully, their victimhood is built up as a red herring for distraction. They imply through self-righteous interviews that if a police operation, abetted by tabloid hysteria, persecuted Thee Temple using contrived abuse allegations, then what other cruel untruths stand to be leveraged against them.[1]

Interestingly, the early 1900s Satanic Panic was very similar to the late 1960s Satanic Panic that caused the Process Church to be associated with Charles Manson and the murders of Sharon Tate and others. They were also associated with the infamous Son of Sam murders and even the assassination of Bobby Kennedy. The Process Church did, perhaps unwisely, contact Manson after his arrest, and knew they were being controversial. As with TOPY, they invited negative publicity and should not have been too surprised when they received it. After their disbandment, both the Process Church and TOPY ended up with ex-members who felt they were damaged by their association with a cult, while others seem to have more positive memories.

Like other would-be cult leaders before him, P-Orridge was a showman, courting controversy and manipulating everyone around him. Bad behaviour was both very real and an act; he may have claimed his poses were ironic, but many took him very seriously. For a while he wielded power as the leader of a cult, and perhaps it is for the best that he dismantled TOPY before he was able to do any more damage (similarly, the Process church was dismantled by its shadowy leader, Mary Ann MacLean).

---

[1] 'Groupthink and Other Painful Reflections on Thee Temple ov Psychick Youth' by Dan Siepmann, 27th September 2019.

Books Consulted

Ford, Simon, Wreckers of Civilisation: *The Story of Throbbing Gristle*, 1999.

Janisse, Kier-La, and Corupe, Paul, *Satanic Panic: Pop-Cultural Paranoia in the 1980s*, FAB Press, 2016.

Keenan, David, *England's Hidden Reverse*, SAF Publishing, 2003.

P-Orridge, Genesis, *Esoterrorism, Selected Essays 1980-1988*, UV Press, 1989.

ditto, *Thee Psychick Bible*, Feral House, 2006.

ditto, *Nonbinary*, Abrams Press 2021.

Reynolds, Simon, *Rip It Up and Start Again*, Faber and Faber, 2005.

Rushkoff, Douglas, and others, *Painful But Fabulous: The Life and Art of Genesis P-Orridge*, Soft Skull Press, 2002.

Tutti, Cosey Fanni, *Art Sex Music*, Faber & Faber, 2018.

Online Resources Consulted

Darlington, Andrew, 'Genesis P Porridge: From COUM to Throbbing Gristle and Beyond', Eight Miles Higher Blog, 25th May 2017

Hagen, Olav (interviewer): 'Coil: Lust's Dark Exit', Electric Dark Space, 1991

O'Dell, Alaura (Paula P-Orridge), Outsideleftmusic, outsidleft.com

'Surviving Genesis', Alaura O'Dell (Paula P-Orridge) talking to Alan Rider, Outsideleftmusic, outsidleft.com

Siepmann, Dan: 'Groupthink and Other Painful Reflections on Thee Temple ov Psychick Youth', 27th September 2019

Conclusion

Conclusion

Apart from the novelty of their beliefs, I think my interest in 'alternative' and 'new' religions and cults derives from a hope to understand why intelligent people will often embrace ideas that are not just resistant to proof, but for which good evidence exists to show they are mistaken. It has always struck me that when presented with the most extravagant claims, especially those unencumbered by tradition, discussion should be easier and understanding clearer. I have to admit that it isn't.

Lobsang Rampa first attracted followers in the West because his book, *The Third Eye*, was based upon religious and cultural practices with which Westerners were unfamiliar, and about which they had a tendency to romanticise. When Lobsang Rampa was exposed as Cyril Henry Hoskin, he disappointed a large number of his readers. Sales of his books will have been seriously damaged, and because he went on to promote so many alternative ideas derived from non-Buddhist religions, pseudo-science, crypto-zoology, etc, for a whole generation he was considered a crank. Rampa's original publisher, Secker & Warburg may have acted with little integrity at first, but they later dropped their author. There were, however, other publishers like Corgi who had no qualms about promoting Rampa's ideas. Consequently, new generations have had to assess Rampa for themselves without necessarily knowing his back-story.

Common sense suggests that anyone who makes wild claims and is then found out in a deception, should not be trusted, but there will always be those who *want* to believe and will make excuses for obvious charlatans, wilfully disregarding evidence that does not suit them. After his exposure, Rampa seems to have continued to appeal to those who, having reasons for accepting one kind of supernatural, mystical or pseudo-scientific phenomenon are predisposed to believe in *all* the alternative thinking offered to them. If they are sure that crystals can heal, then why not use dream-catchers, consult terrestrial zodiacs and

Conclusion

attempt to travel on the astral plane? Such passionate believers in New Age ideas have their counterparts among modern day conspiracy theorists who, because they feel they have reason to believe a particular nefarious activity has been conducted by a certain agency, go on to consider no other conspiracies too unlikely. It is irrational, but there appears to be something appealing to people about having esoteric or hidden knowledge; being one of the few 'in the know' seems to offer comfort, even if the knowledge is inherently frightening.

In many ways, Rampa was a 'one-off'. He was a fantasist who, like L. Ron Hubbard, may well have come to believe in his own fictions. At least Rampa made few demands on his readers, other than thirty pence for his latest paperback. Rampa oversaw his own increasingly threadbare cult of personality, but this would never have been enough for Hubbard. The founder of Scientology was obviously not content with being recognised simply as the man who added an e-meter to psychoanalysis, making it fashionable and accessible. It is remarkable that any-one would believe the outrageous science-fiction elaborations he concocted to underpin Scientology, but we have the benefit of hindsight and Wikileaks. Such cults invariably impart their esoteric revelations piecemeal and as initiation develops and followers become more enmeshed, they seem unable or unwill-ing to make critical judgments. No doubt this is, in part, because it would mean admitting that all they had invested up to that point had been worthless.

Rampa and Hubbard were almost certainly aware they were creating fictions, but one cannot say this with such assurance about Olumba Olumba Obu. He may well have believed in his own divinity right up to the year 2000, at which point he was certain the world really would end violently and only he and his followers would be saved. That his various pronouncements prior to the millennium do not always stand up to scrutiny does not necessarily mean he was intending to deceive, and he does seem to have otherwise preached peace and love while not ask-ing very much more of anyone than that they believe him to be the final incarnation of Christ. It was really only after he failed

Conclusion

his self-imposed Armageddon test that the integrity of Obu and the administration of the Brotherhood are all called into question. Why did more followers not turn away when the very basis of their faith was discovered to be in error? Once again, it would have been difficult for them to acknowledge that everything they had invested up to that point had been a waste of time; and nobody wants to admit they have been deceived. When the Brotherhood decided to re-interpret the words of Obu, effectively re-writing their own history, followers were willing to go along with this because so much else that Obu had taught continued to make sense. When offered the choice between believing they had failed to understand the words of the great man, or admitting he had misled them, they chose the former.

My researches into Thee Temple ov Psychick Youth have been, in some ways, the most revealing to me, even though TOPY may not have been the most convincing or successful mystical/ magical cult. TOPY sought to tick off as many of the obvious activities on the 'cult checklist' as possible, and its cynical use of manipulative techniques does seem to have damaged some members. However, many came through the experience unscathed, while others even remember their time with nostalgic affection. This led me to question whether or not I was making too much of TOPY as a 'cult' and whether the chapter should even be included. It was while reading around the subject that I came across Timothy Wyllie's *Love Sex Fear Death*, and went on to watch Neil Edwards' 2015 documentary on the Process Church, *Sympathy for the Devil*, and the 2016 *Dangerous Minds* interview with Wyllie.

Wyllie's contention that if he had his time again, knowing what he knows now, he might still join the Process Church, shifted my perspective on not just cults, but on faith in general. It now strikes me that more time might be given to considering what faiths offer people, even outlandish and potentially dangerous cults, rather than trying to engage with believers over those aspects of belief that have no basis in verifiable reality, and perhaps condemning them as simply gullible.

Conclusion

It is hard-wired into our brains that we should try to make sense of the world around us. Indeed, it is probably a biological necessity. And it is only natural that we should also want to have knowledge of that which is beyond our lived experience. Systems of faith offer answers (comforting or otherwise) to such questions, whether they be traditional world religions, new religious movements, pseudoscience or what appear to be crackpot cults. It is understandable that some believers tend towards tradition, while others look to more contemporary charismatic denominations, (whether their leaders are sincere or otherwise). Our sympathy towards the wide range of different answers on offer will depend upon our culture, our education and our personal experience.

We will most likely be drawn to certain explanations because they ring true for us. The degree to which we might interrogate the information offered depends upon each individual, and it takes bravery when confronted with the idea that you might be wrong, or have even been misled, to dispassionately consider the evidence. It takes a great strength of character to recognise and admit any error, and even more courage to walk away from a belief system if it has been an important part of your life. Exiting your church will potentially cause rifts with friends and family, and the loss of real benefits accrued while living with that belief. This wrench does not just occur in repressive cults, but also within the most benign systems of belief, as well as secular institutions and organisations.

General Reading

Drury, Nevill, *The New Age: Searching for the Spiritual Self*, Thames & Hudson, 2004.

Evans, Christopher, *Cults of Unreason*, Harrap, 1973.

Shermer, Michael, *Why People Believe Weird Things*, Freeman, 1997.

Sladek, John, *The New Apocrypha: A Guide to Strange Sciences and Occult Beliefs*, Hart-Davis Macgibbon, 1973.

Wilson, Colin, and John Grant, *The Directory of Possibilities*, Webb & Bower, 1981.

Index

'A Few Words on Lobsang Rampa' by David Mitchie, 76
Ablett, Mrs, 31
Abominable Snowman, 5, 70, 121, 136
Adam (biblical figure), 176
Aftenposten, 209
Akashic Record, 78, 79, 128
Akpan, Cyrinus O., 189
All Authors Are Equal by Frederic Warburg, 3, 7-11, 13-18, 33, 40, 57, 65, 67, 124, 128
AllMusic.com, 245
Almond, Marc, 228
Alternative TV, 227
Amadi, G.I.S., 171, 179
'Purity and Power', 171, 185
Ambo Street, 34, 165, 190
Anderson Report (Australia), 209, 213
Anger, Kenneth, 235
Aparicio, Luis Manuel Da Luz, 116
Archibong, Christ Shepherd Edet, 188, 190
Art Sex Music by Cosey Fanni Tutti, 243
As It Was! by T. Lobsang Rampa, 27-29, 31, 34, 36-37, 40, 52, 62-63, 65, 91, 99, 106, 126, 127
Atlantis, vi, 79, 110, 114, 135, 137
August Pentecostal Assembly Weekly Gospels by Olumba Olumba Obu, 175, 178, 181
Autumn Lady by Mama San Ra-ab Rampa, 88
Balance, John, 228, 233, 235, 238, 239, 240, 242, 243
Bare-Face Messiah by Russell Miller, 207
Baribeau, Pierre
Les chandelles de Lobsang Rampa, 114
Barker, Gray, 23, 24, 89, 90, 112
They Knew Too Much About Flying Saucers, 90
Bayne, Murdo MacDonald
Beyond the Himalayas, 73
BCS Journal, 173, 177, 181

Beach Boys, 239
Beatles, The, 111
'Tomorrow Never Knows', 111
Beckley, Timothy Green, 107
Silencers, Mystery of the Men in Black, 108
Subterranean Worlds Inside Earth, 108
Beheim-Schwarzbach, Martin
'The Pseudo-Tibetan', 59
Ben Edair (Rampa's house in Howth), 20, 41, 47
Bentine, Michael
Potty Time, 233
Bergin, Gray, 103, 104
Bernard, Theos, 71
Bess, Georges, 122
Bethsaida, 177
Beyond Seven Years in Tibet by Heinrich Harrer, xiv, 17, 26, 38
Beyond the Himalayas by John Geddie, 71
Beyond the Himalayas by Murdo MacDonald Bayne, 73
'Beyond the Lost Horizon' by Dr R.A. Gilbert, 72, 120
Beyond The Tenth by T. Lobsang Rampa, 79, 90, 112
Bharati, Agehananda, xiv, 17, 75, 77, 115, 120
'Fictitious Tibet', xiv, 17, 77
Biakpan, Emon Anneyeng (*The New World Language*) by Apostle E.K. Ukpat, 185
Biakpan, Nigeria, 172, 173, 185
Birmingham Post, The, 53, 66
Blake, William
Marriage of Heaven and Hell, The, 135
Blavatsky, Helena, 77, 78, 79, 125, 132, 133
The Secret Doctrine, 78
'Blind faith in the third eye', *Sunday Times*, 123
Bonham-Carter, Mark, 9

264

Index

Book of Forgotten Authors, The by Christopher Fowler, 114
Bookseller, The, 1, 86, 87
Boothby, Guy
  Dr Nikola, 72
Bouthillette, Karl-Stéphan
  Relire T. Lobsang Rampa, 129
Boxall, Mr, 32
Boyd, Andrew, 251
Brain-washing by L. Ron Hubbard, 214
Bramwell, David
  'On the Art of Deception', 14
British Psychological Society, 216
Brooks, Cyrus, 7-9, 14, 26, 38, 39-40, 47, 81, 82, 85, 126
Brotherhood of the Cross and Star, viii, 164-200, 261
Brotherhood of the Cross and Star, A Sociological Case Study by Friday Michael Mbon, 178, 179
Brown, James, 229
Brown, Ossian, 241
Buckingham Palace, 43
Buckley, Michael
  Eccentric Explorers, 101
Burgess, Clifford, xiv, 25-31, 33, 35, 38, 41, 49-50, 58, 85, 145, 148, 155, 158
Burks, J. Arthur
  Great Mirror, The, 73
Burroughs, William, 227, 232, 248
Butler, Kennth, 122
Buttercup. *See* Rouse, Sheelagh
Calabar, Nigeria, 165-166, 168, 172, 174, 187, 190, 195
Calgary, The Unknown City by James Martin, 105
Campbell, Brud, 21
Campden, Anne, 35, 36, 38, 59, 66
'Can You Please Crawl Out Your Window?' by Bob Dylan, 111
Candlelight by T. Lobsang Rampa, xiii, 26, 36
Candler, Edmund, 10, 71
  The Unveiling of Lhasa, 71
Carruthers, Brian, Q.C., 49
Carter, Chris, 231
Cave of the Ancients by T. Lobsang Rampa, 110
Caycedo, Alfonso, 118
Chakpori, Tibet, 1, 28
Chang, Professor Chen-Chi, 59
  'Tibetan Phantasies', 59

'Changing the World' by Danny Goring, 189
Channing, Mark
  Nine Lives, 73
Chapman, Dr, 21
Chapman, F. Spencer, 71
Chapters of Life by T. Lobsang Rampa, 138
Chen. *See* Rampa, T. Lobsang
Choegyal, Tendzin, 116
Choki, Pema, 13, 14
Chorazin, 177
Christmas Pentecostal Assembly Weekly Gospels by Olumba Olumba Obu, 176
Christopherson, Peter ('Sleazy'), 226, 227, 228, 229, 231, 233, 238, 239, 241, 243
Church of Satan, 239
Church of Scientology, The, viii, 199, 207-208, 211, 213, 217, 221, 223
Churchill, Winston, 2
'Citizens of the World' (television programme), 96
Cleopatra, Miss (cat), 93
Coil, 239
Collins, William (publisher), 8
Compulsions Analysis (precursor of The Process Church), 199
Corgi, vii, 19, 82, 83, 87-88, 106, 259
Cosa Nostra (band), 240
COUM Transmissions, 231, 243
Couture, André, 130
Crass, 230
Creighton, Gordon, 112
  'Tibetan Connection, The', 112
Crisp, Quentin, 253
Cross River State, Nigeria, 165
Crouch, A.P.
  Wife from the Forbidden Land, A, 72
Crowley, Aleister, vi, 218, 229, 234, 253
  Strategem, The, 240
Cults of Unreason by Christopher Evans, vii, 32, 207
Current 93, 239
CVLT Nation, 245
Daily Express, 8, 11-12, 14, 21, 35, 50-51, 53, 56-58, 110, 157, 159, 191
Daily Mail, xiv, 21, 23, 26, 33, 41, 43-48, 51, 54-58, 86, 110, 136, 147, 153

Index

Daily Mirror, 53, 122
Daily Telegraph, 4, 5
Dalai Lama (fourteenth), 116, 117, 118
Dalai Lama (thirteenth), 2, 16, 69, 119, 148
Dalai Lama's Cat, The by David Mitchie, 75
Dangerous Minds (interview), 199, 261
Darkness and Light by Olaf Stapledon, 73
Darkness Over Tibet by Theodore Illion, 73
Darmadoday, 129
Das, Sarat Chandra, 10, 70, 71
   Journey to Lhasa and Central Tibet, 11, 70, 71
David-Néel, Alexandra
   Magic and Mystery in Tibet, 79
   My Journey to Lhasa, 71, 79
Dazed, 245
December Pentecostal Assembly Weekly Gospels by Olumba Olumba Obu, 185
Der Spiegel, 5, 58, 75
Der Stern, 20, 38, 54, 58, 68, 69, 117
Desjardins, Arnaud, 118
Devil's Guard, The by Talbot Mundy, 73
Dhammika, Shravasti
   Strange Case of the Three-eyed Lama, The, 19
Dianetics, 206, 208, 217, 219, 221
Dianetics: The Modern Science of Mental Health by L.Ron Hubbard, 206, 207
Die Zeit, 58, 59
Dillon, Michael, 84-86, 115, 125
Dingle, Edwin John
   My Life in Tibet, 71
Dispatches (Channel Four documentary), 251, 252
Ditko, Steve, 122
Doctor from Lhasa by T. Lobsang Rampa, 22-24, 29, 80, 82-84, 86-89, 137
Doctor Strange (fictional character by Steve Dikto), 122
Dondup, Lama Mingyar (fictitious character), 2, 106, 108
Doors of Perception, The by Aldous Huxley, 111, 135, 163
Doubleday and Company, 3, 80
Dovers, The

'The Third Eye', 111
'Dovers, The, open their Third Eye' by Jon Savage, 111
Doyle, Arthur Conan
   Return of Sherlock Holmes, The, 72
Dr Nikola by Guy Boothby, 72
Dreamachine (Gysin), 232
Dreams Less Sweet by Psychic TV, 228
Dreamworld Tibet by Martin Brauen, 3
Dutton, E.P. (publisher), 8, 9, 18
Dylan, Bob, 111
   'Can You Please Crawl Out Your Window?', 111
Eastern Science Fiction Association, 208
Eccentric Explorers by Michael Buckley, 101
Ecclesiastes 12:6, 78
Edwards, Neil
   Sympathy for the Devil, 261
Eichman, Adolf, 97
Ejedawe, Matthew, 189
Ekanem, Asukwo, 189
Ekpu, Ray, 173
Ekuk (prayer group), 174
Eljah (biblical figure), 176
'Enduring Fascination with Lobsang Rampa, The' by David Mitchie, 76
England's Hidden Reverse by David Keenan, 233, 235, 238, 240-241, 243, 246
Enoch (biblical figure), 176
Errington, Louise, 251, 252
Esalen Institute, 132
Eshbach, Lloyd Arthur, 208
Esoterrorism, Selected Essays 1980-1988 by Genesis P-Orridge, 233
Evans, Christopher, 32
   Cults of Unreason, vii, 32, 207
Evans, Jennifer. *See* Errington, Louise
Everlasting Gospel, The by Olumba Olumba Obu, 170, 174, 176
Evetts, Ian, 244
Eye, E.B., 174
'Fair Game, Secrecy, Security, and the Church of Scientology in Cold War America' by Hugh B. Urban, 209
Fairbairn, Nicholas, M.P., 232
Fairweather, Eileen, 251
Fashionable Philosophy and other Sketches by Laurence Oliphant, 72
Feeding the Flame by T. Lobsang Rampa, 89, 90, 94, 95, 99, 104

266

Index

Fergusson, Alex, 226-228, 232, 238
Final Academy (event), 227
First Transmission by Psychic TV, 236, 251, 253
Flowmotion (fanzine), 227, 228
'Flying into Space' by T. Lobsang Rampa, 23, 89
Flying Saucer News Bookstore, 107
Flying Saucer Review, 23, 24, 89, 112
Flying Saucers (magazine), 89
Force the Hand of Chance by Psychic TV, 228, 232
Foster Report (Great Britain), 209, 213
Fowler, Christopher
  Book of Forgotten Authors, The, 114
Freeman, Pearl, 48
Freud, Sigmund, 133
Gabriel (member of the Brotherhood), 166, 167, 168
Gasmantell, Spydeee. *See* Evetts, Ian
Geddie, John
  Beyond the Himalayas, 71
Geff Rushton. *See* Balance, John
Geographical Journal, 70
Gibbs-Smith, Charles, 9, 39
Gibran, Kahlil, 125
Gilbert, Dr R.A., 72, 74, 120
  'Beyond the Lost Horizon', 72, 120
'Godstar' by Psychic TV, 239
Going Clear by Lawrence Wright, 221
Gollancz (publisher), 8
Goring, Charlie, 164
Goring, Danny, viii, 163-166, 168-170, 193, 195, 198
  'Changing the World', 189, 193
  'Love is the Answer', 164
Goring, George, 163, 164, 165
Goring, Jeremy, 188, 193, 194, 196
Goring, Rosemary, 163, 166
  'Brotherhood for Beginners', 173
Grace, The World of Rampa by Sheelagh Rouse, 20, 127
Graydon, William Murray
  Lama's Secret, The, 73
Great Mirror, The by J. Arthur Burks, 73
Greenpinkamber' (song), 163
Greywhiskers, Mrs Fifi (cat), 88, 95, 119
Grimston, Robert de, 199
'Groupthink and Other Painful Reflections on Thee Temple ov

Psychick Youth' by Dan Siepmann, 243-245, 248, 254
Guardian, The, 245
Gurdjieff, George, 133
Gysin, Brion, 232
Habitat 67, 92, 96, 106
Haçienda (Manchester), 232
Hagen, Olav
  'Coil, Lust's Dark Exit', 243
Hale, Robert (publisher), 8
Hall, Tommy, 111
Harrer, Heinrich, 16-17, 26, 38, 50, 68-71
  Beyond Seven Years in Tibet, xiv, 17, 26, 38
  'My Seven Years in Tibet', 70
  Seven Years in Tibet, 16, 70
Hart-Davis, Rupert, 16
HCO Bulletin, 220
Heard, Gerald, 110, 111, 125, 134
  'Can This Drug [LSD] Enlarge Man's Mind?', 110
Heath, A.M., 7, 9, 26, 39, 82
Hecht, Ernest, 86
Herald-Journal (Spartanburg), xiii
Hergé
  Tintin in Tibet, 121
Hermetic Order of the Golden Dawn, 234
Hermit, The by T. Lobsang Rampa, 79
HERO, 245
Hillary, Sir Edmund, 136
Hilton, James
  Lost Horizon, 74
Hitler, Adolf, 96, 97
Hodgkinson, Liz, *Reincarnation, The Evidence*, xiv
Hoffmann, Professor Helmut, 5
Holy Circle. *See* Ekuk (prayer group)
Horam, Sussex, 165
Hoskin, Cyril. *See* Rampa, T. Lobsang
Hoskin, Eva (Rampa's mother), 28, 29
Hoskin, Joseph (Rampa's father), 27-29
Hoskin, Sarah. *See* Rampa, Mama San Ra-ab
Hoskin, William Henry (Rampa's grandfather), 27
Howard, Dana
  My Flight to Venus, 113
  Strange Case of T. Lobsang Rampa, The, 113
Howden, Jane, 240

Index

Hubbard, L. Ron, 125, 204, 207-208, 210-222, 260
    Brain-washing, 214
    Dianetics, The Modern Science of Mental Health, 206, 207
    Ron's Journal 67, 221
Humm, R., and Co (Garage, Plymouth), 28
Huxley, Aldous, 110, 111, 134, 135, 163
    Doors of Perception, The, 111, 135, 163
Iburene, Pastor Lovina Amangala, 191
i-D, 245
Illingworth-Butler, Mrs Winifred, 47
Illion, Theodore
    Darkness Over Tibet, 73
    In Secret Tibet, 73
Illustrated London News, The, 83, 84
In Secret Tibet by Theodore Illion, 73
Ireland's Eye, 21
Irwin, John, 55, 66, 155
Isherwood, Mrs Margery, 47
Jarman, Derek, 235
Jehova's Witnesses, 186, 206
Jesse, Mrs Betty, 104
Jesus (biblical figure), 28, 164, 175-179, 183- 184, 193-195
Jivaka, Lobzang. *See* Dillon, Michael
Jodorowsky, Alejandro
    White Lama, The, 122
John the Baptist (biblical figure), 177, 179
Jones, Jim, 243
Journey to Lhasa and Central Tibet by Sarat Chandra Das, 70, 71
Jours de France, 3
'Joy' by Psychic TV, 239
Jung, Carl, 133
'Just Drifting' by Psychic TV, 228, 229
Kat (Janice Ahmed), 235
Keenan, David, 235, 241, 242, 246
    England's Hidden Reverse, 233, 235, 238, 240, 241, 243, 246
Kemerovo (Russia), 118
Kemp, Daren
    New Age, A Guide, 131
Kemp, Ray, 210
Kennedy, Robert F., 254
Kensington News, 35, 59, 66
Kevin, S.A.
    Universal Love, The, 177, 178
King, Stephen
    Salem's Lot, 227

Kirkus, 25, 4
Kirlian photography, 137
Kuan, Dr Carl. *See* Rampa, T. Lobsang
Kuan, Sanya. *See* Rampa, Mama San Ra-ab
Kuan-suo. *See* Rampa, T. Lobsang
Kukkolos, Dmitry Vladimirovich, 119
'Lama of Suburbia, The' by Sarah Penicka, 115
Lama's Secret, The by William Murray Graydon, 73
Landon, Perceval, 10, 70-71
    Lhasa, 70-71
LaVey, Anton, 239
Leadbeater, Charles Webster, 79
Leadmill (Sheffield), 239
Leary, Timothy, Metzner & Alpert
    Psychedelic Experience, The, 111
'Leave Your Body Behind' by The Thirteenth Floor Elevators, 112
Ledauc, W., 118
Lennon, John, 111
Les chandelles de Lobsang Rampa by Pierre Baribeau, 114
Ley Lines, vi, 113
Lhasa and its Mysteries by Laurence Austine Waddell, 71
Lhasa by Perceval Landon, 70, 71
Lhasa, Tibet, 5, 6, 10-13, 15-16, 68-69, 76, 128
Liberté, La, 118
Library Journal, 82, 4
Life of Brian by Monty Python, 166
Light of the World, The by Olumba Olumba Obu, 178, 182
Living with the Lama by T. Lobsang Rampa, 88, 95
Loftus, Mr, 21
Lopez, Donald S., Jr, 71, 120, 121, 128
    Prisoners of Shangri-La, 4, 15, 19, 38, 71, 115, 120, 129, 146
Los Angeles Daily News, 204
Los Angeles Science Fantasy Society, 208
Los Angeles Times, 196, 197
Lost Horizon by James Hilton, 74
'Love is the Answer' by Danny Goring, 164
Love Sex Fear Death, The Inside Story of the Process Church by Timothy Wyllie, 199, 261
Lovecraft, H.P., vi
Lundborg, Patrick, 112

Index

Macdonald, Alexander
   Through the Heart of Tibet, 72
Machen, Arthur, vi
MacLean, Mary Ann, 199, 254
Macrae, Elliott, 8-9, 11-16, 18, 117, 126
'Mad Organist, The' by Psychic TV, 233
Magic and Mystery in Tibet by Alexandra David-Néel, 79
Maharishi Mahesh Yogi, 111, 136
Manson, Charles, ix, 234, 237, 239, 254
Marley and Me by Don Taylor, 135
Marley, Bob, 135
Marpa, 128
Marriage of Heaven and Hell, The by William Blake, 135
Martin, James
   Calgary, The Unknown City, 105
Maslow, Abraham, 133
Maxwell, Pat, 41, 42, 43, 47, 53
   Stories Behind My News Pictures, 41, 53
Mayer, Jean-François, 118
Mayoral House (Plympton, Devon), 27
Mba, Kanu, 174
Mbon, Friday Michael, 178, 179
   Brotherhood of the Cross and Star, A Sociological Case Study, 178, 179
McCormick, Ken, 80, 81, 82
Medical Lama. See Doctor from Lhasa
Medlicott, Hugh, 41, 45, 47, 55, 127, 147, 153
Megson, Neil Andrew. *See* P-Orridge, Genesis
Melchizedek (biblical figure), 176
Men in Black, 90, 108
Merwin, Sam, 208
'Message from the Temple' by Psychic TV, 228, 230
Michie, David
   'A Few Words on Lobsang Rampa', 76
Miller, Henry, 80, 81, 82, 125
   Stand Still Like the Hummingbird, 125
Miller, Henry, A Personal Archive, a sale catalogue compiled by Jackson and Ashley, 80
Miller, Russell
   Bare-Face Messiah, 207
Mitchie, David

The Dalai Lama's Cat, 75
'The Enduring Fascination with Lobsang Rampa', 76
Monty Python
   Life of Brian, 166
Morning of the Magicians by Louis Pauwels, 97
Morris, John, 17
Moses (biblical figure), 176
Moskowitz, Sam, 208
Mundy, Talbot
   Devil's Guard, The, 73
   Old Ugly Face, 73
   Om, the Secret of Ahbor Valley, 73
   Thunder Dragon Gate, The, 73
Mutton, Karen, 32, 108, 114
   T. Lobsang Rampa
New Age Trailblazer, 114
My Flight to Venus by Dana Howard, 113
My Journey to Lhasa by Alexandra David-Néel, 71, 79
My Life in Tibet by Edwin John Dingle, 71
'My Seven Years in Tibet' by Heinrich Harrer, 70
My True Story by T. Lobsang Rampa, 90
My Visit to Agharta by T. Lobsang Rampa, 108, 114
My Visit to Venus by T. Lobsang Rampa, 89, 100, 107
Myrvang, Rudy, 209
Naughton, Dr. *See* Dillon, Michael
Never Despair, by Gilbert Martin, 2
New Age, A Guide by Daren Kemp, 131
New Heaven and New Earth by E.B. Eyo, 177
New York Review, 80
New Yorker, The, 211, 245
Newby, Eric, 47, 51, 52, 53, 67, 86, 124
   A Short Walk in the Hindu Kush, 51
   Traveller's Life, A, 47, 51, 53, 65, 67, 124
Newswatch, 189
Nexus (magazine), 114
Nine Lives by Mark Channing, 73
Nkor (Brotherhood member), 193
Nkpa, Prophet Enu Enu, 172
Noah (biblical figure), 176
Norgay, Tenzing, 136
O'Dell, Alaura. *See* P-Orridge, Paula

269

Index

O'Grady, Mr and Mrs, 21, 102
Observer Magazine, 251, 252
Obu, Ajah (daughter of Olumba Olumba Obu, 189
Obu, Ibum (daughter of Olumba Olumba Obu, 189, 190
Obu, Olumba Olumba, 162-184, 186-196, 260, 261
    'A Special Message from Leader Olumba Olumba Obu', 184
    August Pentecostal Assembly Weekly Gospels, 175, 178, 181
    Christmas Pentecostal Assembly Weekly Gospels, 176
    December Pentecostal Assembly Weekly Gospels, 185
    Everlasting Gospel, The, 170, 174, 176
    'I Am That I Am', 173
    Light of the World, The, 178, 182
    Our Lord Jesus Christ the Alpha and Omega, 173, 192
    Prophets' Handbook, 173
    'Reign of Love by 2000 AD, The', 193
    Supernatural Teacher, The, 177, 180-181, 192
Obu, Onoghen (daughter of Olumba Olumba Obu, 189
Obu, Rowland (son of Olumba Olumba Obu, 170, 188-190, 194-196
Old Ugly Face by Talbot Mundy, 73
Oliphant, Laurence
    Fashionable Philosophy and other Sketches, 72
    'Sisters of Thibet, The', 72
Om, The Secret of Ahbor Valley by Talbot Mundy, 73
Ordo Templi Orientis, 234
Oriental Art (magazine), 15
Otumesin, Prophetess Otemegan, 172
Our Lord Jesus Christ the Alpha and Omega by Olumba Olumba, Obu, 173, 192
Ouspensky, P.D., 133
Outsideleftmusic, 244
'Ov Power' by Psychic TV, 229
Oxford Capacity Analysis test, 206, 209, 212, 215-217, 223
Pallis, Marco, 15-16, 26-27, 47, 50, 69-71, 152
Parker Russell, Tim, 168
Parker, Rosalie, 163, 165-166, 168

Parsons, 'Jack' Whiteside, 218
Pattinson, Sarah Anne. *See* Rampa, Mama San Ra-ab
Pauwels, Louis, 97
    Morning of the Magicians, 97
Pavlov, Ivan, 133
Penicka, Sarah
    'Lama of Suburbia, The', 115
Penrith Observer, 30, 66
People's Temple, The (Jonestown), ix
PG Tips
    Unexplained Mysteries of the World, 131
Pitchfork, 245
Pitt, John (*Psychic Times*), 31
Plympton (Devon), 27, 51, 128, 145, 147, 154, 157
Polanski, Roman, 239
PopMatters, 245
P-Orridge, Caresse, 238
P-Orridge, Genesis, viii, ix, 226-229, 231-249, 251-254
    Esoterrorism, Selected Essays 1980-1988, 233
    Thee Psychick Bible, 237, 242, 246
P-Orridge, Paula, 228, 238, 244
    'Surviving Genesis' (by Alaura O'Dell), 244
Porter, Clint, 105
Potala Palace, Lhasa, Tibet, 5, 6, 68, 72, 117
Potty Time by Michael Bentine, 233
Power of Prayer, The by T. Lobsang Rampa, 90
Prabhavananda, Swami, 111
Price, Albert (incorrect identity for Rampa), xiv
Prisoners of Shangri-La by Donald S. Lopez, Jr, 4, 15, 19, 38, 71, 115, 120, 129, 146
Process Church of the Final Judgment, The, ix, 199, 234, 239, 243, 254, 261
Prophets' Handbook by Olumba Olumba, Obu, 173
'Pseudo-Tibet, The' by Martin Beheim-Schwarzbach, 59
Psychedelic Experience, The by Leary, Metzner & Alpert, 111
Psychic Times, 31
Psychic TV, viii, 227-233, 235-236, 239-240, 242, 249, 251-252
    Dreams Less Sweet, 228
    First Transmission, 236, 251, 253

Index

Force the Hand of Chance, 228, 232
'Godstar', 239
'Joy', 239
'Just Drifting', 228, 229
'Message from the Temple', viii, 228, 230
'Ov Power', 229
'Roman P', 239
'Stolen Kisses', 229
'The Mad Organist', 233
Themes, 233
Psychick Bible, Thee by Genesis P-Orridge, 237, 242, 246
'Purity and Power' by G.I.S. Amadi, 171, 185
Queen Elizabeth II, 43
Quietus, The, 245
Rampa Story, The by T. Lobsang Rampa, 19, 21-22, 38, 52, 60-61, 63-65, 79, 82, 86-88, 111, 126
Rampa, Imposteur ou initié? by Stanké, Alain, 92, 96
Rampa, Mama San Ra-ab, 19, 21-22, 30-31, 33-36, 39, 42, 45-46, 48, 52-54, 60, 64-66, 88, 105-106, 127, 146-147, 150, 158-159
Autumn Lady, 88
Tigerlily, 27, 33
Rampa, T. Lobsang, vi, vii, 259
As It Was!, 27-29, 31, 34, 36-37, 40, 52, 62-63, 65, 91, 99, 106, 126-127
Beyond The Tenth, 79, 90, 112
Candlelight, xiii, 26, 36
Cave of the Ancients, 110
Chapters of Life, 138
Doctor from Lhasa, 22-24, 29, 80, 82-84, 86-89, 137
Feeding the Flame, 89, 90, 94-95, 99, 104
'Flying into Space', 23, 89
Hermit, The, 79
Living with the Lama, 88, 95
My True Story, 90
My Visit to Agharta, 108, 114
My Visit to Venus, 89, 100, 107
Power of Prayer, The, 90
Rampa Story, The, 19, 21-22, 38, 52, 60-61, 63-65, 79, 82, 86-88, 111, 126
'Saucers over Tibet', 23, 89
Third Eye, The, 1-10, 15, 18-19, 21, 23-26, 37, 40, 42-43, 45,

47, 52-53, 57-60, 64, 68-70, 73-75, 78-83, 85-89, 98, 109-110, 112, 114-115, 117-118, 120-122, 125, 128-129, 135, 146-147, 149, 153-155, 157, 160, 259
Thirteenth Candle, The, 104
Tibetan Sage, 106
Wisdom of the Ancients, vi, vii, 90, 99, 138
You—Forever, 111, 122
'Rampa, T. Lobsang—Lama, Mystic and Plumber' (Radio 4 documentary), 38
Randi, James, 104
Encyclopedia, An, of Claims, Frauds, and Hoaxes of the Occult and Supernatural, xiv
Reich, Wilhelm, vi, 133
Reincarnation, The Evidence by Liz Hodgkinson, xiv
Relire T. Lobsang Rampa by Karl-Stéphan Bouthillette, 129
Rene Clair (shop), 35, 36
Return of Sherlock Holmes, The by Arthur Conan Doyle, 72
Reynolds, J.N., 137
Reynolds, Marcus, 239
Reynolds, Simon
Rip It Up and Start Again, 229, 244
Richardson, Hugh, 4, 5, 26, 47, 146, 152
Rider, Alan, 244
Rigberg, Jim, 107
Rip It Up and Start Again by Simon Reynolds, 229, 244
'Roman P' by Psychic TV, 239
Ron's Journal 67 by L. Ron Hubard, 221
Rouse, John, 39, 46, 47, 48
Rouse, Sheelagh, 20-23, 39, 41-45, 47-52, 56, 58, 85-86, 88, 92, 96, 102, 105-106, 108, 110, 124-125, 127, 147, 150-151, 154-155, 157-158
Grace, The World of Rampa, 20, 127
Twenty-Five years with T. Lobsang Rampa, 20, 21, 23, 39, 48, 49, 50, 51, 107, 124
Royal Sanitary Institute (London), 29
Salas, Senor, 91
Salem's Lot by Stephen King, 227
Satanic Panic, 251, 253, 254
Saucerian Bulletin, 23, 89

Index

Saucerian Press, 24, 82
Saucerian Records, 90
'Saucers over Tibet' by T. Lobsang Rampa, 23, 89
Savage, John
  'The Dovers open their Third Eye', 111
Save a Cat League, 89
School of Oriental Studies at London University, 15
Scientology, Church of, vii, viii, 260
Seaside Post, 105
Sebastian, Mr, 228, 234
Secker & Warburg, 1, 3-4, 6, 13, 51, 80, 87, 157, 259
Secret Doctrine, The by Helena Blavatsky, 78
Secrets of the Aura. See You—Forever self-titled, 245
Seven Years in Tibet by Heinrich Harrer, 16, 70
Shalom (Brotherhood member), 194, 195
Shambhala, 74
Shangri-La, 74
Shipton, Eric, 136
Short Walk in the Hindu Kush, A by Eric Newby, 51
Siepmann, Dan, 244, 253
  'Groupthink and Other Painful Reflections on Thee Temple ov Psychick Youth', 243-244, 245, 248, 254
Sierksma, F.
  Tibet's Terrifying Deities, 121
Silencers, Mystery of the Men in Black by Timothy Green Beckley, 108
'Sisters of Thibet, The' by Laurence Oliphant, 72
Smythe, Jeremiah (fictional name for Clifford Burgess), 49
Snellgrove, Dr David, 15, 47, 152
Snow Lion Newsletter, 64
Son of Sam murders, 254
Souvenir Press, 80, 82, 83, 86, 87
Spare, Austin Osman, 235
  Starlit Mire, The, 240
'Special Message from Leader Olumba Olumba Obu, A' by Olumba Olumba Obu, 184
Sphere (magazine), 119
SPIN, 245
Sri Ramakrishna, 125
Stables, Gordon

War on the World's Roof, 72
Stand Still Like the Hummingbird by Henry Miller, 125
Stanké, Alain, 64-65, 92-94, 96-97, 99, 100, 102-103, 116-117, 123-125
  Rampa, Imposteur ou initié?, 92, 96
Stapledon, Olaf
  Darkness and Light, 73
Stevens, Matthew Levi, 227
Stolen Grand Lama, The, by Claverdon Wood, 72
'Stolen Kisses' by Psychic TV, 229
Stories Behind My News Pictures by Pat Maxwell, 41, 53
Strange Case of T. Lobsang Rampa, The by Dana Howard, 113
Strange Case of the Three-eyed Lama, The by Shravasti Dhammika, 19
Strategem, The by Aleister Crowley, 240
Stubbs, David, 244
Sturgeon, Theodore, 207
Subterranean Worlds Inside Earth by Timothy Green Beckley, 108
Sun (Nigeria), 182
Sunday (BBC Radio Four programme), vii
Sunday Concord, 178, 182
Sunday Times (Sri-Lanka), 123
Supernatural Teacher, The by Olumba Olumba Obu, 177, 180, 181, 192
'Surviving Genesis' by Alaura O'Dell (Paula P-Orridge), 244
Sutherland, Stacy, 111
Sutton, Lorraine, 32
Symmes, John Cleves Symmes, Jr, 137
Sympathy for the Devil by Neil Edwards, 261
T. Lobsang Rampa, New Age Trailblazer by Karen Mutton, 114
Tadalinka, Miss (cat), 93
Tagesspiegel, 5
Take Two Club (Attercliffe), 239
Tate, Sharon, 239, 254
Tatler, The, 48
Taylor, Don
  Marley and Me, 135
Taylor, Greg 'Foxtrot Echo', 244
Teegeeack (Scientology's secret name for planet Earth), 219, 221
Temple of Thelema (Crowley), 218
Temple ov Psychick Youth, viii, ix, 228-232, 234-249, 252-254, 261

Index

Temple Ov Psychick Youth Newsletter, 230

Thames Ditton, 34, 60, 62, 63, 65, 66

Thee Grey Book by Temple ov Psychick Youth, 233

Themes by Psychic TV, 233

Theosophical Society, 79, 132

Theosophy, 71, 77, 78

Theroux, Louis, 207

They Knew Too Much About Flying Saucers by Gray Barker, 90

Third Eye, The by T. Lobsang Rampa, 1-10, 15, 18-19, 21, 23-26, 37, 40, 42-43, 45, 47, 52-53, 57-60, 64, 68-70, 73-75, 78-83, 85-89, 98, 109-110, 112, 114-115, 117-118, 120-122, 125, 128-129, 135, 146-147, 149, 153-155, 157, 160, 259

'Third Eye, The' by The Dovers, 111

Thirteenth Candle, The, by T. Lobsang Rampa, 104

Thirteenth Floor Elevators, The, 112

'Leave Your Body Behind', 112

Throbbing Gristle, 231, 232, 233, 243

Through the Heart of Tibet by Alexander Macdonald, 72

Thunder Dragon Gate, The by Talbot Mundy, 73

Tibet, David, 228, 233-234, 238-239, 241

Tibet's Terrifying Deities by F. Sierksma, 121

Tibetan Book of the Dead, 111

'Tibetan Connection, The' by Gordon Creighton, 112

'Tibetan Phantasies' by Professor Chen-Chi Chang, 59

Tibetan Sage by T. Lobsang Rampa, 106

Tigerlily by Mama San Ra-ab Rampa, 27, 33

Time (magazine), 19, 21, 40, 41, 42

Times Literary Supplement, 4, 87

Times, The, 26

Tintin in Tibet by Hergé, 121

Tiny Mix Tapes, 245

Tomorrow (journal), 59

TOPYNA, 247, 248

Touch-Stones, Rampa's tranquiliser, 99

Traveller's Life, A by Eric Newby, 47

Tutti, Cosey Fanni, 231, 243

Art Sex Music, 243

Twenty-Five years with T. Lobsang Rampa by Sheelagh Rouse, 20-21, 23, 39, 48-51, 107, 124

UFO Review, 90

Ukpat, Apostle E.K., 185

Biakpan, Emon Anneyeng (The New World Language), 185

Unexplained Mysteries of the World, PG Tips, 131

Universal Love, The by S.A. Kevin, 177, 178

University of Chungking, 6

Unveiling of Lhasa, The by Edmund Candler, 71

Urban, Hugh B.

Fair Game: 'Secrecy, Security, and the Church of Scientology in Cold War America', 209

Vice Media, 245

Victoria and Albert Museum, 9, 39

von Däniken, Erich, vi, 113, 137

Waddell, Laurence Austine, 10

Lhasa and its Mysteries, 11, 71

War on the World's Roof by Gordon Stables, 72

Warble-in-Tun (public house), 169

Warbleton, Sussex, 165

Warburg, Frederic, 6, 11-12, 16, 32, 38, 47, 51-52, 65-66, 87, 124, 126, 128, 155

All Authors Are Equal, 7-11, 13-18, 33, 40, 57, 65, 67, 124, 128

Warburg, Pamela, 9, 11

Watson, Lyall, 113

Western Morning News, xiii

Weybridge (Surrey), 30, 31, 62, 65, 146

White Lama, The by Alejandro Jodorowsky, 122

Wiesenthal, Simon, 97

Wife from the Forbidden Land, A by A.P. Crouch, 72

Wikileaks, 221

Wilde, Oscar, 253

Will, The (Nigeria), 191

Williams, Okpalla, 189

Wilson, Colin, vi

Directory of Possibilities (with John Grant), vi

Wilson, Mrs Pat (teacher), v

Wire, The, 244

Wisdom of the Ancients by T. Lobsang Rampa, vi, vii, 90, 99, 138

273

Index

Wood, Claverdon
   Stolen Grand Lama, The, 72
Wood, Mrs, 39
Worm (collective), 231
Wright, Lawrence
   Going Clear, 221
Wyllie, Timothy, 199, 261
   Love Sex Fear Death, The Inside Story of the Process Church, 199, 261

Xenu (extraterrestrial ruler of a 'Galactic Confederacy'), 207, 213, 219, 220, 221, 222
Yeti. *See* Abominable Snowman
You—Forever by T. Lobsang Rampa, 111, 122
Younghusband Mission to Tibet, 71